Dismissing Jesus

Dismissing Jesus

How We Evade the Way of the Cross

DOUGLAS M. JONES

Foreword by
PETER J. LEITHART

CASCADE *Books* · Eugene, Oregon

DISMISSING JESUS
How We Evade the Way of the Cross

Cascade Books
An Imprint of Wipf and Stock Publishers
199 W. 8th Ave., Suite 3
Eugene, OR 97401

www.wipfandstock.com

ISBN 13: 978-1-62032-535-3

Cataloging-in-Publication Data

Jones, Douglas M.

Dismissing Jesus : how we evade the way of the cross / Douglas M. Jones.

xii + 288 p. 23 cm. Includes bibliographical references.

ISBN 13: 978-1-62032-535-3

1. Spiritual life—Christianity. 2. Christian life. I. Title.

BV4501.2 .J587 2013

Manufactured in the U.S.A.

for Paula
the best is still ahead

Contents

Foreword

Doug Jones has taught me more than I can remember. I got a refresher in Western philosophy sitting in on his philosophy class when I first arrived at New St. Andrews College (NSA). In lectures on Trinitarian theology, aesthetics, the ethics of jokes, theology of the body, Sabbath, and festivity, Doug's habit of raising more questions than he answered left students and other faculty inspired, bewildered, always begging for more. I wasn't the only one to learn much from him about Nietzsche; for several years, self-styled *Uberwenches* stalked the NSA campus, smart women not to be messed with. Not everything Doug tried to teach me has stuck: To this day, I cannot bring myself to regard *Finnegans Wake* as a novel, much less a masterpiece, though Doug convinced me it was worth my time to mine Joyce's inexhaustible vein of neologisms.

Of all the things I have learned from Doug, none has been so revolutionary for me, or for Doug, as his recent work on political theology, economics, and the way of the cross. Doug shook me out of a complacent neoconservatism and forced me to examine how often our economic habits are liturgies to Mammon. During the depths of the recent recession, I caught myself breathing a sigh of relief at news reports that the Dow was rising again. I would never have recognized that sigh as the idolatry it is without Doug's provocations.

Doug begins with a meditation on the mystery of persuasion. I am unpersuaded of several of the central arguments in *Dismissing Jesus*. As Doug says, Abraham was no Pharaoh, but the Bible describes him as a man of wealth, and at the climax of the Abraham narrative the sons of Heth declare him a "great prince" (Gen 23). Jesus says that the "broad way" leads to destruction, but Doug seems to think most Christians are on the "broad way," that runs the risk of promoting a two-tiered church. I would like Doug to offer a more precise definition of "violence," and

I think the topography of maturation from Old to New is less smooth than Doug maps it. Doug is not a pacifist, but he needs to explain why not. I wonder if Doug has given weight to the way the patriarchal narratives, the life of David, the career of Jesus, and the history of the church progress from weakness to power. I would like to see Doug integrate Acts more intimately into his reading of Luke.

Doug has always been a jolly provocateur. There was the time he celebrated April Fool's Day by parking a friend's pickup in a neighboring town with a "For Sale" sign in the windshield. On another April 1, he joined with students to hack into the NSA web site and post pictures of the torture chamber in the cavernous basement of the library. Doug assumed the role of college President, wielding a whip against unruly students.

Dismissing Jesus too is a provocation, though no joke. Doug identifies and invites us to remove the blinders that seduce us from the way of our crucified and risen Lord. Ultimately he calls the church to be more fully herself, a community devoted to seeking Jesus's kingdom and trusting the Father for the rest, a communion in the Spirit that is for that reason a communion in all of God's good gifts, a fellowship that is herself a graced economy. His book is unsettling; frequently it is unsettling in just the way Jesus is. Doug's barbs sink deep, and, persuaded or not, every reader will profit from a slow, receptive engagement with this book.

Peter J. Leithart
Peniel Hall
Moscow, Idaho

Preface on Persuasion

Ten years ago I would have dismissed this book rather quickly, after reading just a few paragraphs. I would have thought it missed the importance of beauty and joy and laughter, in the way I narrowly conceived them then.

Twenty years ago I would have dismissed this book with just a glance at the table of contents and back cover, for what I would have judged as a minimizing of the power of doctrine. It would not have meshed with my assumption of a worldview through which every answer clicks out automatically. I would also have held my nose at its tone. And its categories would have seemed alien territory, a different Christian tradition, too uncomfortable for my comfortable Reformed truths. What good could come from anywhere off my farm?

Thirty years ago, if I even would have picked up this book, I would have quickly denounced it as Marxist crap masquerading as Christian faith, completely hopeless and dangerous, lying about the whole gospel. I would have said that it lacked conservative hardness.

I can't see any way I could have broken through to my earlier selves. They had barricaded themselves too well.

Persuasion is a terribly strange thing. It has to overcome our personality types, our histories, our ages, all our past friends and safe influences, and our willingness to reconsider. We dismiss books and authors for lacking the right feel or for not sounding like our friends. It's an impossible task. Persuasion is magic or more like an unbelievable accident. We have to be standing at just the right intersection at the exact moment of time, tilting our head in just one direction to see what we need to see. It's astounding we're ever persuaded of anything new. I guess that's why most of us tend to stick forever with views we embraced in high school or college.

Then Kierkegaard's clown complicates the issue beyond all hope:

> It happened that a fire broke out backstage in a theater. The
> clown came out to inform the public. They thought it was just
> a jest and applauded. He repeated his warning, they shouted
> even louder. So I think the world will come to an end amid
> general applause from all the wits, who believe that it is a joke.[1]

---

1. Oden, *Parables*, 3.

PART ONE

What Is the Way of the Cross?

1

Overview of the Way of the Cross

I am spiritually blind. Conservative Christian and blind. I am one of the many who followed the broad path and said to Jesus "I will follow you" but did "not sit down first and count the cost" (Luke 14:28). I have taught and pastored and misled many sincere Christians—congregants, students, my family—for decades, preaching cheap grace and missing the weightier matters of the law. "Whoever of you does not forsake all that he has cannot be My disciple" (Luke 14:33). "Whoever does not bear his cross and come after Me cannot be My disciple" (Luke 14:27).

I am the rich young ruler Jesus addressed. I have a car, several computers, lawn sprinklers, a tiled shower, a full pantry, air conditioning, a nice outdoor deck, plenty of books, and I've spent years sincerely trying to figure out theological questions—"Good teacher, what shall I do to inherit eternal life?" (Luke 18:18). Bonhoeffer commented on the rich young ruler's strategy: "Keep on posing questions, and you will escape the necessity of obedience."[1]

Why read on, then? Why read a book by the spiritually blind? Maybe, because I am not alone. I suspect you, like me, are a rich young ruler. Most of us in the West are. It's our most common shape. At least, Jesus "looking at him, loved him" (Mark 10:21). Maybe there's hope for us.

So, I am blind but arguing with myself, with us. I write to persuade myself out of blindness, with a plea to the Spirit. I long for a second chance, now later in life. Maybe the Spirit can get through to me. Of

1. Bonhoeffer, *Cost*, 73.

course, most of us rich, young rulers don't consider ourselves wealthy or blind. It's always the people above us, the blatantly greedy and cruel, whom Jesus had in mind, not us innocuous and insipid followers. And it's always secularists or people in other Christian traditions who are blind. Never us.

But when Scripture addresses God's people, it portrays spiritual blindness as rather normal. It's regular, common, cutting across Old and New Testaments. Moses promised the Israelites "I know after my death you will become utterly corrupt, and turn aside from the way which I have commanded you" (Deut 31:29). A psalmist lamented "They do not know. . . . They walk about in darkness" (Ps 82:5). Isaiah declared, "who is blind but my servant?" (Isa 42:19) and "His watchmen are blind, they are all ignorant; they are all dumb dogs" (Isa 56:10). Jesus was frustrated by both opponents and followers: "blind leaders of the blind. And if the blind leads the blind, both will fall into a ditch" (Matt 15:14). And even just a few short years after the crucifixion, resurrection, and Pentecost, Christ told his own people, "I will vomit you out of My mouth. Because you . . . do not know that you are wretched, miserable, poor, blind, and naked" (Rev 3:16,17). Blindness everywhere. God's people have a high probability of blindness.

How would you know if you were spiritually blind? It's not obvious. Imagine, for a moment, that you are actually among the majority of us who are spiritually blind. You walk about in darkness, but you think you see clearly. Imagine you're one of the nice, well-meaning churchgoers, who has nice Christian ideas in your head. Imagine you were one of the people Isaiah spoke to, the ones who sacrificed diligently and properly (Isa 1:11), you appeared before the Lord regularly (Isa 1:12), attended worship meetings and festivals (Isa 1:13), you offered many prayers (Isa 1:15), and you might even have been one of the few who were disciplined enough to fast regularly (Isa 58:3). That's exactly the sort of person who was and is most likely to be blind. We are those who so often totally miss what God has called his people to do. Can we imagine being so sincere and well-meaning and diligent and yet hear God say to us "When you spread out your hands, I will hide My eyes from you; even though you make many prayers, I will not hear" (Isa 1:15)? "I have had enough" (Isa 1:11). Rather, we tend to assume mere middle-class niceness and decency protects us from blindness. But it's that decency that makes us the most likely to be blind.

So how could we know if we're spiritually blind? The Old Testament prophets thought they could get through to us with pointed denunciations. Some of us respond to denunciations by looking more and more inward. We hope that greater introspection will lead to truth. But that, too, is often a path of blindness. Most truth is not that mysterious and subjective. Just as Moses said, "for this commandment which I command you today is not too mysterious for you, nor is it far off" (Deut 30:11). And it's not as complicated as struggling to get a small gnat from a drink and accidentally swallowing a beast (Matt 23:24). In the end, Christ's message is pretty straightforward and obvious. You don't need five hundred years to figure it out. "Whoever does not bear his cross and come after me cannot be my disciple." It's not hard to see. In fact, spiritual blindness assumes that truth is easy to see and obey. It's so easy we have to manufacture obstacles in order to "miss it." We don't want to see it. I don't want to see it.

That's what I want to argue about in this book. Here's a short version of my thesis: The dominant form of Christian living is one designed to shield us from Jesus's explicit priorities. How is it that the vast majority of Christians set aside Jesus's obvious and revolutionary call so easily? How do we make disobedience and blindness so normal and acceptable?

Here's a longer version of the same thesis: *Certain deeply and widely cherished assumptions about Christ, society, and our selves block us from seeing Jesus's call, and we must escape these blinders before we can walk Jesus's path again. When we do that, we'll see that the gospel of Christ is not primarily about getting into heaven or about living a comfortable, individually-pious middle-class life. It is about being free from the ancient, pervasive, and delightful oppression of Mammon in order to create a very different community, the church, an alternative city-kingdom here and now on earth by means of living and celebrating the way of the cross—the reign of joyful weakness, renunciation, self-denial, sharing, foolishness, community, and love-overcoming-evil.*

We simply do not want the way of the cross to be what life is *all* about. It would mean that what most often passes for Christianity is largely a lie, a deception designed to keep us from the way Jesus. But how could a majority get it wrong? That seems so unlikely. I'll come back to that.

This book is divided into three parts. The first and main part aims to get clear about the way of the cross itself. We have to understand the way of the cross before we can evade it. The second part focuses on several key, contemporary reasons why we can't see the way of the cross, and it tries to undermine each. The third part offers a brief, constructive vision about what a healthy local and international church would look like if it took up the cross of Christ. It's a new world with ancient roots. The final chapter describes the sort of ancient spirituality required for the kingdom work to proceed.

I somehow stumbled into talk of the way of the cross late in life, decades after doing the typical evangelical thing, and I'm still not there. I certainly wasn't looking for it, and it's certainly not some unique angle I made up. It has always been a stream within the Christian church, and it's a tradition that beautifully cuts across all denominations and traditions. Within each prominent Christian tradition, you can find longtime defenders of the way of the cross. They're usually pushed off to the side, often ignored, often suppressed, while the major institutions and teachers continue fussing and fighting about the broad and easy way. The way of the cross is sometimes described as "radical" but it's just normal Jesus. The "radical" label frees us from taking it seriously. The way of the cross stands out clearly in the early church. But we also see it through the early Middle Ages in various expressions of monasticism. Later we see it in the Waldensians, St. Francis, Wycliffe and the Lollards, Hussites, Vincent de Paul, Thomas a Kempis, and many more. In modern times, we find expressions of the way of the cross in Dostoevsky, Tolstoy, Eberhard Arnold, Nikolai Berdyaev, Peter Maurin, Dorothy Day, Howard Thurman, Andre Trocme, Jacques Ellul (both from my own Reformed tradition), Clarence Jordan, and, of course, the Lutheran Dietrich Bonhoeffer, the author of the most important theology book of the last two or three hundred years—*The Cost of Discipleship* (1937). That's the book that many of us have long had on our shelves but never got around to reading. It is not a perfect book, but it is profoundly simple, exasperating, timeless, and revolutionary. It aims, after all, to be just a simple restatement of Jesus's most basic teaching—the way of the cross.

Bonhoeffer recognized the long tradition of the way of the cross. He offered this famous insight about the rise of monasticism as a protest movement, once the "broad way" had settled into the church after Constantine.

> Here on the outer fringe of the church was a place where the
> older vision was kept alive. Here men still remembered that

grace costs, that grace means following Christ. Here they left
all they had for Christ's sake, and endeavored daily to practice.[2]

Bonhoeffer added that the false turn came when the church represented monasticism "as an individual achievement which the mass of the laity could not be expected to emulate."

> By thus limiting the application of the commandments of
> Jesus to a restricted group of specialists, the Church evolved
> the fatal conception of the double standard—a maximum and
> a minimum standard of Christian obedience. . . . [T]he fatal
> error of monasticism lay not so much in its rigorism (though
> even here there was a good deal of misunderstanding . . .) as
> in the extent to which it departed from genuine Christianity by
> setting up itself as the individual achievement of a select few,
> and so claiming a special merit of its own.[3]

The way of the cross turned into something marginal, something radical, and so Jesus's basic, normal way was sidelined throughout most of the church. Jesus's way diverged from the "normal" Christian way. Jesus's path somehow became freakish. The Sermon on the Mount was tamed and declawed.

And, strangely, none of these results should be surprising. Jesus predicted this marginalizing of himself within the church. After all, he gave all those famous warnings about the "narrow way." What other words have been so ignored and explained away? Sure, some Christian traditions, way-of-the-cross traditions understood these passages, at least in part. But most of our traditions have to twist and turn to get away from that pointed warning in order to make the faith fit with Western notions of bigness and success. Wall Street can't do anything in a narrow way.

What could be more straightforward, though? "Narrow is the gate and difficult is the way which leads to life, and there are few who find it" (Matt 7:14). This language should always and immediately make us skeptical of the huge manifestations of "Christianity," whether it's evangelical academic institutions, sprawling megachurches, or St. Peter's Basilica. Something is amiss. It doesn't mean that God can't work through whatever the broad way is, but, at least, we shouldn't grant automatic awe to these expressions. They are most likely misleading.

2. Ibid., 46.

3. Ibid., 47.

To explain the "narrow way," Jesus added that premonition of his own future sidelining: "Many will say to Me in that day, 'Lord, Lord, have we not prophesied in Your name, cast out demons in Your name, and done many wonders in Your name?' And then I will declare to them, 'I never knew you; depart from Me, you who practice lawlessness!'" (Matt 7:22, 23). In other words, they missed it. They were doing good, churchy things, even supernatural things, but these Christians missed Jesus's way. The "many" will do all sorts of broad-path behavior, even activities of the Spirit—preaching, prophesying, exorcism, and miracles. The many even have some manifestations of God's Spirit working on their side, and yet they have missed the way of Jesus. Missed it completely, notice. Again, Jesus's way isn't obscure. After all, his warning comes at the end of the Sermon on the Mount. That's the way of the cross, when it's not been suppressed and gutted. In my circles, we got pretty good at dismissing the narrow-way passages, and I'll return to interact with those moves in the second part of the book.

Dostoevsky offered one of the most telling explanations about the sidelining of the way of the cross in his presentation of the Grand Inquisitor in the *Brothers Karamazov*. Dostoevsky puts the story in the mouth of the atheistic brother, Ivan, and uses it with great irony as an attack on Christ. In Ivan's story, Christ returns to earth during the height of the Spanish Inquisition. The head of the Inquisition, the Grand Inquisitor, recognizes Jesus walking around the town and has him arrested. In prison, the Grand Inquisitor tells Jesus that he will burn him at the stake as the worst heretic. Why? Because, after 1500 years, the church had finally fixed Jesus's *mistake*. Jesus's error, says the Grand Inquisitor, was requiring too much freedom and responsibility from his followers. In Satan's temptation, Christ had repudiated all the ways that constrain freedom— miracle of bread, mystery of faith, and the power of domination. Instead of such terrible freedom, the church had given Christ's followers happiness. Instead of the way of the cross, the church had relieved believers of the burdens of responsibility, conscience, disciplines, of going against the cultural grain, and given them the happiness of rule-following.

In the midst of the account,[4] the Grand Inquisitor tells Jesus, "you overestimated mankind." "Man is created weaker and baser that you thought him!" "It was impossible to leave them in greater confusion and torment than you did, abandoning them to so many cares and insoluble

4. Dostoevsky, *Brothers Karamazov*, 249ff.

problems. Thus you yourself laid the foundation for the destruction of your own kingdom." That's why the church has "corrected your deed."

The Grand Inquisitor recognizes the centrality of Satan's temptation of Christ. Christians often take that temptation as trivial filler. But the Inquisitor sees that "now that fifteen centuries have gone by, we can see that in these three questions everything was so precisely divined and foretold, and has proved so completely true, that to add to them or subtract anything from them is impossible."

Christ rejected the three central offers "that would have furnished all that man seeks on earth, that is: someone to bow down to, someone to take over his conscience, and a means for uniting everyone at last into a common, concordant, and incontestable anthill."

The church fixed that misdeed. Instead of the way of the cross and its frightening freedom, the church created an easier way that delivered the masses "from their great care and their present terrible torments of personal and free decision." And at the last day, the easy-way church will stand strong against Jesus and say "Judge us if you can and dare." The Grand Inquisitor ends with the telling observation to Jesus, "I joined the host of those who have *corrected your deed.* I left the proud and returned to the humble, for the happiness of the humble. What I am telling you will come true, and our kingdom will be established. Tomorrow, I repeat, you will see this obedient flock, which at my first gesture will rush to heap hot coals around your stake, as which I shall burn you for having come to interfere with us."

So, what exactly is this narrow way of life, this way of the cross? Notice, first, that Jesus characterized it as a *way*, a path, a road on which we travel and do things. A way is biased toward action rather than mere thinking. For most of us, being a Christian has meant holding Christian ideas in our heads. Christianity is just a view, a worldview by which we judge everything else. Sure, these ideas also serve as rules and shape some of our behavior, but for the most part we live the typical middle-class life, with all its worries, activities, and rituals—all the things Jesus warned us against.

We first find the language of a "way" describing Jesus's mission at his birth. Jesus was said to be the one who will "guide our feet into the way of peace" (Luke 1:79). Others acknowledged that he taught "the way of God" (Matt 22:16; Luke 20:21). Jesus himself observed that John the Baptist also taught "the way of righteousness" (Matt 21:32). But "difficult is the way" (Matt 7:14). And he who entered "some other way" was a thief (John 10:1). Most importantly, Jesus said, "I am the way" (John 14:6).

In the book of Acts, the language of the "way" does more work. The word grows and becomes a label for the whole gospel of Christ. Paul was said to be hunting "any who were of the Way, whether men or women" (Acts 9:2). He confessed that he "persecuted this Way to the death" (Acts 22:4). Apollos knew something of the "way of the Lord" (Acts 18:25), but Aquila and Priscilla "took him aside and explained to him the way of God more" (Acts 18:26). In Ephesus, opponents "spoke evil of the Way" (Acts 19:9) and later "there arose a great commotion about the Way" (Acts 19:23). Before the governor, Paul explained that he worshiped the God of his fathers, "according to the Way which they call a sect" (Acts 24:14), and, after Paul's explanation, Felix had a "more accurate knowledge of the Way" (Acts 24:22). As ancient Christians understood it, a way suggests a journey of transformation, with steps and maturing of soul and community. In contrast, one can embrace a system of belief and never mature, except in fine-tuning of doctrines. As many have noted, a system of belief is different than a way of transformation. Most of us rest happy within a system of belief, century after century.

For the apostle Paul, the whole message of the Way gets summarized in terms of the cross of Christ: "I determined not to know anything among you except Jesus Christ and Him crucified" (1 Cor 2:2). For many Christians, Paul's claim simply means he's only concerned with blood atonement. But in context, Paul hasn't been talking about blood or forgiveness at all. He's been discussing weakness. In fact, just following his claim about Christ crucified, Paul explains it as social "weakness" (1 Cor 2:3), not atonement.

What is the way of the cross, then? It is first and foremost a genuine way, a course of action, not merely a set of ideas. And, as noted, it's a course of action that has been recognized with marvelous consistency across many centuries and traditions and denominations. Agreement over the basic way of the cross is certainly a miracle. But as noted, it's not hard to see. It's just the Sermon on the Mount taken seriously. It should be obvious. Dietrich Bonhoeffer's life began to open up to him when he realized this.

In 1935, Bonhoeffer wrote his brother about how his theological studies had turned from mere academic work to "something completely different from that."

I now believe I know at least that I am at least on the right
track—for the first time in my life. And that often makes me
very glad . . . I believe I know that inwardly I shall be really
clear and honest only when I have begun to take seriously the
Sermon on the Mount. Here is set the only source of power
capable of exploding the whole enchantment and specter [Hit-
ler and his rule]. . . . The restoration of the church will surely
come from a sort of new monasticism which has in common
with the old only the uncompromising attitude of a life lived
according to the Sermon on the Mount in the following of
Christ. I believe it is now time to call people to this.[5]

For Bonhoeffer, and many others in the way of the cross tradition, we see
this move, a shift of the Sermon on the Mount and Sermon on the Plain
from being peripheral, afterthoughts to standing at the center. And the
whole Christian world shifts around a new axis.

Expositors of the way of the cross have explained it in many ways,
often in bits and pieces. I had a hard time finding something attempting
a more comprehensive summary of it, so that's what I'm trying. Other
advocates will and have chosen other language or categories to do so. But
it's basically the same thing. I'll summarize the way of the cross in terms
of seven subordinate ways that make it up. Here is the basic list, and later
sections of the book will trace each of these ways through scripture.

The way of the cross is made up of these paths:

Way of Weakness: In the history of his saving work, the Lord primarily and regularly works through various kinds of human weakness rather
than through power and wealth. He uses the aged, the lame, the enslaved,
the few, the poor, the women, the shameful ones. This doesn't mean that
God excludes the powerful, wealthy, and "healthy" (Luke 5:31). These
just aren't the focus of God's reign. Most importantly, death on the cross
in the first century was a despised and shameful way of death. It was the
way Romans utterly humiliated and killed the hope of those hoping to
resist its rule. The way of the cross, then, sides, first, with the weak and
shameful. Everything begins around this.

Way of Renunciation: From Eden to Revelation, the continuous
enemy of God's work is some incarnation of the spirit of domination,
selfishness, power, greed, ostentation, pageantry, exceptionalism, and
greatness—way of the Serpent, Sodom, Canaan, Egypt, Assyria, Babylon,
Persia, Greece, Rome, and all those who kiss up to them. Jesus labels this

5. Kelly and Nelson, *Bonhoeffer*, 424.

demonic mixture "Mammon" and "the World." The evil of Mammon is not money itself, but the broader cult of domination, unsacrificial wealth, violence, and greatness. The way of the cross continually renounces the delicious ways of Mammon and seeks to overthrow all its expressions. But modern life glorifies domination, selfish wealth, and greatness.

Way of Deliverance: The chief goal of God's work is not to populate heaven with holy thinkers but to create a living, holy community on earth, and this means that the main thrust of God's work, from the start, has been to deliver people from the various oppressions of Mammon, both fleshly and spiritual. Without neglecting any subordinate duties and callings, God's people aim first and foremost to emancipate enemies and friends from the domination of sin, demons, and the perennial rulers of Mammon. The way of the cross is the continual mission of Exodus. It takes seriously—"mercy, not sacrifice."

Way of Sharing: The earth is the Lord's, and Father, Son, and Spirit give life and freedom to one another. Once delivered, God's people incarnate God's life of sharing by sacrificial living so that all in the community have enough, a sharing that characterized original sabbath life—"Every man had gathered according to each one's need" (Exod 16:18), demanded by the prophets (Isa 58), revived by Christ and the apostles—"distributed to each as anyone had need" (Acts 4:35), and pictured in the Lord's Supper. But modern Western life is not organized around self-denial and sacrifice. We're happy to do generosity on the side, giving out of our abundance, but Jesus rejected the life of charity.

Way of Enemy Love: God is love, and he is also patient, training his Old Covenant people out of the one-time relevant but immature ways of violence, hatred, and war against enemies into the new life of loving our enemies, blessing not cursing, and overcoming evil with good—the "way of peace" and peacemaking. The way of the cross does "not war according to the flesh. For the weapons of our warfare are not carnal but mighty" (2 Cor 10:3, 4). Modern life rushes to bow to the god Mars, calling on us to respect and support the butchery and enslavement of civilians and manufactured enemies.

Way of the Foolishness: The way of Mammon or the World appears undeniable, rational, effective, superior, but the way of the cross recognizes that God works in mysterious, unpredictable, and surprising ways. It takes a special way of seeing to understand the unpredictable truth of God's ways. This way of perceiving contrary to common sense, scripture calls "faith." It is a perception of "unseen things" and a way of walking "not by sight." This contrary-to-sight perception distinguishes the great heroes of the faith, like Abraham, the prophets, Christ, and the apostles. Faith is not just a belief in a supernatural truth or an easy way into heaven, but a costly way of living contrary to the World—"do not be conformed to this world, but be transformed" (Rom 12:2). Faith is not simply believing that Jesus is the divine savior but a total way of life, a way opposed to the seemingly obvious and automatic rules of the World and Mammon.

Way of Community: The way of the cross thrives only in a dedicated body of believers, not heroic individuals. Jesus has delegated his mission on earth to his body, the church, the center of worship and effective ceremony. The way of the cross fails if it is not lived in community. It is not designed for loners. Jesus's way assumes a community of love and commitment and burden bearing. It requires great sacrifice and self-denial out of love for others in the body. The way of the cross is deeply communal because, in the end, it seeks to incarnate the love and loyalty of Father, Son, and Spirit on earth. The way of the cross seeks to make Trinity here and now. That is God's mission for us.

But these paths are not my life. (Yet.) The way of the cross is not the typical middle-class, Christian way. In fact it's at odds with it. A church that lived this way would quickly undermine everything dear to our way of life—mortgages, jobs with no kingdom relevance, the assumption of constant ease, military glories, clothing made by wage-slaves, being the greatest among our peers, and the cool relief of blindness. The great Christian observer Nikolai Berdyaev once noted, that typical, Christian, middle-class life is "dominated by money and social position [and] a complete disregard of the human personality." It is

> the fortress of virtues, principles, patriotism, family, property, Church, State, morality. It can also be the champion of freedom, equality, and fraternity. But such falsehood and falsification are a most terrible manifestation of universal evil. The devil is a liar. Thus a negation of spirit must masquerade itself as a defense of spirit, atheism may assume the form of a piety, a contempt for freedom and equality may manifest itself as a championship of them.[6]

Now, so far this is mere assertion. You're simply not allowed to believe it. But that's not the question. The question isn't whether middle-class life is a manifestation of the cult of Mammon. The question is *would you*

---

6. Berdyaev, *Spirit*, 110.

be willing to give it up if it were? What if becoming a follower of Christ actually required you to give up your modest middle-class life? Would you follow him? What if Christ required you to take on a life of shame and disapproval by contemporary criteria? Would you do it? That's not the sort of question we're used to hearing. But it was a common challenge from Jesus. And not just for one, lone rich young ruler.

Jesus repeatedly called his followers to take up their crosses. We have to remember he did this before his disciples even knew he would end up on a cross. Most often, we understand "taking up our cross" to mean that, yes, we have to bear with modern, middle-class frustrations and anxieties, our burdens. Bills and children. Sigh. We automatically soften the edges of Christ's challenge, but first-century disciples couldn't. "'Crucify that slave,' says the wife. . . . 'What a fool you are! Do you call a slave a man?'"[7] Cicero famously observed, "[T]he very word 'cross' should be far removed not only from the person of a Roman citizen but from this thoughts, his eyes and his ears. . . . Indeed, the very mention of [it], that is unworthy of a Roman citizen and a free man."[8] "Riches buy off judgment, and the poor are condemned to the cross."[9]

In the first century, execution on a cross meant gross public shame. It was, after all, the "slave's punishment."[10] To take up your cross, then, meant embracing public and political shame and class humiliation. It meant embracing the full scorn of Mammon. It meant that whoever the strong and wealthy ruling powers were, they would find you weak, pathetic, foolish, tiresome, and useless. That's what Jesus called his disciples to—a ridiculous counterculture, not respected, not a mover-and-shaker, impressively credentialed, and cool.

"Do you not know that friendship with the world is enmity with God?" (James 4:4). As Bonhoeffer chided, "The world goes on in the same old way. . . . [L]et the Christian live like the rest of the world, let him model himself on the world's standards in every sphere of life, and not presumptuously aspire to live a different life under grace from his old life under sin."[11] Middle-class Christians automatically translate such exhortations into questions about Christian ideas alone. Sure, we say, we have

7. Cited in Hengel, *Crucifixion*, 58.
8. Ibid., 42.
9. Ibid., 60.
10. Ibid., 51ff.
11. Bonhoeffer, *Cost*, 44.

very different ideas than the secularists and evolutionists and "liberals." We even say things just to drive liberals crazy. It's fun to offend secularists, some even say. That's our way of the cross. Count us in. We believe crazy things, but that's the limit of being countercultural. We still work, advertise, and seek profit like everyone else. We cheer smart bombs and want sharp houses, just like the rest. We're not crazy, after all. We're proud to believe crazy things. We dare not side with slaves. We dare not lose our middle-class respectability.

"If anyone desires to come after Me, let him deny himself, and take up his cross daily, and follow Me. For whoever desires to save his life will lose it, but whoever loses his life for My sake will save it" (Luke 9:23).

"And he who does not take his cross and follow after Me is not worthy of Me. He who finds his life will lose it, and he who loses his life for My sake will find it" (Matt 10:38,39).

"If anyone desires to come after Me, let him deny himself, and take up his cross, and follow Me. For whoever desires to save his life will lose it, but whoever loses his life for My sake will find it. (Matt 16:24,25; cf. Mark 8:34)

"Then Jesus, looking at him, loved him, and said to him, 'One thing you lack: Go your way, sell whatever you have and give to the poor, and you will have treasure in heaven; and come, take up the cross, and follow Me'" (Mark 10:21).

"And whoever does not bear his cross and come after Me cannot be My disciple" (Luke 14:27).

"I determined not to know anything among you except Jesus Christ and Him crucified" (1 Cor 2:2).

He who does not take on the scorn and shame of Mammon is not worthy of Me. And that's just what happened in the early and later church. Those who embraced the way of the cross—the way of weakness, renunciation, deliverance, sharing, enemy love, foolishness, and community—have produced joy and rich community and fierce persecution. Just as Jesus promised.

Now I'll work through some of the biblical evidence for each of the ways that make up the way of the cross.

2

The Way of Weakness

"The quest may be attempted by the weak with as much hope as the strong. Yet such is oft the course of deeds that move the wheels of the world: small hands do them because they must, while the eyes of the great are elsewhere."

—Gandalf, *Fellowship of the Ring*

"Let us work with a new love in service of the poor, looking for the most destitute and abandoned among them. Let us recognize that before God they are our Lords and masters, and we are unworthy to render them our small services."

—St. Vincent de Paul

Nero's chief advisor, Seneca, urged the young Roman emperor to speak this way: "Have I of all mortals found favour with heaven and been chosen to serve on earth as vicar of the gods? I am the arbiter of life and death for the nations; it rests in my power what each man's lot and state shall be: by my lips fortune proclaims what gift she would bestow on each human being: from my utterance peoples and cities gather reasons for rejoicing; without my favour and grace no part of the whole world can prosper."[12]

Conservative historian William Russel Mead cheered the United States in a similar, more modern way, describing the U.S. as "a society that is ruthlessly practical in the way that everything gets reduced to profit and loss. It's Darwinian. The winners become more powerful. . . . The choice we give people is either you learn to play our game by our rules or you get left behind and become impotent and poor. . . . We are still the best thing going."[13]

Jesus instituted a vastly different kind of kingdom. He called for a kingdom of weakness in contrast to the way of power and domination. As the Lord told Paul, "My strength is made perfect in weakness" (2 Cor 12:9). Paul elaborated this way of weakness for the Corinthians:

> For you see your calling, brethren, that not many wise according to the flesh, not many mighty, not many noble, are called. But God has chosen the foolish things of the world to put to shame the wise, and God has chosen the weak things of the world to put to shame the things which are mighty; and the base things of the world and the things which are despised God has chosen, and the things which are not, to bring to nothing the things that are, that no flesh should glory in His presence. (1 Cor 1:26–29)

Not the powerful or wealthy. God has chosen weak things for his kingdom. God has chosen despised things on which to focus his work. We often quickly spiritualize or intellectualize this text. We turn it into a claim about Christian ideas and how Christian ideas might seem foolish in a secular culture. But Paul talked about actual people in Christ's kingdom, those there in the Corinthian congregations. He asked them to look around and notice that the other people with them were not highly educated, powerful, aristocratic, cool, or prestigious. Instead, they were drawn primarily from the underclass—the weak—the same sort of underclass that followed Jesus around (Matt. 4:24, 25).

But Paul wasn't introducing something new by saying that God sided with weakness. It wasn't even something introduced by the New Testament. It started at the Fall.

---

12. Wengst, *Pax*, 47.

13. Mead, PBS, May 23, 2003.

Three persons received curses at the Fall, but one took more of a back seat—Adam, the male. God cursed Adam with toilsome work and sweat. But the central conflict in all of history was symbolized as a battle between Satan and Eve, Satan and bodily weakness. We might expect God to fight his enemy by means of his best masculine fighters, those with serious upper-body strength. But no. "I will put enmity between you and the woman, and between your seed and her seed" (Gen 3:15). Eve would struggle as Israel and the church. The symbolism of Adam seems to be almost completely left out of this great redemptive struggle to come. God identified his people in terms of a woman, a woman who would later produce a very new and different kind of Adam.

Centuries later, when God worked through a new Eve, he chose even more weakness. He chose a poor peasant woman, Mary. And Mary knew God's preference for weakness. Through her, she realized, God "has put down the mighty from their thrones, and exalted the lowly. He has filled the hungry with good things, and the rich He has sent away empty" (Luke 1:52,53).

The theme of weakness shows itself in the connection between Eve and Mary, but not just there. We see it clearly in the patriarchs of Genesis, beginning with Abraham. Often, we too easily classify Abraham as a rich man in modern terms, but he wouldn't have stood out that way in his time. To be rich in Abraham's time, you needed to have the power of permanence, the wealth to stay in one place, preferably with a giant pyramid. The rich didn't wander the Middle East like gypsies. In fact, Yahweh's initial call of Abram to abandon his home would have sounded as frightening as Jesus's call "whoever of you does not forsake all that he has cannot be My disciple" (Luke 14:33).

Ancient wealth lay in one's inheritance. It waited in a father's house. And that is what the Lord called Abram to give up: "Get out of your country, from your family, and from your father's house" (Gen 12:1). God called Abram to break from all the safety and security of his inheritance. He called Abram to weakness. The book of Hebrews highlighted this, too: "By faith Abraham obeyed when he was called to go out to the place which he would receive as an inheritance" (Heb 11:8). It was a call to ancient poverty, to travel without a home in the way Jesus would later do—"Foxes have holes and birds of the air have nests, but the Son of Man has nowhere to lay His head" (Matt 8:20).

Certainly Abram had possessions, but those alone didn't make him rich. Notice, even with the limited possessions mentioned in Genesis 12,

Abraham still ran out of simple necessities like food. The truly rich didn't run out of food. Instead, Abram fled to the truly wealthy and substantial country, Egypt, to find food (Gen 12:10). Next to the wealth of Pharaoh, Abram was weak and vulnerable. Abram had to guard his life with a half-truth about his wife. It is only after this encounter that the Lord started seriously adding to Abram's wealth, and it was wealth that God transferred from rich rulers to the weaker Abram (Gen 13:2).

Abraham revealed the relative weakness of God not only in his interactions with Pharaoh and King Abimelech but also in his choices. When conflict broke out between Abraham's herdsmen and his nephew Lot's, Abraham proposed dividing into different lands, and Abraham didn't demand the better land. Lot "lifted his eyes and saw all the plain of Jordan, that it was well watered everywhere. . . like the garden of the LORD" (Gen 13:10), and Lot took the better land. In a similar lack of greed, later, when Abraham rescued Lot's family (Gen 14), Abraham refused a reward for the deliverance. The king of Sodom tried to give Abraham riches, but Abraham replied, "I have raised my hand to the LORD, God Most High, the Possessor of heaven and earth, that I will take nothing, from a thread to a sandal strap, and that I will not take anything that is yours, lest you should say, 'I have made Abram rich'" (Gen 14:22, 23).

But the larger focus on Abram's weakness showed in his old age: "And Abram was seventy-five years old when he departed from Haran" (Gen 12:4). Paul highlighted Abram's weakness in terms of a dead body: "And not being weak in faith, [Abraham] did not consider his own body, already dead (since he was about a hundred years old), and the deadness of Sarah's womb" (Rom 4:19). God's strength would be revealed through the weakness of old age.

On top of these forms of weakness, Abraham had great love for gross sinners. Perhaps he was too merciful. Even after the Lord reminded Abraham of Sodom and Gomorrah's great sin—"their sin is very grave" (Gen 18:20)—Abraham interceded and sought mercy for some of them. He even had the beautiful boldness to remind God of his own standards— "Far be it from You to do such a thing as this, to slay the righteous with the wicked, so that the righteous should be as the wicked; far be it from You! Shall not the Judge of all the earth do right?" (Gen 18:25).

All these weaknesses together made Abraham a special friend of God. His initial giving up of his wealth and security, his relative weakness before kings, his weakness of age, his deliverance of the enslaved, his generosity and lack of greed, and his too soft mercy combined to mark

Abraham as a man given to God's way of weakness. Because of this, by Jesus's time, Abraham had been seen as the patron saint of weakness and poverty. When Jesus told the story of the poor man, Lazarus, and the rich man who dismissed the way of weakness, we see the poor man after his death in the embrace of none other than Abraham. Weakness had joined with weakness. And Abraham's hard exhortation to the powerful man reflected Abraham's own priorities: "Son, remember that in your lifetime you received your good things, and likewise Lazarus evil things; but now he is comforted and you are tormented" (Luke 16:25). Abraham comforted the weak against the wealthy. Did Abraham reach the levels of weakness that culminate in Jesus? No. Abraham was no homeless foot-washer, like Jesus. But he pointed in the direction of Jesus. He was the beginning of a trajectory that gets clearer and clearer. God begins dealing with us where we are.

Abraham set an early model of weakness, but God continued to fill out that picture more and more throughout redemptive history. Among the patriarchs, God chose Isaac, the son of old age, over Ishmael, the "wild man" and fighter whose "hand shall be against every man, and every man's hand against him" (Gen 16:12). Then Isaac himself had two sons, one of which, Esau—"by your sword you shall live" (Gen 27:40)—and Esau would be the father of a people "stronger" than his brother's descendants. Yet, the weaker, smoother brother, Jacob, would rule over the older brother, Esau (Gen 25:23; 27:40). The last would be first. Then the weaker brother, Jacob, would serve as a slave for fourteen years to win his wife. And in Jacob's holy wrestling, God explicitly weakened him, touching "the socket of his hip; and the socket of Jacob's hip was out of joint. . . . and he limped on his hip" (Gen 32:25, 31). Then Jacob's one-time youngest son, Joseph, was seemingly conquered by his stronger, older brothers and sold into slavery. But again the last would be first because God raised Joseph out of slavery to rule Egypt and deliver his stronger brothers from death. Later, when Joseph's two sons were to receive a blessing from their grandfather Jacob, Jacob followed God's weakness habit and blessed the younger in place of the older. Joseph objected to making the last first, but Jacob explained, "I know, my son, I know. He also shall become a people, and he also shall be great; but truly his younger brother shall be greater than he" (Gen 48:19). From this angle, Genesis becomes the opening story showing how "God has chosen the weak things of the world to put to shame the things which are mighty" (1 Cor 1:27).

The story of weakness doesn't end in Genesis, though. The book of Exodus starts with God's people in a very weak condition. God's people were in the lowest social class—slaves—"the children of Israel groaned because of the bondage, and they cried out; and their cry came up to God because of the bondage" (Exod 2:23), and God Himself had planned for them to be there (Gen 15:13, 14), even using Joseph to enslave much of Egypt (Gen 47:13–25). Even with all of Joseph's power, God used him to create a people enslaved and weak.

Given Joseph's high authority, God could have easily had his people installed in the Egyptian hierarchy for centuries. He could have moved them to rule all aspects of Egyptian life, triumph in their power, construct great buildings, and dominate the Middle East militarily. But instead, he chose for them the path of slavery and weakness. And He would remind them of their slavery throughout the rest of their history.

We also see the path of weakness in the choice of Moses as leader. His life began not in nobility but in a desperate, bulrush basket, an act of his mother and sister, another instance of the promise to Eve about the triumph of women's weakness (Gen 3:15). Sarah and Rebekah had served in this role earlier, sustaining God's promise through old age and cunning, and in Exodus we find it in the midwives' civil disobedience, as well as the scheming of Moses's mother and sister.

Born to a slave family, Moses rose to the highest ranks among the Egyptian elites, only to flee in exile and shame when he tried the way of power and killed an Egyptian oppressor. Pharaoh didn't appreciate this and, in turn, "sought to kill Moses" (Exod 2:15). In short, the Lord changed Moses from a privileged Egyptian elite into a shamed exile.

In the ensuing struggle between slaves and exceptional power, the Lord sided with the slaves. The Lord had "heard their cry because of their taskmasters" and known their "sorrows," so he came to "deliver them out of the hand of the Egyptians" (Exod 3:7). The Israelites, at that time, were certainly no grand prize. The Israelites were already entranced with Egyptian gods (Ezek 20:5ff), even in their slavery. Everything in Egypt's culture pointed to the truth that the highest powers of the universe sided with the triumphs of Pharaoh and strength. Even the Israelites must have believed that cultural propaganda. So step-by-step, plague-by-plague, the Lord turned Egypt upside down and made the last, first and the first, last. The slaves walked out of Egypt with riches, and the rich and powerful sank, drowned under the waters of the sea.

The books of Deuteronomy and Joshua continue God's favoring of the weak. The whole invasion of Canaan is sometimes portrayed as a superpower genocide of the poor villages of Canaan. But Moses described it differently. The Israelites were the weak pastoralists taking on a Canaan full of powerful cities and militaries. The Hittites and others, Moses said, were "seven nations greater and mightier than you" (Deut 7:1). Canaanite cities resembled those of Mesopotamia, in which a bureaucracy "hoarded wealth" and "became an upper class of power and prestige which could oppress the lower classes and use the wealth for personal gain." Canaanite cities "favored the accumulation of wealth" in which, typically, "a wide gap developed between upper-class rich and lower-class poor. Land proprietors did not forgive debts" and "slaves were retained permanently."[14]

Then Moses added, even more explicitly, "The Lord did not set His love on you nor choose you because you were more in number than any other people, for you were the least of all peoples" (Deut 7:7). This divine preference for the least or the weakest foreshadows Jesus's language that "he who is least in the kingdom of God is greater than he" (Luke 7:28).

In various ways, the preference for weakness shows up among Israelite's judges, too. God's dealings with Gideon stood out as the most explicit and symbolic picture of the divine slogan "My strength is made perfect in weakness" (2 Cor 12:19). God had raised up the Midianites to oppress the Israelites for their unfaithfulness, and Gideon complained to the Lord's angel about this—"Did not the LORD bring us up from Egypt? But now the LORD has forsaken us and delivered us into the hands of the Midianites" (Judg 6:13). The angel told Gideon that God had called him to save the Israelites from Midianite oppression. But Gideon responded weakly: "he said to Him, "O my Lord, how can I save Israel? Indeed my clan is the weakest in Manasseh, and I am the least in my father's house." Another Moses. The reader can predict which way this deliverance will go.

Gideon moved against the Midianites with around thirty-two thousand Israelites, but the Lord objected that that was too many for the way of weakness. So the Lord told Gideon, "The people who are with you are too many for Me to give the Midianites into their hands, lest Israel claim glory for itself against Me, saying, 'My own hand has saved me'" (Judg 7:2). By a series of criteria, Gideon whittled his forces from thirty-two thousand to a mere three hundred. Then Gideon overcame

14. Gnuse, *Steal*, 56.

the oppressors by the foolishness of noisemaking. That's the Lord's way, and it also served as a picture of the coming shift between Old and New Covenants, a shift from military means to a lack of material weapons.

Israel cycled through phases of idolatry, oppression, and divine deliverance, again and again, and they grew weary of the way of weakness, weary of their calling as the weakest and "least of all peoples" (Deut 7:7). They desired to be an exceptional nation, full of worldly power and triumph. But the book, 1 Samuel, where the Lord, with sadness, allowed his people to pursue the path of power, begins with one last voice for the way of weakness, a woman's voice, of course. Hannah knew the ways of the Lord, and the Lord finally answered her prayers and gave her Samuel, a prophet and last judge for Israel. When Hannah weaned her son and dedicated him to the Lord, she sang of God's special favor for the weak, in a way that foreshadowed Mary, centuries later, a song of how the last will be made first:

> The bows of the mighty men are broken,
>   And those who stumbled are girded with strength.
>
> Those who were full have hired themselves out for bread,
>
> And the hungry have ceased to hunger. . . .
> He raises the poor from the dust
> And lifts the beggar from the ash heap,
> To set them among princes
> And make them inherit the throne of glory. (1 Sam 2:4, 8)

Hannah's son Samuel grew up into the offices of prophet and judge, and he even led Israel through another of those weakness battles, in which the Israelites didn't have to fight at all, where the Lord overcame the enemy Philistines, with thunder and fear (1 Samuel 7).

In their idolatry, though, the Israelites grew weary of miraculous, glory-less battles and called on Samuel to give them worldly power and pomp like the pagan nations around them—they wanted a true Middle-Eastern king. A carnal military was much more visible and realistic than Yahweh's mysterious magic.

The Israelites spoke frankly to Samuel, saying, "Look, you are old, and your sons do not walk in your ways. Now make us a king to judge us like all the nations" (1 Sam 8:5). This displeased Samuel, but the Lord wanted to allow it. The Lord explained that Israel's insult was not directed at Samuel: "Heed the voice of the people in all that they say to you; for they have not rejected you, but they have rejected Me, that I should not reign over them" (1 Sam 8:7). The Lord even warned them of the tyranny such kings will inflict upon the Israelites—forced military and royal service, land confiscations, increased taxation—"And you will cry out in that day because of your king whom you have chosen for yourselves, and the LORD will not hear you in that day" (1 Sam 8:18). But the people were entranced with the way of strength: "No, but we will have a king over us, that we also may be like all the nations, and that our king may judge us and go out before us and fight our battles" (1 Sam 8:19, 20). Note, they specifically wanted battles of visible strength.

This whole episode cast a shadow over all the history of Israel's kings, even the good ones. The Lord never repeals his lament "They have rejected Me," and it frames the whole interlude of the kings. Samuel certainly didn't forget it. At the coronation of Israel's first king, Samuel mentioned the dark shadow of the people's choice once again:

> Then Samuel called the people together to the LORD at Mizpah, and said to the children of Israel, "Thus says the LORD God of Israel: 'I brought up Israel out of Egypt, and delivered you from the hand of the Egyptians and from the hand of all kingdoms and from those who oppressed you.' But you have today rejected your God, who Himself saved you from all your adversities and your tribulations; and you have said to Him, 'No, set a king over us!'" (1 Sam 10:17–19)

In the narrative, the symbolism changed instantly. Instead of symbols of weakness, we see Saul—"taller than any of the people from his shoulders upward. . . . You see there is no one like him among all the people? So all the people shouted and said, 'Long live the king!'" (1 Sam 10:23, 24).

It's true, the Lord wanted and planned for a king (Deuteronomy 17), but that was a king of weakness, without a great military or wealth (Deut 17:16ff.), unlike the Israelite kings who regularly imitated the forbidden kingship of Egypt (Deut 17:16). In fact, we learn later, the king the Lord ultimately sought was King Jesus, the master of the way of weakness. Jesus is the truest standard of kingship, and all the Old Testament kings failed to meet his model. Along the way, though, we see the hints of the way of weakness even among the kings, especially, with King David.

David certainly seemed to be God's favorite person in the Old Covenant, "a man after God's own heart" (Acts 13:22), and yet even David didn't ultimately embrace Christ's way of kingship, though David saw through a glass darkly at times. David himself started off as a picture of weakness. The Lord rejected all David's older and stronger brothers since the Lord did at their appearance or "physical stature" (1 Sam 16:7).

We see the way of weakness clearly in David's courage against Goliath. Just as God used Abraham's weakness of age, so He used David's weakness of youth. Carnal Saul judged by the eye of strength: "You are not able to go against this Philistine to fight with him; for you are a youth, and he a man of war from his youth" (1 Sam 17:33). Goliath, too, dismissed David's weakness: "Am I a dog, that you come to me with sticks?" (1 Sam 17:43). Still, David grew even weaker. He abandoned the armor given him and slung a stone through the giant's forehead. In the midst of all this, David confessed the way of weakness: "Then all this assembly shall know that the LORD does not save with sword and spear" (1 Sam 17:47).

We also see the way weakness in David's best, later moments, in the Psalms. David seemed to have something of an obsession with the weak and poor. It stood out because it contrasted with much in the age of the kings who acted so much like Pharaohs.

> But you, O God, do see trouble and grief;
> you consider it to take it in hand.
> The victim commits himself to you;
> you are the helper of the fatherless. (Ps 10:14)

> "For the oppression of the poor, for the sighing of the needy,
> Now I will arise," says the LORD. (Ps 12:5)

> I know that the LORD will maintain
> The cause of the afflicted,
> And justice for the poor. (Ps 140:12)

During the abject failure of the experiment with the kings, the Lord raised up his prophets, who, like David and Moses, had a special focus on the oppression of Israel's weak and poor. We often tend unwittingly to think of the prophets as coming after the era of kings, but that's an illusion of a table of contents. God raised up the prophets as a constant, corrective voice against the kings. The prophets are God's voice against the way of the kings, the way of power and strength, a way he has permitted and used, even though the whole enterprise remained a perennial expression of "they have rejected Me" (1 Sam 8:7).

Against the oppressions of the various kings and wealthy elites, the Lord spoke through Isaiah, Jeremiah, Ezekiel, Amos, Malachi, and the others. Isaiah told the wealthy, despite their nice, clean worship, their hands were "full of blood" (Isa 1:15) and that they needed to "seek justice, rebuke the oppressor; defend the fatherless, plead for the widow" (Isa 1:17). He told them the "plunder of the poor is in their houses" (Isa 3:14), and that the Lord wanted them to "to share your bread with the hungry, And that you bring to your house the poor who are cast out; when you see the naked, that you cover him" (Isa 58:7).

Similarly, Jeremiah rebuked the kings and wealthy for having "grown fat, they are sleek" while "they do not plead the cause. . . of the fatherless; yet they prosper, and the right of the needy they do not defend. Shall I not punish them for these things?' says the LORD" (Jer 5:28, 29). He ordered them: "do not oppress the stranger, the fatherless, and the widow, and do not shed innocent blood in this place" (Jer 7:6). Ezekiel compared Jerusalem to Sodom, that great pagan city who refused to care for its poor: "Look, this was the iniquity of your sister Sodom: She and her daughter had pride, fullness of food, and abundance of idleness; neither did she strengthen the hand of the poor and needy" (Ezek 16:49). Amos declared that the wealthy "sell the righteous for silver, and the poor for a pair of sandals" (Amos 2:6) and "swallow up the needy, and make the poor of the land fail" (Amos 8:4). Zechariah prophesied, "Execute true justice, show mercy and compassion, do not oppress the widow or the fatherless, the alien or the poor" (Zech 7:9, 10). Malachi warned, "I will come. . . against those who exploit wage earners and widows and orphans, and against those who turn away an alien" (Mal 3:5), and the examples continued. Over and over, the prophets called the people to see and act in terms of Yahweh's way of weakness, his way of making the last, first and the first, last. He wanted the world turned upside down, a revival of the Exodus against the way of power.

In the end, though, Israel did not have the spiritual power or maturity to live the way of weakness (Jer 31:31; Heb 8:8). Israel was God's son, but the Lord needed a new, mature Son after His own heart. The prophets had seen this new Son in the distance. Isaiah saw this coming man who would "not fail nor be discouraged, until He has established justice in the earth. . . . a light to the Gentiles, to open blind eyes, to bring prisoners from prison" (Isa 42:4, 7).

This Jesus most clearly came teaching the way of weakness. Though He was a noble and owned the whole world, with armies of angels at his call, Jesus didn't come with any of those means. Instead, he came with weakness, without prestige and power: He "made Himself of no reputation, taking the form of a bondservant" (Phil 2:7). As the apostle Paul said, "our Lord Jesus Christ, that though He was rich, yet for your sakes He became poor, that you through His poverty might become rich" (2 Cor 8:9). This was nothing new. Abraham, Moses, and the prophets had walked this path. But the way of weakness certainly became more explicit in Jesus.

Jesus described his new political realm on earth as one opposite from the prevailing domination and oppression. In the way that God raised Israelite slaves and lowered Pharaoh, so too, Jesus's kingdom would be a place in which weakness triumphed, where "the first will be last, and the last first" (Matt 19:30; 20:16; Mark 10:31). And Jesus's kingdom would be worldwide in scope: "They will come from the east and the west, from the north and the south, and sit down in the kingdom of God. And indeed there are last who will be first, and there are first who will be last" (Luke 13:29). But Jesus's disciples had a very difficult time in recognizing what a different kingdom Jesus wanted. Throughout Jesus's ministry, his apostles continued blindly to argue among themselves about their own greatness and relevance in the kingdom. One time Jesus asked them what they had been arguing about, "but they kept silent, for on the road they had disputed among themselves who would be the greatest. 'If anyone desires to be first, he shall be last of all and servant of all'" (Mark 9:34, 35).

The way of weakness is opposite the way of fame and relevance. It is to follow Jesus's model, the way of the bondservant, the way of the rich becoming poor to raise others. Jesus began his ministry with offensive claims. He said he didn't bring a universal message for everyone. His kingdom wasn't going to focus on those who were "first" in the eyes of the world. He didn't come to serve the so-called healthy and righteous. Jesus came to focus on the weak. The rich and powerful might come along, too, though it would be very difficult for them to be happy in his kingdom on earth (Matt 19:23).

Jesus stated his concern for the weak and poor most explicitly. In his opening speech, Jesus quoted Isaiah, saying simply that he came "to preach the gospel to the poor" (Luke 4:18). In his Sermon on the Plain, Jesus framed the way of weakness by again focusing on the materially poor and class differences:

> Blessed are you poor,
> For yours is the kingdom of God.
>> Blessed are you who hunger now,
> For you shall be filled. . . .
>> But woe to you who are rich,
> For you have received your consolation.
>> Woe to you who are full,
> For you shall hunger. (Luke 6:20ff)

Jesus wasn't afraid to speak in terms of class differences or to side with the weak and powerless. That's what God had done from the start. It was the way of weakness that characterized Yahweh's distinctness. As James would say later, "Has God not chosen the poor of this world to be rich in faith and heirs of the kingdom which He promised to those who love Him?" (Jas 2:5).

For Jesus, everything revolved around weakness. He didn't spend much time preaching to the wealthy and powerful. He didn't set up seeker-friendly moments to entice the rich to listen while they drank their coffee. He was kind once to a powerful centurion, loving an enemy, but the centurion didn't afterwards follow Jesus around Palestine like the poor and sick did. Jesus overwhelmingly focused his ministry on the poor. In Galilee, Jesus preached "the gospel of the kingdom" and went about "healing all kinds of sickness. . . . They brought to Him all sick people who were afflicted with various diseases and torments, and those who were demon-possessed, epileptics, and paralytics; and He healed them. Great multitudes followed Him." (Luke 4:23, 24).

For a worried John the Baptist, Jesus summarized his work in terms of messianic service to the poor: "Go and tell John the things which you hear and see: The blind see and the lame walk; the lepers are cleansed and the deaf hear; the dead are raised up and the poor have the gospel preached to them. And blessed is he who is not offended because of Me" (Matt 11:4–6). Later, Peter also summarized Jesus's ministry as focused on the oppressed: "God anointed Jesus of Nazareth with the Holy Spirit and with power, who went about doing good and healing all who were oppressed by the devil, for God was with Him" (Acts 10:38).

When the socially powerful Pharisees complained about Jesus eating with sinners and unclean outcasts, Jesus explained, somewhat sarcastically, that his ministry wasn't directed at the strong and healthy, like the well-off Jewish leadership: "Those who are well have no need of a physician, but those who are sick. I have not come to call the righteous, but sinners, to repentance" (Luke 5:31, 32; Mark 2:17). Jesus's "prejudice" against decent "middle-class" folks is hard to hear, and we often ignore it. We insist that the gospel should go to everyone indiscriminately, well, especially those with decent jobs. In most of our middle-class denominations, when we want to plant a church, we generally find a nice, suburban place with enough middle-class families to support a full-time pastor. In other words, we go directly contrary to Jesus's pattern. He went to the unhealthy first. We ignore the weak. He intentionally avoided trying to minister to the wealthy and powerful. They didn't enter his interests much at all. And when they did, he urged them to become second-class citizens in the kingdom, and let the weak and outcast fill the center. "I thank You, Father, Lord of heaven and earth, that You have hidden these things from the wise and prudent and revealed them to babes" (Luke 10:21). James described the work of the wealthy in the church in terms of humiliation: "Let the lowly brother glory in his exaltation, but the rich in his humiliation, because as a flower of the field he will pass away" (Jas 1:9, 10).

The way of weakness isn't just being kind to the poor. It isn't charity. It is identification. It is being united with the poor, as Jesus was. He "made Himself of no reputation" (Phil 2:7). "He became poor" (2 Cor 8:9). Jesus reveals his radical indwelling of the poor, his incarnation as the poor, most strikingly in the notorious and unnerving passage about final judgment in Matthew 25.

> When the Son of Man comes in His glory, and all the holy angels with Him, then He will sit on the throne of His glory. All the nations will be gathered before Him, and He will separate them one from another, as a shepherd divides his sheep from the goats. And He will set the sheep on His right hand, but the goats on the left. Then the King will say to those on His right hand, "Come, you blessed of My Father, inherit the kingdom prepared for you from the foundation of the world: for I was hungry and you gave Me food; I was thirsty and you gave Me drink; I was a stranger and you took Me in; I was naked and you clothed Me; I was sick and you visited Me; I was in prison and you came to Me." (Matt 25:31ff.)

The passage deserves long and thoughtful meditation, but that's beyond my purpose here. It is a passage that has shaken Christians for centuries, at least those willing to take it seriously. Here, Jesus declared so much of what Christians talk about as relatively unimportant. Why didn't he mention key beliefs like justification and regeneration or even atonement?

Jesus's words, here, are the culmination of the way of weakness. In this passage, we see Him in the place of the poor: "For *I* was hungry and you gave *Me* food; *I* was thirsty and you gave *Me* drink; *I* was a stranger and you took *Me* in; *I* was naked and you clothed *Me*." Jesus didn't picture himself as an everyman. He doesn't play the role of the rich noble, the sergeant, the banker. He was the weak one, the one without food, drink, home, and clothing. Jesus is the poor, in this passage, with no guarded qualifications even about the nature of these poor, how they got that way, what mistaken beliefs they hold.

Though Jesus worked as a carpenter for a while, he finally received a slave's execution. He was executed in the manner of the poor, especially lower-class political revolutionaries of the day. Paul said of Christ that "He was crucified in weakness" (2 Cor 3:4). The way of Jesus is the way that puts the last at the center. It allows us rich to be second-class citizens in the kingdom, or less. It is a world turned upside down. "For though He was crucified in weakness, yet He lives by the power of God. For we also are weak in Him, but we shall live with Him by the power of God toward you" (2 Cor 3:4). "My strength is made perfect in weakness" (2 Cor 12:9). "God has chosen the weak things of the world to put to shame the things which are mighty" (1 Cor 1:27). The way of weakness is the way after God's own heart. The way of weakness is the way of the cross.

3

The Way of Renunciation

"Fall'n Cherub, to be weak is miserable."

—BEELZEBUB, *PARADISE LOST*

"In these three questions all of subsequent human history is as if brought together into a single whole and foretold."

—IVAN KARAMAZOV ON SATAN'S TEMPTATION OF CHRIST

The life is in the blood. But U.S. founding father Alexander Hamilton identified money as blood: "Money is, with propriety, considered as the vital principle of the body politic; as that which sustains its life and motion and enables it to perform it most essential functions."[1]

Jesus grew out of a divine root, to a branch, a vine. But financial historian Niall Ferguson explains, "money is the *root* of most progress. . . . [T]he ascent of money has been essential to the ascent of man. . . . [F]inancial innovation has been an indispensable factor in man's advance from wretched subsistence to the giddy heights of material prosperity that so many people know today."[2]

1. Hamilton in Kesler, *Federalist*, 184.
2. Ferguson, *Ascent*, 2. Emphasis added.

Jesus claimed to be the source of life. But Thomas DiLorenzo says, "Free-market capitalism, based on private property and peaceful exchange, is the *source* of civilization and human progress."[3]

These thinkers do hit on important truth, though. They correctly invoke biblical metaphors for the divine categories of money and profit. Jesus did the same: "No one can serve two masters; for either he will hate the one and love the other, or else he will be loyal to the one and despise the other. You cannot serve God and mammon" (Matt 6:24). Jesus didn't deny that the money was a god. That god even had a name—Mammon. Jesus affirmed Mammon as the sole, serious competitor to the Trinity.

The authors above are also right to limit money to blood, roots, and source. Money is essential to Mammon, but it's not the whole story. Money is the blood of Mammon, but it's not all of Mammon. It's not the brain or heart or fist of Mammon. Other things fill those functions.

Jesus understood the antithesis or contrast between God's way and Mammon's way as the most fundamental distinction in all of life and history. He didn't divide the world into Left vs. Right or liberal vs. conservative or the envious vs. entrepreneurs or Muslim vs. Christian. Jesus didn't make Mammon just a side temptation for a few, the way most Christians do. Typical Christians tend to shrink Mammon into one of many small idols. We reduce it, as an equal, alongside Aphroditean Sexuality, Hephaestean Technology, Baccanalian Passion, Promethean Science, Gaian Mysticism, the Leviathan State, and others. Herbert Schlossberg did something like this in his influential *Idols for Destruction* (1980), one of those books that looked full of life in its time but has since shown itself to be simply a recitation of Reagan-era categories.

For Jesus, Mammon wasn't one idol among many equals. Jesus never spoke of any other god in the way he spoke of Mammon. He singled it out as the direct competitor to God. He never contrasted the idols of sexuality or knowledge or the earth in such stark opposition to God. Jesus never said you cannot serve Sexuality and God or Knowledge and God, though those were idols, too. Why did Jesus give such a high and central place to Mammon, out of all the gods? That question seems fundamental, and if we can't answer it then we've misunderstood something basic to Jesus's way of life. Because of that we have to have a good grasp of what Mammon is and isn't.

3. DiLorenzo, *Capitalism*, 1. Emphasis added.

Following others in church history, I want to recognize Mammon as a divinity much more encompassing than mere money. Jesus and the apostles used money. But if we let Jesus fill in the meaning of Mammon by watching what he considers the fundamental divide throughout his ministry, as well as recognizing the same pattern in the Old Testament, then we can understand why Jesus marked out Mammon as the central opponent to his way of life and community. And that's why the way of cross has the way of renunciation central to it. The way of renunciation is a conscious rejection of the way, path, and system of Mammon. Christ's cross precludes the system of Mammon. You cannot bear both. To see this, let's return to the Garden of Eden, since Mammon was first revealed there.

The Genesis account of the fall gives us a frame but omits some interesting details. We know the Serpent in the garden was more cunning than any beast of the field. And we can also see how desire, specifically the longing for food and beauty played into the temptation: "when the woman saw that the tree was good for food, that it was pleasant to the eyes" (Gen 3:6).

We don't learn much there, though, about the nature of the Serpent. What drove him? What specific way of life did he assume? We learn those details in other places. The most important source for this is the prophet Ezekiel. In the prophecies spread across chapters 26–28, Ezekiel denounced the king of Tyre, but in that castigation, the Lord revealed the Serpent's way in Eden, too. Ezekiel spoke *through* the king of Tyre to angelic Satan, in the garden:

> Because your heart is lifted up,
> And you say, 'I am a god. . . .
>
> You were the seal of perfection,
>
> Full of wisdom and perfect in beauty.
> You were in Eden, the garden of God;
> Every precious stone was your covering. . . .
>
> You were the anointed cherub who covers;
> I established you;
> You were on the holy mountain of God;
> You walked back and forth in the midst of fiery stones.
> You were perfect in your ways from the day you were created,
> Till iniquity was found in you.
> Therefore I cast you as a profane thing
> Out of the mountain of God;

And I destroyed you, O covering cherub. (Ezek
28:2,12,14,15,16)

Within this Edenic context, then, we find the prophecy speaking of the
king of Tyre as something of an incarnation of the Serpent, of Satan.

Tyre was terribly famous in the ancient world. But it wasn't famous
the way, say, Persia and Rome were, for devouring, trampling, and breaking (Dan 7:23). Phoenician Tyre was known for sailing, and with that
sailing they traded all around the Mediterranean, establishing colonies
and trading posts all the way to Spain. Through this extensive entrepreneurial spirit, Tyre grew very wealthy over the centuries.

> When your wares went out by sea,
> You satisfied many people;
> You enriched the kings of the earth
> With your many luxury goods and your merchandise. (Ezek
> 27:33)

Tyre enriched kings all over the Mediterrean, and it satisfied the world
with quite a fashionable and cosmopolitan trade in, as Ezekiel listed it—
silver, iron, tin, lead, bronze, horses, mules, ivory, ebony, emeralds, purple clothes, embroidery, fine linen, corals, rubies, wheat, millet, honey,
oil, balm, wine, wool, cane, lambs, rams, goats, woven cords, gold, and
slaves—all of these "were in your marketplace" (Ezek 27:24).

> With your wisdom and your understanding
> You have gained riches for yourself,
> And gathered gold and silver into your treasuries;
> By your great wisdom in trade you have increased your riches.
> (Ezek 28:4, 5)

Notice that Tyre didn't gain this wealth by imperial conquest or even
dishonesty. It gained it by "wisdom," business wisdom. The Lord didn't
rebuke Tyre for imperial slaughter. They were simply good at merchan-
dizing and sales, the best at wealth creation in the Mediterranean. And,
yet, the Lord still categorized it as an incarnation of *Satan*. This wise and
crafty business acumen, this wealth creation, still led the Lord to see Satan in Tyre, "Full of wisdom and perfect in beauty. You were in Eden. . . .
I cast you as a profane thing, out of the mountain of God."

Satan was Tyre, and the ways of Tyre were in Eden. We rarely as-
sociate riches and successful merchandising with Satan. We know Satan

primarily as a deceiver (John 8:44) but not as a wildly successful wealth creator. But that's the interesting connection we find in Ezekiel. This helps us better understand the centrality of Mammon as an enemy of Christ. Mammon isn't some lesser antagonist. Mammon is another name for Satan himself. That's why we can't serve God and Mammon. It's the same dichotomy Paul mentioned later: "what accord has Christ with Belial? Or what part has a believer with an unbeliever? And what agreement has the temple of God with idols?" (2 Cor 6:15).

Ezekiel's characterization of Satan in terms of impressive wealth and greed helps make more sense of the fall in Eden. Commentators have seen all sorts of sins in the fall, and most of the time they leave the disobedience rather abstract. We sometimes describe the prohibition against eating the Tree of Life as replaceable by any command; it "might" have been a command against lying or murder or some form of sexual practice. But in the larger frame of God vs. Mammon, it's telling that the test comes as a challenge about consumption and its limits, much like we see later with Israel in the wilderness, the challenge of abundant manna with a prohibition against hoarding (Exodus 16). In Eden, the Lord laid out a vast quantity of good things for Adam and Eve: "Of every tree of the garden you may freely eat" (Gen 2:16). The Lord provided much more than they needed. He placed only one limit upon their desire: "but of the tree of the knowledge of good and evil you shall not eat" (Gen 2:16). Many foods were available, but Adam and Eve had to control their desire for eating one prohibited good. In a similar way, the Lord would "rain bread from heaven" for Israel (Exod 16:4) so that they could eat "to the full" (Exod 16:8), with a simple limit on consumption: "Let every man gather it according to each one's need" (Exod 16:16). More on this later. In both Eden and the wilderness, the people imitated Satan's greed. Neither the abundance in Eden nor manna was enough. They had to have more. Most important, both cases focused on fullness and food. They were both contests over self-denial. They were both contests for loyalty to God or Mammon, and in both cases, Mammon won.

The Mammon we're called to renounce involves desire and self-aggrandizement. It involves beauty and prestige. It involves wealth creation and wisdom. And it also increasingly involved violence. Notice the causal connection between wealth and violence, even for relatively peaceful Tyre: "By the abundance of your trading, you became filled with violence within, and you sinned" (Exod 28:16). Tyre's trade wasn't even dishonest. Nice, peaceful, wealth creation produced an overflow of violence within

Tyre. And Tyre drew mercenaries and soldiers from the surrounding lands, "Those from Persia, Lydia, and Libya, were in your army as men of war; they hung shield and helmet in you" (Ezek 27:10). In the end, Tyre's wealth created violent terror:

> O renowned city,
> Who was strong at sea,
> She and her inhabitants,
> Who caused their terror to be on all her inhabitants! (Ezek 26:17)

Tyre was an incarnation of Mammon. It was the spirit of the Serpent in the garden. It was the spirit of unsacrificial wealth, self-interest, and greed, a longing for greatness and prestige, a grasping for power, the power of domination and violence.

In other words, it was a very ancient and common way of life. Mammon is a whole social system, not just coins in our pockets. It is the opposite of the way of the cross, and that's why Christ calls on us to renounce it. He himself openly renounced the systems of Mammon at a key moment—in his temptation in the wilderness. We often privatize or spiritualize Satan's temptation of Christ. It becomes a quaint, disjointed moment in our thinking. But history truly turns on that encounter between Christ and Mammon. As noted, Dostoevsky recognized the centrality of Christ's tri-fold temptation. Dostoevsky has his conscious defender of the broad way of destruction, the Grand Inquisitor, observe about Satan's three temptations:

> For in these three questions all of subsequent human history
> is as if brought together into a single whole and foretold; three
> images are revealed that will take in all the insoluble historical
> contradictions of human nature over all the earth. This could
> not have been seen so well at the time, for the future was
> unknown, but now that fifteen centuries have gone by, we can
> see that in these three questions everything was so precisely
> divined and foretold, and has proved completely true, that to
> add to them or subtract anything from them is impossible.[4]

Christ's temptation provided the most expanded explanation of the system of Mammon, which is what we expect since the antagonism between Christ and Satan is naturally central to redemptive history. Matthew and

4. Dostoevsky, *Brothers*, 252.

Luke gave different orders to Satan's temptations, but both laid out the same fundamental features of Mammon's whole system of life.

Just prior to this temptation, we find a revelation of Father, Son, and Spirit at Christ's baptism. The Spirit descended on Christ and drove him out into the wilderness, one of many echoes of the Exodus account. In the wilderness, Satan raised many temptations, but we learn only of the three—bread, the kingdoms of this world, and the spectacular deliverance from a Temple jump.

But what are these temptations? At first, they seem a bit disconnected and arbitrary. In fact, they overlap and fill out each other. They are fuller expressions of the temptations first found in Eden, as well as those that stumbled Israel throughout her history. If we resist turning them into mere personal and private lures for one individual, then we can see their communal nature. Satan's temptations are first and foremost a clash of kingdoms, not private piety.

Jesus had been fasting for forty days, and he was hungry. Satan came along and offered him bread. But not exactly. Satan didn't just wave some bread in front of Jesus. Instead, he suggested that Jesus use his supernatural power to remove his hunger. Use divine magic to turn desert rocks into loaves. But Jesus wasn't out in the wilderness for private, spiritual experiences. He was out there representing Adam and Israel. He was on a mission as a corporate person, a community. In that reality, Satan sought to lure Jesus-the-community by appeal to self-interest. Take care of your immediate, self-focused needs first, before accomplishing the mission. Be foremost a community of self-interest and self-focus.

And Jesus responded to Satan with the words of a community spokesman, not an individual. Jesus cited Deuteronomy 8—"not by bread alone"—where Moses explained to the people of Israel that God led them through the wilderness to test them and prove that God, not Egypt, would provide sufficient food for everyone (Exodus 16) if they lived according to his communal code. Returning to Egypt's ready supply of food was a constant temptation for the Israelites—wonderful Egypt where "we sat by the pots of meat and when we ate bread to the full" (Exod 16:3).

Satan's temptation was also the more general temptation to let the stomach rule the community. Stomach-rule is another way of describing simple greed, that is, the desire for more than is needed (Exod 16:16–18). The apostle Paul spoke of belly-rule in contrast with the way of Christ: "For those who are such do not serve our Lord Jesus Christ, but their own belly" (Rom 16:18), and he described the "enemies of the cross of Christ" as those "whose god is their belly . . . who set their mind on earthly things. For our citizenship is in heaven" (Phil 3:18–20). Satan urged Christ and his community to embrace the way of greed and self-interest, but Jesus said he would not be ruled by his stomach alone, since seeking God's kingdom first produced much more, and bread, too. Jesus renounced the kingdom of self-interest.

Satan's temptation, then, wasn't simply bread for a hungry man. It was a temptation about systems and communities. It was the same temptation given to the Israelites. Would Jesus receive God or Mammon's supply of manna? Jesus knew that God would provide bread in due time, and so he rejected Egypt's way. That's similar to the dichotomy we hear later, when Jesus's disciples worried about the five thousand followers without food. The disciples wanted to send them "into the villages" to "buy themselves food," but Jesus said, "They do not need to go away. You give them something to eat" (Matt 14:15, 16). God provided loaves and fish through his own kingdom.

And yet the temptation was subtler than that, too. Satan wasn't offering bread the way Egypt did. Satan suggested that Jesus himself perform magic on the stones. This angle involved an appeal to easy, efficient solutions rather than the need for wilderness suffering. Henri Nouwen observed, "I would not have been able to reject the magical gift of making the dusty stone-covered streets [of Lima] into places where people could pick up any of the thousands of rocks and discover they were croissants, coffee cakes or fresh-baked buns."[5] But the easy path doesn't build the right sort of community. It doesn't build a community of self-sacrifice and virtue. Jesus rejected it.

So Satan tried another tactic, another angle on the same subject. In the second temptation, Satan took Jesus out of the wilderness to the center of financial corruption at that time, the Temple in Jerusalem. Jesus would later describe it, following Jeremiah, as a "den of thieves" (Luke 19:46), a place where the people were constantly robbed and exploited. Still, it was an impressive architectural presence, a place of ordered beauty and grandeur, a spectacle and a sight to behold. That's one of the features at the core of this second temptation—sight and spectacle.

Paul characterized the Christian faith with the statement, "we walk by faith, not by sight" (2 Cor 5:7). It is a path that does "not look at the things which are seen, but at the things which are not seen" (2 Cor 4:18).

5. Nouwen, *Name*, 30.

In contrast to Jesus's way, the Roman world was a society of sight. Every idolatrous society is. Idolaters set up temples and statues of their gods to assure followers that the god or goddess is present, and great fear descends if an idol is smashed.

Satan's call for Jesus to throw himself off the Temple into the arms of angels would have been a great spectacle. The Romans would have loved that sort of circus. Even the Jewish leadership was hungry for visible idols—"a wicked and adulterous generation seeks after a sign" (Matt 16:4). Jesus's objection to the visible isn't so much against pictures for the uneducated as it is against Mammon's obsession for external criteria of greatness. Jumping off the Temple to be rescued by angels is an empty, external spectacle. It wouldn't have revealed Jesus's character or virtue. It would be simply a show of surfaces. That's Satan's way. Mammon loves an external show of prestige and credibility. It loves bureaucratic credentials and the glitz of greatness. It loves the seriousness of marble columns and shiny war medals. None of that requires an inner life or deep habits of goodness and empathy. It's all surfaces and lies, whited sepulchers with dead men's bones. Jesus hated those expressions of Mammon's greatness. In the Sermon on the Mount, all of Jesus's denunciations of showy, external religion are denunciations of Mammon's understanding of greatness and spectacle. Jesus called for a kingdom of genuine virtue, not empty greatness.

That's why the apostles' fights over "who was the greatest" among them were so significant (Mark 9:34; Luke 9:46; 22:24). We often dismiss those fights as simple immaturity, but they're important manifestations of Mammon. They show us how hard it is to purge the Mammon habit. It's deep within our lives. We've been catechized in the pursuit of greatness from our birth, especially Americans. We long to be the greatest, the most successful, the most relevant, the most popular and admired. Nouwen observed, "Jesus refused to be a stunt man. He did not come to prove himself. He did not come to walk on hot coals, swallow fire, or put his hand in the lion's mouth to demonstrate that he had something worthwhile to say."[6]

Jesus's answer to the second temptation of Mammon was to quote Moses again—"You shall not tempt the Lord your God" as you tempted Him in Massah (Deut 6:16). The omitted reference to Massah points us back to a revealing moment. In Massah (Exodus 17), the Israelites

6. Ibid., 55.

angered God by calling for a Mammon spectacle. They demanded to walk by sight. They had been walking in the absence of God in the wilderness, and they finally asked, "Is the LORD among us or not?" (Exod 17:7). Their faith had been undermined in Egypt, the land of great spectacle and sphinxes and giant pyramids. In the wilderness, God had called them to abandon the imperial show of Mammon, and they resisted—"Why is it you have brought us up out of Egypt?" (Exod 17:3).

In Jesus's temptation, Satan lured Jesus with the promise of great credibility and convincing spectacle. Jesus could have been the most lauded leader in Palestine. After all, who wouldn't believe in Jesus if he would just follow all the Roman or Sadducees' rules for greatness, standing on the Temple, confirming its legitimacy, having the angels rescue him? Forget all this talk of shame and the cross. The Sadducees might even give you a degree, and the Pharisees might introduce you to their friend Caesar. But Jesus had none of it. That was the way of death. Mammon's greatness and prestige was a lie. Jesus renounced the system of Mammon once again. No greed. No greatness.

As mentioned, Satan's temptations overlapped. The first two—greed and greatness—were simply different angles on the same system of Mammon. Likewise, Satan's third temptation—all the kingdoms of the world— is just Satan again attempting to lure Jesus with the system of Mammon. This third temptation was more ham-fisted. Instead of the subtleties of greed and greatness, Satan blatantly offered the system of Mammon as a whole—the kingdoms of the world (Matt 4:18)—the realm of domination and violence. In fact, Satan seems to have shown Jesus something like a moving picture of kingdoms, states, and empires throughout time: "taking Him up on a high mountain, [he] showed Him all the kingdoms of the world in a moment of time" (Luke 4:5). In a moment of time, past and future. Certainly Satan showed Jesus an overview of the dominant empire, then, Rome, but he also showed "all the kingdoms"—Egypt, Assyria, Babylon, Persia, Tyre, Greece, China, the Holy Roman Empire, Spain, Portugal, Britain, Germany, the Soviet Union, and the United States. Satan owned them all—"All this authority I will give You, and their glory; for this has been delivered to me, and I give it to whomever I wish" (Luke 4:6). In a very important sense, they are all Tyre, all Satanic.

All Satanic? We instinctively resist such a conclusion, especially those of us who identify with some of these nations. Certainly *our* nation has to be benevolent and well-meaning at heart. Some of these kingdoms even seemed to grew out of Christian roots. Christ wouldn't call

all nations or empires Satanic, would he? Surely, "Christian" nations do plenty of good.

But consider the Roman Empire itself. It certainly did plenty of good. It certainly trumpeted its own good works throughout the Mediterranean, and it went to great pains to propagandize everyone that it was the source of peace and order and blessing. Certainly many in the ruling classes benefited from Roman domination. But it's significant that the prophet Daniel didn't describe Rome in the laudatory spin of Pax Romana. Daniel described Rome as "exceedingly dreadful, with its teeth of iron and its nails of bronze, which devoured, broke in pieces" (Dan 7:19), an empire that "shall devour the whole earth, trample it and break it in pieces" (Dan 7:23). Then in the Book of Revelation, we see Rome most explicitly described as a Satanic beast. Satan the dragon persecuted God's people (Revelation 12), and then that dragon empowered an imperial beast that fit Daniel's description: "the dragon gave him his power, his throne, and great authority" (Rev 13:2), and "all the world marveled and followed the beast. So they worshiped the dragon who gave authority to the beast; and they worshiped the beast, saying, 'Who is like the beast? Who is able to make war with him?'" (Rev 13:3, 4). Satan empowered the Roman Empire, and all its subordinates, like its Herodian puppets in first-century Palestine. It was an incarnation of Satan, the spirit of violence and domination.

This is what Satan offered Jesus—Mammon kingdoms. Sometimes the comeback to these sorts of inferences is that Jesus rejected Satan's property here because he wanted to conquer and not receive it as a gift. In the background of that sort of response is the hope that Jesus would own all those kingdoms happily and then reform them, perhaps like a Constantine is said to have done. Perhaps Jesus did want to take them. After all, in Revelation and elsewhere, we learn that at a certain point heaven rejoiced, "The kingdoms of this world have become the kingdoms of our Lord and of His Christ, and He shall reign forever and ever!" (Rev 11:15). Hence, some say that Jesus really wanted to rule in the pattern of Rome and Babylon, once they belonged to him. But what's interesting is that if you follow the narrative of Revelation, we don't see Jesus or the saints redeeming and reforming the Satanic beast. Jesus didn't baptize the kingdoms of the world and hold them close to his heart. No, he destroys the beast and everyone connected with it. That's what Jesus did with Satan's former property. And those nations and kings who repented didn't continue in their old way of life, they surrendered their glory to

Christ's kingdom (Rev 21:24), a surrender foreseen by Isaiah (Isaiah 60). In a similar image, Daniel 2 describes the effect of the first coming of Christ, not as a restoration of the grand idol made up of empires, not a continuation of their normal way of life, but as a destruction of empires— "And in the days of these kings the God of heaven will set up a kingdom which shall never be destroyed; and the kingdom shall not be left to other people; it shall break in pieces and consume all these kingdoms, and it shall stand forever" (Dan 2:44). Christ's kingdom destroyed and replaced Satan's kingdoms. It's a completely different way of rule.

The reason that Jesus destroyed Satanic kingdoms is that the kingdoms of this world run according to entirely alternative way of life. One can envision this divide many ways, but the simplest might be to recognize that Jesus seeks to organize his empire around Triune love—God is love, after all, but nations and empires don't even attempt to do that. States slice and bomb. They are institutions that by their nature focus on external obedience and order. They cannot look on the heart. They do not attempt to live by love, especially not love of enemies that was so central to Jesus's life. States excel at breaking things and people, pushing them into outward order, forcing surface conformity. The goal of Jesus and the whole New Testament aims another direction entirely. He aims for an obedience of the heart, a faith of internal virtues grounded in love. The kingdoms of this world have always been horrible at that. It's against their nature.

Jesus wanted something completely different from the violence and domination of past, present, and future kingdom, nations, and empires. He wanted a radical alternative, a new sort of kingdom, and so his way of life, his empire—the church—would struggle against the kingdoms of this world forever. One cannot serve God and Mammon; one cannot serve Christ and the kingdoms of this world. So Jesus rejected Satan's offer of the tools of domination and violence, with all their false glory and honor. And Jesus's rejection was, once again, communal, as he cited Moses against Satan: "You shall worship the Lord your God, and Him only you shall serve" (Deut 6:13). Jesus recognized the lure of worldly domination as that from a different god. To embrace worldly domination was to reject the rule of God and follow "the gods of the peoples who are all around you" (Deut 6:14). Jesus overcame as the new Moses for a new people.

Greed, greatness, and domination—those are the three temptations. Richard Rohr summarized these three temptations more helpfully as the three Ps: the need for prestige, power, and possessions. The three Ps of Mammon permeate Jesus' teaching:

> In the Sermon on the Mount, Jesus says there are three basic obstacles to the coming of the Kingdom. These are the three P's: power, prestige and possessions. Nine-tenths of his teaching can be aligned under one of those three categories. I'm all for sexual morality, but Jesus does not say that's the issue. In fact, he says the prostitutes are getting into the Kingdom of God before some of us who have made bedfellows with power, prestige and possessions (see Matthew 21:31–32). Those three numb the heart and deaden the spirit, says Jesus.[7]

These three demands make up the way of Mammon. Jesus renounced them, and his renunciation finally clarifies so much in the Old Covenant. We can finally see why Jesus described Mammon as so central an opponent. We can follow the three traits (or variations on them) through the Old Covenant, and we find that the system of Mammon has always been the chief opponent of God's plan. We find greed, greatness, and domination not just in Tyre, but in the Garden of Eden. And from there, the system of Mammon incarnated itself time and again throughout the Old Covenant—Cain against Abel, Noah's opponents, the Tower of Babel, Sodom and Gomorrah, Egypt, Assyria, Babylon, Medo-Persia, Greece, and Rome. It was always God versus Mammon.

The same continues throughout the New Testament. Mammon didn't vanish after Jesus's temptation. It wasn't just incarnated in Rome. Rome had beaten and seduced first-century Jewish leadership, turning even the temple into a den of thieves. The land was full of devils. In the end, all the forces of Mammon joined together to crucify Jesus. Then almost immediately, the apostles in the book of Acts clashed with the forces of Mammon over and over. They, too, had to imitate Jesus in renouncing Mammon. And this struggle culminated very explicitly in the book of Revelation, where again, the chief enemy of the church is a Tyre, a Babylon, another incarnation of Mammon—"Babylon the great is fallen, is fallen, and has become a dwelling place of demons, a prison for every foul spirit, and a cage for every unclean and hated bird! For all the nations have drunk of the wine of the wrath of her fornication, the kings of the earth have committed fornication with her, and the merchants of

7. Rohr, *Radical*, 18. Compare also Rohr's helpful and challenging discussions on this point in *Things Hidden*; *Falling Upward*; and, with John Feister, *Hope Against Darkness*.

the earth have become rich through the abundance of her luxury" (Rev 18:2ff).

The way of the cross is not just the way of weakness, not just a siding with the powerless and the poor. It also finds great strength in a determined and conscious renunciation of the system of Mammon, the way of prestige, power, and possessions. By themselves, these two aspects of the way of the cross—the way of weakness and of renunciation—might appear passive, reserved, merely intellectual. That's not the way of Jesus, though, and so we'll consider the next aspect of the way of the cross, the way of deliverance. It will fill out the way of weakness and renunciation with more explicit and constructive action.

The final vision of Matthew 25 captures the way of renunciation, too. We saw previously how Matthew 25 revealed the way of weakness, but in this vision the blessed community is not focused on gaining big houses, secure careers, and large weapons. The community of Matthew 25 doesn't have Mammon's values in mind at all. They face the other direction entirely, toward Christ: "I was naked and you clothed Me; I was sick and you visited Me; I was in prison and you came to Me" (Matt 25:31ff).

4

The Way of Deliverance

"Jesus had come not only to change hearts but to restore Israel. He had to change institutions as well as hearts in order to restore God's justice in the world."

—ANDRE TROCME

"It is only for your love alone that the poor will forgive you the bread you give to them."

—ST. VINCENT DE PAUL

Almost every aspect of modern Christianity assumes that the faith is first and foremost a set of ideas to be believed. That's it. Sure, we encourage some marginal action on the side, but that's not truly important, not central. Our worship is primarily about explaining and singing ideas, our schools focus on transferring ideas, our evangelism spreads ideas, our apologetic tries to persuade others of ideas, community means chatting with people who share our ideas, our entry into heaven requires holding the right ideas in our heads. In centuries past, this strange obsession with ideas simply went by the name of Gnosticism—the ancient heresy that ideas and intellect are more important than bodies and people and actually doing something. We even have a safe, approved word to hide our new Gnosticism—"worldview."

Many Christian traditions have spent the last few decades fine-tuning what it means to have a Christian worldview. It seems to be all we're good at. Notice that *viewing* can take place at a nice, safe distance. You don't need to be involved or get your hands dirty. It would just be awkward to call it a Christian worldsmell or worldtouch. Those would require closeness and bodies. We just want a Christian set of ideas, and sight has long served as the favorite sense of Gnostics throughout history.

Defenders of worldview thinking (I'm a chief sinner here) said we were really more interested in the "world" part of that word. We wanted to encourage Christians to think of all areas of life in obedience to Christ. We wanted to discourage compartmentalization of the faith or synthesis with pagan ideas. But scripture had plenty of language that already did that—lordship, faithfulness, idolatry, and the like. The "world" part of "worldview" was, in fact, rather redundant. But the "view" part quietly allowed us to avoid real work and sacrifice. It allowed us to be thinkers rather than doers of the word. "Worldview" sounded holy and intellectual, and it permitted us to be holy without actually doing what Jesus said. Some of us helped build entire colleges and churches around Gnosticism, "worldview" as the core. God be merciful. I also suspect that Gnostic or worldview thinking is a class issue. It easily falls out of satisfied, middle-class life. After all, we don't have to struggle to access hot water or chicken, so there's not much to do anyway. We might as well sit and talk about ideas. Yeah, we conclude, that must be what Jesus was really concerned with after all. And so "worldview" became all we did, over and over.

But what if, as a thought experiment, we weren't allowed to talk about ideas? What if we were only allowed to act without words? A famous slogan, apparently misattributed to St. Francis, but still very much on target, puts it this way: "Preach the gospel, and sometimes use words." Imagine going further and living with an actual constraint against words in our ministries. Imagine we could only evangelize by actions. Of course, scripture doesn't require that, but the thought experiment highlights how deep our Gnosticism is. Most of us would be completely lost. Nothing we do is geared for serious action.

Interestingly, Jesus actually came close to a constraint like this. He said, "By this all will know that you are My disciples, if you have love for one another" (John 13:35). Imagine taking that observation seriously. Love is action. This exhortation from Jesus suggests that we will win the world primarily by love, not words. He doesn't say people will be persuaded by our smart books refuting atheism and Buddhism. He doesn't say people will flood the church because of cleverly explained worldviews. It's just love. It's just action. Imagine if Christians made a concerted effort to shut up and act, instead of talking and writing books like this one. We'd quickly be far more advanced along the path to maturity. Alas.

That's what the way of the cross exhorts us to. The way of the cross involves the paths of weakness and renunciation, as we've seen, but it also involves a reprioritizing of action over words. It involves a particularly focused action—deliverance. Deliverance becomes the model for everything else, the model for setting any other priority.

Christians like me know that scripture teaches the priority of action over words. We can quote the verses: "These people draw near to Me with their mouth, and honor Me with their lips, but their heart is far from Me" (Matt 15:8–9; Isa 29:13). "Be doers of the word, and not hearers only, deceiving yourselves" (Jas 1:22). "Let us not love in word or in tongue, but in deed and in truth" (1 John 3:18). We memorize these sorts of verses, but then because we assume the Christian faith is mainly about ideas anyway, we count believing and thinking as major actions, and we gut the commands.

Contrary to all this, the way of the cross embraces the primacy of action, of doing over believing. I'd even argue that this comes from the central thesis of all of scripture. Do we often think about scripture's main thesis? I don't think it's difficult to find, but it would disrupt much of modern Christian living, if we took it seriously. A trait of a main thesis for a literary work involves many things, but certainly it is often repeated more than other claims, and it has to shape the rest of the story. In other words, what is the main point God wants us to live and be? I see only one serious candidate that fits in so many ways, and it's this: "I desire mercy and not sacrifice." Nothing else captures the personality and goals of God as much as this paradoxical claim. It not only reveals the depths of Father, Son, and Spirit, it explains the transition between the Old and New Covenants and mission of the church. Consider some of its manifestations in scripture:

"So Samuel said: 'Has the LORD as great delight in burnt offerings and sacrifices, As in obeying the voice of the LORD? Behold, to obey is better than sacrifice, And to heed than the fat of rams. For rebellion is as the sin of witchcraft, And stubbornness is as iniquity and idolatry.

Because you have rejected the word of the LORD, He also has rejected you from being king" (1 Sam 15:22, 23).

"To do righteousness and justice is more acceptable to the LORD than sacrifice" (Prov 21:3).

"Sacrifice and offering You did not desire; my ears You have opened. Burnt offering and sin offering You did not require. Then I said, 'Behold, I come; In the scroll of the book it is written of me. I delight to do Your will, O my God, And Your law is within my heart'" (Ps 40:6–8).

"For You do not desire sacrifice, or else I would give it; You do not delight in burnt offering. The sacrifices of God are a broken spirit, A broken and a contrite heart—these, O God, You will not despise" (Ps 51:16, 17).

"To what purpose is the multitude of your sacrifices to Me? says the LORD. I have had enough of burnt offerings of rams and the fat of fed cattle. I do not delight in the blood of bulls. . . . Bring no more futile sacrifices; incense is an abomination to Me. . . . Your hands are full of blood. . . . Cease to do evil, learn to do good; seek justice, rebuke the oppressor; defend the fatherless, plead for the widow" (Isa 1:11ff).

"Hear, O earth! Behold, I will certainly bring calamity on this people—the fruit of their thoughts, because they have not heeded My words nor My law, but rejected it. For what purpose to Me comes frankincense from Sheba, and sweet cane from a far country? Your burnt offerings are not acceptable, Nor your sacrifices sweet to Me" (Jer 6:19, 20).

"For I desire mercy and not sacrifice, And the knowledge of God more than burnt offerings" (Hos 6:6).

"I hate, I despise your feast days, And I do not savor your sacred assemblies. Though you offer Me burnt offerings and your grain offerings, I will not accept them, nor will I regard your fattened peace offerings. Take away from Me the noise of your songs, for I will not hear the melody of your stringed instruments. But let justice run down like water, And righteousness like a mighty stream" (Amos 5:21–27).

"Shall I come before Him with burnt offerings, with calves a year old? Will the LORD be pleased with thousands of rams, ten thousand rivers of oil? Shall I give my firstborn for my transgression, the fruit of my body for the sin of my soul? He has shown you, O man, what is good; And what does the LORD require of you but to do justly, To love mercy, And to walk humbly with your God?" (Mic 6:6–8).

"'Why does your Teacher eat with tax collectors and sinners?' When Jesus heard that, He said to them, 'Those who are well have no need of a physician, but those who are sick. But go and learn what this means: "I desire mercy and not sacrifice." For I did not come to call the righteous, but sinners, to repentance'" (Matt 9:13).

"Have you not read in the law that on the Sabbath the priests in the temple profane the Sabbath, and are blameless? Yet I say to you that in this place there is One greater than the temple. But if you had known what this means, 'I desire mercy and not sacrifice,' you would not have condemned the guiltless. For the Son of Man is Lord even of the Sabbath" (Matt 12:1–8).

"For it is not possible that the blood of bulls and goats could take away sins. Therefore, when He came into the world, He said: 'Sacrifice and offering You did not desire, but a body You have prepared for Me. In burnt offerings and sacrifices for sin You had no pleasure. Then I said, 'Behold, I have come—in the volume of the book it is written of Me—to do Your will, O God.' Previously saying, 'Sacrifice and offering, burnt offerings, and offerings for sin You did not desire, nor had pleasure in them' (which are offered according to the law), then He said, 'Behold, I have come to do Your will, O God.' He takes away the first that He may establish the second" (Heb 10:1–18).

The Lord packs so much into this simple phrase. Yet it's not simple. On the surface it actually seems false. It seems to suggest that God never commanded ritual sacrifices and liturgical codes. But he most certainly did in a very public way for centuries. So we take him to mean that he was aiming for something deeper, more mature than the mere letter of the law.

The law, after all, was about shaping a different kind of community than Egypt's (Mammon). Its goal was social and communal. The law was a mere stepping stone toward the mature community the Trinity wanted. That new community was to be a people of action, with the key actions being mercy and justice—"Seek justice, rebuke the oppressor; defend the fatherless, plead for the widow."

In what should be one of the most troublesome New Covenant teachings for modern Christians, the apostle James summarized all of faith in this way: "Pure and undefiled religion before God and the Father is this: to visit orphans and widows in their trouble, and to keep oneself unspotted from the world" (Jas 1:27). True religion. James identified what God wants with simple acts of mercy, caring for widows and orphans. It's a stunning bit of poetry in its simplicity and power. James simply gave us another way of saying that the Lord wants mercy, not sacrifice. And he didn't want it in a worldly way. The Lord wants this within the faith he delivered. But why would acts of mercy be the main point of scripture? Because they're the main mission of God. He stooped to help us, the weak and enslaved. The goal of Father, Son, and Spirit is to make Trinity on earth, with humans, and that would mean rescuing us from Mammon, creating a community of giving, serving, and mercy to one another. That's how we image the Trinity on earth, and that's why God's mission through Moses and the prophets was to "desire mercy and not sacrifice." Jesus not only taught this saying, he embodied it at every point, showing mercy and healing and restoring Trinity on earth. The church is called to imitate his work.

Notice, though, that phrase's prioritizing of action. It's not a call to feel sorry for people or to think good thoughts about distressed people. Those are as bad as empty rituals. The Trinity calls for actual merciful actions right at the center of our communal life, more central than ritual, worship, liturgy, fine-tuned doctrine, evangelism, education, and more. Doing mercy is what should characterize us most. It should be the thing we're known for. And when the New Covenant church imitates the ritualism and mere intellectualism of ancient Israel, then God grows angry with us, too—"To what purpose is the multitude of your sacrifices to Me?"

Doing mercy and justice is best captured in the recurring biblical language of *deliverance*. The way of deliverance has always been the way of God, and it needs to be his people's main feature, too. The way of deliverance is the action of liberating enslaved people. It is the action of freeing God's oppressed in body and spirit.

Abraham was the first model of deliverance. Various pagan kings in and around Sodom and Gomorrah had entered into war with one another (Genesis 14). Abraham's nephew Lot had followed the path of Mammon and chosen to live in Sodom, a place "like the land of Egypt" (Gen 13:10). In the midst of the battles, Sodom fell, and the opposing kings looted it, kidnapping many of its people, typically for slavery. When Abraham heard of this, he became a deliverer: "he armed his three hundred and eighteen trained servants" and attacked the kidnappers in pursuit of Lot. He "brought back all the goods, and also brought back his brother Lot and his goods, as well as the women and the people" (Gen 14:16). Abraham overcame an incarnation of Mammon and delivered his family. As father of the faith, Abraham's act of deliverance stood as a model to imitate from that time forward. The friend of God was an imitator of God.

Abraham's great-grandson, Joseph, would also follow Abraham's path as a deliverer of his people. Like Abraham, Joseph began in a state of weakness, slavery, and God raised him up to rule over a Mammon kingdom. In that position, God used him both to deliver his people and return them to Canaan (and also to set up their later slavery) (Genesis 47–50). In the midst of Joseph's service, we also see God training the other brothers away from the ways of domination toward the way of mercy and deliverance. Joseph's brothers had enslaved him, but when Joseph tested them by pretending to threaten the new youngest brother, Benjamin, Judah did the right thing and offered himself in the place of weakness: "please let your servant remain instead of the lad as a slave to my lord, and let the lad go up with his brothers" (Gen 44:13). Judah's father Jacob later blessed Judah using the language of deliverance—"Your hand shall be on the neck of your enemies" (Gen 49:8).

Of course, then, Moses became the main model of deliverance. The greatest act of divine mercy was God's deliverance of Israel from Egypt. Scripture continually points back to that God-defining act. That act of deliverance became the main description of God's character throughout the Old Covenant, and it's no accident that the Trinity places the work of the Son right in the middle of a celebration of the Exodus, Passover. Christ's work was a new exodus story. It was a new act of deliverance.

In Moses's primal act of deliverance, God overcame the incarnation of Mammon in Egypt. He had sent his people through the oppression of slavery and then heard their cry—"Then the children of Israel groaned because of the bondage, and they cried out; and their cry came up to God because of the bondage. So God heard their groaning" (Exod 2:24) and he saw "the oppression of My people" and "I know their sorrows" (Exod 3:7). "So I have come down to deliver them out of the hand of the Egyptians" (Exod 3:8).

After the exodus, the divine theme of deliverance didn't vanish. It remained the main act. During the history of the judges, we repeatedly see God's work of deliverance for his people, in the same pattern as Moses: "And when the LORD raised up judges for them, the LORD was with the judge and delivered them out of the hand of their enemies all the days of the judge; for the LORD was moved to pity by their groaning because of those who oppressed them and harassed them" (Judg 2:18).

The theme of deliverance gained new strength in David's era. We read earlier of David's devotion to the weakest, but now note how that gets expressed specifically in terms of deliverance. David was a new Moses:

All my bones shall say,
    "LORD, who is like You,
Delivering the poor from him who is too strong for him,
    Yes, the poor and the needy from him who plunders
him?" (Ps 35:10)

For He will deliver the needy when he cries,
    The poor also, and him who has no helper.
 He will spare the poor and needy,
    And will save the souls of the needy. (Ps 72:12, 13)

Defend the poor and fatherless;
    Do justice to the afflicted and needy.
Deliver the poor and needy;
    Free them from the hand of the wicked. (Ps 82:3, 4)

Who executes justice for the oppressed,
    Who gives food to the hungry?
    The LORD gives freedom to the prisoners.
The LORD opens the eyes of the blind;
    The LORD raises those who are bowed down;
    The LORD loves the righteous.
The LORD watches over the strangers;
    He relieves the fatherless and widow;
    But the way of the wicked He turns upside down. (Ps
146:7–9)

Why was David so focused on singing about delivering the weak and poor? Certainly we can say David was a new Abraham and a new Moses. But something more seemed to be at work. This focus on the weak and poor was a distinctive characteristic of Yahweh, as we've seen. David lived that life, too. Perhaps this best makes sense of the description of David as a "man after God's own heart" (Acts 13:22; 1 Sam 13:14). We normally take that phrase in generic ways—that David was faithful, repentant, grateful, loved God's law, etc. But those don't pick out David in any unique way. Noah was all those things, too, as were Moses and Abraham. Something unique in David won that special designation. The Psalms show us that David put greater emphasis on delivering the weak than anyone else in the Old Covenant. Even Moses had to be pushed in that direction, but David spoke of it from the heart. In other words, despite all of David's epic failures, God truly delighted in him because, like God, David heard the groaning of the poor and had Exodus deep in his heart. More than any other, David was "a man after God's own heart" of deliverance.

The Mosaic code returned as a rebuke to much of the era of Israel's kings. In many ways, the prophets represented the voice of Moses against the kings. For example, the slavery laws of Leviticus focused on release from slavery and an outright prohibition on chattel or unpaid slavery for the covenant people of God. When selling land was no longer possible, sometimes God's people would sell themselves into servitude. The Levitical or jubilee code put very interesting constraints on this move of desperation:

> And if one of your brethren who dwells by you becomes poor,
> and sells himself to you, you shall not compel him to serve as a
> slave. As a hired servant and a sojourner he shall be with you,
> and shall serve you until the Year of Jubilee. (Lev 25:39, 40)

Here scripture marked a key difference between indentured servitude for pay and chattel slavery for no pay. It strictly prohibited the latter among covenant members. God's people may not enslave other believers. They had to pay them and then release them. In addition to a required release from indentured servitude at the jubilee, Israelites also had to release believing servants after six years (Exod 21:2–11; Deut 15:12–18). However these six-year and jubilee releases worked out in detail, the key point was that covenant people could not chattel-enslave other covenant people (though they could chattel-enslave noncovenant people from the surrounding nations). This difference would certainly motivate noncovenantal slaves to convert and be circumcised, as Abraham showed (Gen 17:23). Making them believers in this way would also grant them the rights of sixth-year and jubilee releases. The reason God opposed chattel slavery for his people went back to the exodus: "For they are My servants, whom I brought out of the land of Egypt; they shall not be sold as slaves." (Lev 25:42). The way of delieverance is the way of helping believers (first) out of poverty, not having a few "healthy" profit off of them.

That's why slavery in the American south was so abominable. Apologists for southern slavery often went to great lengths to show how southern slave owners successfully led their slaves into the Christian faith, and the numbers bear this out. Millions of African slaves came to Christ during their servitude. And yet that only compounded the injustice of southern slavery because it had powerful believers enslaving other believers in long-term violation of Old Testament law. Southern slavery violated God's commands by (a) not paying believing slaves (Lev 25:39, 40; Jer 22:13), (b) not releasing them after six years (Exodus 21; Deuteronomy 15), (c) not releasing them outright after forty-nine years (Lev 25:40), (d) not allowing abused slaves to flee without punishment (Deut 23:15, 16), and (e) purchasing kidnapped persons in the first place (Exod 21:16), a capital crime even if you weren't the kidnapper. Rather than being analogous to slavery under pagan Babylon or Rome, southern slavery was more akin to that of Jeremiah 34, at which the Lord was furious:

> Therefore the word of the LORD came to Jeremiah from the LORD, saying, "Thus says the LORD, the God of Israel: 'I made a covenant with your fathers in the day that I brought them out of the land of Egypt, out of the house of bondage, saying, "At the end of seven years let every man set free his Hebrew brother, who has been sold to him; and when he has served you six years, you shall let him go free from you." But your fathers did not obey Me nor incline their ear. Then you recently turned and did what was right in My sight—every man proclaiming liberty to his neighbor; and you made a covenant before Me in the house which is called by My name. Then you turned around and profaned My name, and every one of you brought back his male and female slaves, whom you had set at liberty, at their pleasure, and brought them back into subjection, to be your male and female slaves.'" "Therefore thus says the LORD: 'You have not obeyed Me in proclaiming liberty, every one to his brother and every one to his neighbor. Behold, I proclaim liberty to you,' says the LORD—'to the sword, to pestilence, and to famine! And I will deliver you to trouble among all the kingdoms of the earth.'" (Jer 34:12ff)

The Israelites had not only practiced servitude without payment (Jer 22:13), they failed to release their brethren after the sixth year. For a while, they had freed their slaves in a way that pleased the Lord, but then they enslaved them again. By this form of slavery, they had "profaned" God's name, and therefore the Lord sent them destruction and death from foreign powers. For that reason, conservative Christians ought to find much more of a hero in Harriet Tubman than Robert E. Lee.

Something strange for modern ears happens within all these biblical passages about deliverance. The work of actual deliverance on earth became the language for salvation. Consider how the following passages identify actual deliverance on earth with salvation:

"And Moses said to the people, 'Do not be afraid. Stand still, and see the salvation of the LORD, which He will accomplish for you today. For the Egyptians whom you see today, you shall see again no more forever'" (Exod 14:13).

"And say, 'Save us, O God of our salvation; gather us together, and deliver us from the Gentiles'" (1 Chr 16:34).

"You will not need to fight in this battle. Position yourselves, stand still and see the salvation of the LORD" (2 Chr 20:17).

"Draw out the spear, And stop those who pursue me. Say to my soul, 'I am your salvation'" (Ps 35:3).

"But the salvation of the righteous is from the LORD; He is their strength in the time of trouble" (Ps 37:39).

"The One who gives salvation to kings, Who delivers David His servant From the deadly sword" (Ps 144:10).

"In the day of salvation I have helped You; I will preserve You and give You As a covenant to the people, to restore the earth" (Isa 49:8).

"My salvation has gone forth, And My arms will judge the peoples" (Isa 51:5).

"You went forth for the salvation of Your people, for salvation with Your Anointed. You struck the head from the house of the wicked" (Hab 3:13).

Salvation is deliverance. Salvation is exodus. Salvation takes place on earth, in history.

More than any other prophet, Isaiah shaped the text of the New Covenant. He is the most quoted prophet. Our New Testament meanings should make sense, then, in Isaiah's world. Isaiah also focused on deliverance as salvation. In Isaiah 42, a key messianic text demonstrates that the Christ would be a deliverer:

> Behold! My Servant whom I uphold,
>   My Elect One in whom My soul delights!
>   I have put My Spirit upon Him;
>   He will bring forth justice to the Gentiles.
> He will not cry out, nor raise His voice,
>   Nor cause His voice to be heard in the street.
>   A bruised reed He will not break. . . .
>   I will keep You and give You as a covenant to the people,
>   As a light to the Gentiles,
> To open blind eyes,
>   To bring out prisoners from the prison,

> Those who sit in darkness from the prison house. (Isa
> 42:1–3, 6–7)

God's anointed would be a man of action more than a teacher. His mission would be justice, though he wouldn't be a man of violence. He would open eyes and free the imprisoned.

Jesus himself invoked Isaiah to explain his mission. He cited Isaiah 61, and it's a passage very similar to the one above. Its subject is also deliverance in history. It has been rightly called Jesus's inaugural address. It is the gospel, and it explains what the mission of Jesus would be, with the remainder of Luke showing him fulfilling his mission:

> And He was handed the book of the prophet Isaiah. And when
> He had opened the book, He found the place where it was
> written:
> "The Spirit of the LORD is upon Me,
>> Because He has anointed Me
>> To preach the gospel to the poor;
>> He has sent Me to heal the brokenhearted,
>> To proclaim liberty to the captives
>> And recovery of sight to the blind,
>> To set at liberty those who are oppressed;
>> To proclaim the acceptable year of the LORD."
> (Luke 4:17–19)

It says plainly that his mission is to preach to the poor, not the rich. He will heal and deliver and restore. Again, that's the gospel. That's what Isaiah meant. Isaiah himself gave no hint of heaven. It was all about life on earth. How much clearer can it get? Jesus was a deliverer, first and foremost, and that's what his church should be, too. Preaching the gospel means preaching deliverance—action on earth in history. We should assume that salvation means the same thing in the New as it did in the Old Covenant, unless we have reason to think otherwise (and sometimes we will see it include heaven). But the main focus is that salvation is deliverance. Jesus didn't reverse the Old on that point. Why should we?

But in what way did Jesus carry out an actual deliverance in history? Did he overthrow the Roman occupation? Did he drive the puppet Herodians out of Palestine and free the poor from oppression? No, obviously Jesus was not a zealot, like many others at that time. He was not a Patrick Henry. He used other means. As Isaiah said, "a bruised reed He will not break" (Isa 42:3).

Still, he brought a real revolution in history, and he was executed for a political crime. Jesus entered territory occupied by Imperial Rome, and he set up a new kingdom. He went and preached about this kingdom all over Galilee and Judah. That's not the sort of thing you do in a region of Mammon, if you want to stay alive. Preaching the kingdom was a huge provocation to the powers that be, and they thought they made him pay for it. His revolution was not like the zealots'. His revolution was the new kingdom called the church. His deliverance of the poor was to create a new and different community as a superior competitor to Mammon's, in a way similar to Moses' new community as a repudiation of Egypt. In Christ's church, the poor would be delivered, healed, fed, clothed, and united—in other words, they would be saved. The church was to be a genuine place of refuge, free of Mammon.

But that wasn't all. Jesus's deliverance went deeper. Instead of attacking Roman and Palestinian governments with violence, he attacked their source. Remember, Rome and its puppets were incarnations of Mammon. Jesus had to break the power of Mammon to bring true deliverance in history. Jesus had to overcome Satan, in a way Abraham, Joseph, Moses, and David were not able to do. In the first century, to truly take out the "kingdoms of this world," you needed to take out Satan. And that's exactly how the New Testament describes Jesus's work—deliverance.

The apostle John said, "For this purpose the Son of God was manifested, that He might destroy the works of the devil" (1 John 3:8). Christ himself spoke to the apostle Paul about salvation as deliverance: "I will deliver you from the Jewish people, as well as from the Gentiles, to whom I now send you, to open their eyes, in order to turn them from darkness to light, and from the power of Satan to God, that they may receive forgiveness of sins and an inheritance among those who are sanctified by faith in Me'" (Acts 26:17). And Paul himself used the language of deliverance in declaring, "He has delivered us from the power of darkness and conveyed us into the kingdom of the Son of His love" (Col 1:13). More on these passages later. But their deliverance follows the same pattern as the Old Testament. Overcome the tyrant and set up a new kingdom. Overcome Satan-Mammon, and set up the church. That is basic salvation in Old and New Covenants.

But all this has been described without mention of the cross. Why is the way of deliverance also the way of the cross? The cross stands right at the center of this whole process, in the same way an imperfect priesthood and temple stood at the center of the Old Covenant. In fact, we can't understand Christ's cross without understanding a key feature of the Old Covenant priesthood: absorption of evil and sin. The tabernacle and temple absorbed evil. They aimed to exhaust its power and weaken it. Christ did more.

As others have explained, the primary purpose of the Old Testament sacrificial system was to purify or cleanse the tabernacle and temple. The temple was a place that in some mysterious yet true sense bore or absorbed the sins of Israel. The priests would sacrifice animals to purge away Israel's moral stains on God's dwelling place. The priests themselves served as God's representatives, and they absorbed the people's sins through eating of the sacrifices (Lev 10:16, 17). Though many other issues are at stake in this passage, the one that stands out is that by consuming, absorbing the sin offering, the priests "bear the guilt of the congregation" and make atonement for them. In other words, atonement is largely about absorbing sin and evil. That's not the whole story, but it's a big part. More on this in a later chapter.

The cross, then, was the central point of deliverance for God's people because there Christ absorbed our evil and broke the tyrannical reign of Satan. As the writer of Hebrews put it, Christ "Himself likewise shared in the same, that through death He might destroy him who had the power of death, that is, the devil, and release those who through fear of death were all their lifetime subject to bondage" (Heb 2:14, 15). Jesus's death destroyed the power of Mammon and delivered us from the millennia-long domination of Satan's power. Christ overthrew the most powerful emperor, the soul of Tyre, Egypt, and Rome, so we could be free to create a new kingdom, empowered by the Holy Spirit—the church.

The way of the cross is the way of deliverance, of bearing sin, of absorbing sin and evil that drive us, Mammon, and its world powers. And though Christ's work definitively broke the power of sin and the reign of Satan, Christ still calls on us to absorb evil from the world. We are imitators of Christ, and just as he suffered and absorbed evil around him, so we, too, are called to take up our crosses and absorb the sin of the world to weaken it, to break it even more, as Christ's kingdom spreads. As Paul noted, "I now rejoice in my sufferings for you, and fill up in my flesh what is lacking in the afflictions of Christ, for the sake of His body, which is the church" (Col 1:24). In some sense, Paul and other Christians continue to suffer bodily like Christ for the sake of the church. Actual suffering and persecution mysteriously adds something to the church. That body is a temple, after all, and its purpose is to absorb sin and give freedom. It seems this is also in view in Revelation 6, where the martyrs cry to Christ for vengeance—"How long, O Lord . . . until you judge?"—and the answer was: "that they should rest a little while longer, until both the number of their fellow servants and their brethren, who would be killed as they were, was completed" (Rev 6:11). In some obviously lesser, though very important sense, the church's suffering changes history for the better. Absorbing evil advances the kingdom of Christ. Jesus came to destroy the works of Mammon, and deliver people out of its kingdom, and so does the church. The way of the cross is the way of deliverance.

The final vision of Matthew 25 captures the way of deliverance, too. We saw previously how Matthew 25 revealed the ways of weakness and renunciation, and now we see the blessed are a community of deliverance, too. The community of Matthew 25 free people from hunger, thirst, and more: "I was naked and you clothed Me; I was sick and you visited Me; I was in prison and you came to Me" (Matt 25:31ff).

5

The Way of Sharing

"It is difficult to get a man to understand something when his salary depends upon his not understanding it."

—UPTON SINCLAIR

It is amazing how wrong Jesus was about the rich. Jesus said that it was very difficult for people with wealth to enter the kingdom of God (Mark 10:23), but modern America has demonstrated clearly and overwhelmingly that this is not the case. We have churches full of the wealthiest people on the face of the earth, that is anyone who earns more than, say, $500 per month, as common knowledge has it. Anyone who earns that amount (actually anyone who earns over $100 per month), sits in the very upper tiers of the wealthy among international populations. Even lower, middle-class Americans sit among the world elites. Maybe as Dostoevsky's Grand Inquisitor says, certainly "we corrected your deed."

Very few people in North America and the West earn less than $500 or $100 per month. In fact, the vast majority of us earn many, many more times that per month, and we have entered the kingdom without much difficulty at all. Conservative churches are full of wealthy people who are "born again and going to heaven." Most of us certainly have far more wealth than that relative peasant in the Gospels, the so-called "Rich Young Ruler" (Luke 18:18–23; Mark 10:17–27; Matt 19:16–20). He had nothing on us. He didn't have the easily accessible hot water, electricity, diversity of cuisines, technology, transportation, air conditioning, and medicines that we have. If we met him in our circles today, we'd almost certainly consider him a bit of third-world throwback. And yet Jesus was so hard on him, saying that even his relatively poor status couldn't fit into Jesus's kingdom. How could Jesus have been so radically mistaken on such an important issue?

Most of us dismiss the Rich Young Ruler by assuming he had a rather unique and unhealthy, over-obsession with wealth that was quite, quite peculiar to him. We deny that he represented a class of people, us. We say his equal in modern times might be the super-rich, far above us, who have ten cars and a champagne sense of entitlement. Whoever this peculiar, radically unique Rich Young Ruler was, he wasn't us, no way. He was a freak. And anyone who suggests otherwise must be full of envy and very ungrateful, yeah (we'll come back to these handy defenses later).

The fact is that all the twists and turns about the Rich Young Ruler aren't in the text. The Rich Young Ruler is common, not unique. As Berdyaev would say, he was simply part of the normal vacuum of Mammon that we wealthy always incarnate. And Jesus's command itself wasn't unique to this one man. Elsewhere Jesus spoke quite universally to his followers: "whoever of you does not forsake all that he has cannot be My disciple" (Luke 14:35).

But, no, the objector continues, the Rich Young Ruler's problem was that when Jesus said to sell all his things, he "went away sorrowful, for he had great possessions." But we aren't like that. If Jesus asked us to do that, we would do it with great pleasure. In other words, we obey Jesus in principle, in the spirit, and need not in practice.

I'll come back to the many practical questions involved here, but the main question before us now is why is it no longer hard for the wealthy to be in Christ's kingdom? One of the ways we get around Jesus's commands about giving up wealth is that we require Jesus himself to ask it. We believe we would do it if Jesus asked in person, but conveniently that can't happen now. But can you imagine if a pastor asked the congregants to give up all their wealth? We'd shout him down as a cult leader. Even more, what if giving up our possessions were a condition of membership in some church? Would we attend there? What if it were commonly and broadly accepted that becoming a Christian required giving up our possessions? Would we become Christians? At least, then we'd be closer to making sense of Jesus's claim that it's hard for the rich to enter his kingdom. It would also make more sense of Jesus's talk of the narrow way. Membership rolls would certainly be much slimmer. And I suspect far more genuinely poor people would fill churches, those who didn't have or want much anyway.

It's within such questions we can begin to grasp the profundity of the way of sharing as central to the way of the cross. The way of sharing is a different way of life than most of us know, than I know. The way of sharing is not about resentment and a reluctant parting with our things. The way of sharing asks us to imagine a world in which people become more human, more divine without the encumbrances of possessions. It is a world of great freedom and joy. It is not a world where possessions are evil but a world where we rejoice to make sure everyone's needs are met. It is a world where people and personality are far more interesting than things. It is the world of Trinitarian life.

The way of the cross is always the way of the Trinity. We saw that in the way of weakness, the way of renunciation, and the way of deliverance. We're called to follow these paths because they naturally flow out of the life of Father, Son, and Spirit. The way of sharing is no different. I'll come back to this point.

The apostle John gives us the best one-line summary of the way of sharing. It clearly grows not out of resentment or envy but out of deep Trinitarian love. It is not a hatred of possessions but a delight to share deeply to create a merciful community. It is not a call for mere charity but genuine sacrifice. It is a wholesale rejection of the ethic of Mammon. The apostle observed: "But whoever has this world's goods, and sees his brother in need, and shuts up his heart from him, how does the love of God abide in him?" (1 John 3:17).

Here is the heart of a Christian social ethic. It's got nothing to do with state coercion. This is the job of the church. And it stems from the heart, not bureaucratic rules. Here John connects love and property in a simple, profound way. True love makes us want to ensure that every Christian has his or her needs met—food, drink, clothing, housing. And it's a rebuke. If Christians haven't done this, if the church hasn't succeeded with this, then how can we say we have been loving the way God commands? If we haven't taken care of Christian needs, then Christians are still infants in regard to love. That's a bit softer than John. He actually says that the love of God is obviously absent if we haven't done this. In other words, we're deceived about how happy God is with us, if we have yet to share enough to have no Christian poor.

Notice that John didn't say that "whoever has a *great deal* of this world's goods." He's not speaking to the super-rich. He's speaking to everyone with more than one cloak, to put it in first-century terms. Simply put, refusing to share with a fellow Christian is a sign we're not genuine believers. We haven't learned lesson one. John shows that it's a heart issue. Not to share is a failure to indwell one another, a failure in basic empathy that is so central to Trinitarian ethics.

Does this mean we're just to take care of those in our middle-class horizon? No, Paul organized an international relief effort between Christians (2 Corinthians 8, 9). Trinitarian love means that Christians will not be satisfied until the church has made sure that all Christians have their basic needs met, and even then we will want to do more. "But whoever has this world's goods, and sees his brother in need, and shuts up his heart from him, how does the love of God abide in him?" We find the roots of John's minimal ethic in the Old Covenant.

The way of sharing finds some of its initial expression after the exodus. The Lord tried to turn his people away from the seduction of Mammon-Egypt, and he led them through the self-denial time in the wilderness. They were a young, immature people without the fullness of the Spirit, and he showed them mercy, even while they pushed back against his way of life. They complained and yearned for Egypt and its food, and so the Lord provided food for them—bread and meat, manna and quail. But he didn't want them to eat like Egyptians or Americans, thinking of themselves and their own families to the exclusion of everyone else in community. He didn't want them saving up food, storing it for future consumption. He wanted them to share and consider the needs of others first. It was a complete retraining from Mammon's way.

All of this is recorded in Exodus 16, where Moses explained the way of distributing manna as given by the Lord himself:

> "Let every man gather it according to each one's need, one
> omer for each person, according to the number of persons;
> let every man take for those who are in his tent." Then the
> children of Israel did so and gathered, some more, some less.
> So when they measured it by omers, he who gathered much
> had nothing left over, and he who gathered little had no lack.
> Every man had gathered according to each one's need. (Exod
> 16:16–18)

Sharing food. This was the beginning of real community. Making sure each person had his or her basics. That is the beginning of Trinity on earth.

And how did the Lord deal with those who tried to privatize the manna, who tried to look out for their own needs before others? Moses commanded the people not to save any of the manna for the next day but to take just what was needed for each day. Some disobeyed. They tried to save some manna, but God made it breed worms and stink (Exod 16:20). Moses grew angry with them, and then they went back to collecting just their daily bread. This was Israel's first lesson about sharing. "But whoever has this world's goods, and sees his brother in need, and shuts up his heart from him, how does the love of God abide in him?"

The second major lesson about the way of sharing came with the gift of Canaan. God promised his people a gift of land, and he divided it among them according to their tribes. In other words, God was the owner of the land, and he divided according to the needs of the tribes— "So Joshua took the whole land, according to all that the LORD had said to Moses; and Joshua gave it as an inheritance to Israel according to their divisions by their tribes" (Josh 11:23). God did not divide it by allowing homesteaders to race forth and mix their labor with the land and call portions their own. He did not divide it by allowing the strongest to dominate, with the weakest left for slums. He did not allow those with the most entrepreneurial gifts to own it all and then sell it to the slower. The initial distribution was centralized in God's hands, via Joshua, and each tribe received a portion of the promise, an inheritance. The Lord took care of each part of his people. He shared it. "But whoever has this world's goods, and sees his brother in need, and shuts up his heart from him, how does the love of God abide in him?"

But starting Israel's history by making sure each tribe had land wasn't the end. The Lord went on to institute laws which aimed to ensure that Israel could not turn into a Mammon society. He set up land-ownership laws that sought to hinder the promised land from turning into an Egypt, where only a small elite of strongest and most entrepreneurial could work their way into owning most of the land, as Canaanite society before them had done.

In short, the Lord banned any absolutistic notion of private property ownership. Only he was an absolute owner; no one else. The Lord owned the land, and everyone else used it with his permission and constraints. The most radical legislation for protecting widespread land ownership of each tribe was to require lands sold to return to the original tribes every fifty years. This was the jubilee legislation. After the original distribution of land, Israelites would sometimes find themselves falling into poverty and debt, and they would sell off some or all of their family lands in order avoid utter impoverishment. We can imagine they needed to do this sometimes because of bad farming seasons, loss of family labor, or even foolishness. But God had mercy on them. He didn't abandon them to the free market. After forty-nine or fifty years of selling off the original lands, the Lord required the purchasers to return the lands they had purchased from impoverished Israelites.

As the Lord explained in Leviticus,

> The land shall not be sold permanently, for the land is Mine; for you are strangers and sojourners with Me. And in all the land of your possession you shall grant redemption of the land. If one of your brethren becomes poor, and has sold some of his possession, and if his redeeming relative comes to redeem it, then he may redeem what his brother sold. Or if the man has no one to redeem it, but he himself becomes able to redeem it, then let him count the years since its sale, and restore the remainder to the man to whom he sold it, that he may return to his possession. But if he is not able to have it restored to himself, then what was sold shall remain in the hand of him who bought it until the Year of Jubilee; and in the Jubilee it shall be released, and he shall return to his possession. (Lev 25:23–28)

Israel had to own everything loosely. They had to live not as Pharaohs but as Abraham, as "strangers and sojourners." At times, they had to return land to the original owners if the original owners were able to come up with the wealth to do so, even though the lands had been purchased and transferred legally to new owners. And then, even if the original owner couldn't come up with the means to repurchase it, he would receive it back for free at the year of jubilee. The Lord overrode absolutistic private property concerns. They were all sojourners and had to show mercy even to the irresponsible.

In the cities, things were a little different. Sometimes Israelites had to sell their homes within cities for similar reasons of poverty: "If a man sells a house in a walled city, then he may redeem it within a whole year after it is sold; within a full year he may redeem it" (Lev 25:29). But if he couldn't do it within the allotted year, then the house wasn't returned. Still it shows the mercy of return extended even beyond land holdings.

We have no evidence, however, that Israel ever obeyed God's jubilee and its related requirements to rest the land itself. In fact, scripture records that Israel, in a very significant way, returned to Egypt. After years of judges and divine deliverance, Israel again wanted to be like Egypt and the others (1 Samuel 8). They rejected God's ways. They didn't want to be a nation of mercy and sharing. They wanted Mammon's ways. As we've seen, amazingly, the Lord condescended to let them return to the principles of Egypt, but the Lord did not mince words. The rulers' desire for a king like the pagan nations was an idolatrous request, and that permitted idolatry would shadow every bit of royal history that followed.

The shift to a pagan kind of king would be a shift from a sharing community to a self-interested, greedy nation of power. The Lord warned the rulers that their powerful, new kings would turn very militaristic, enslave their sons and daughters, and confiscate their wealth for kingly luxuries—"he will take your male servants, your female servants, your finest young men, and your donkeys, and put them to his work" (1 Sam 8:16). It will be an era of reverse jubilee, and when the people despaired, when "you cry out in that day because of your king whom you have chosen for yourselves, and the LORD will not hear you" (1 Sam 8:18). Despite all the warnings about life under Mammon, the people insisted, "No, but we will have a king over us, that we also may be like all the nations" (1 Sam 8:20).

The years passed, and everything the Lord had promised occurred. Mammon ruled, and despite important high spots, especially with David, the era of the kings was a greedy, bloody failure. The prophets were right. The Lord wanted an entirely different sort of community, an entirely different king. In the end, Moses's way of jubilee-sharing booted the people out of the promised land.

The jubilee provisions concerning land and rest turned out to be far more central and important than anyone understood. These provisions about land were tied to the notion of sabbath rest. God wanted Israel to rest the land and the people. But Israel never did it. They ignored God's prescriptions for the land. To modern ears, these sabbath protections for humans and land might sound like relatively unimportant issues. If it were us, we'd be concerned with all sorts of others sins, especially sexual and intellectual sins, but the Lord saw deeper. As always, the antithesis for him was between God and Mammon.

In the end, God exiled Israel for their disobedience over land and justice: "And those who escaped from the sword he carried away to

Babylon, where they became servants to him and his sons until the rule of the kingdom of Persia, to fulfill the word of the LORD by the mouth of Jeremiah, until the land had enjoyed her Sabbaths. As long as she lay desolate she kept Sabbath, to fulfill seventy years" (2 Chr 36:20–21).

Yahweh exiled his people because they refused to rest the land and return it to its original owners. In Jeremiah's time, they refused to free their slaves. Why would they refuse to do all that? It's the same battle that started in Eden. It was more profitable for the few to keep the land they had acquired. It was more profitable not to rest it. And it was certainly more profitable to have free labor. They disobeyed God because they preferred the way of Mammon. They wanted the ways of Egypt and Babylon. So the Lord sent them there. God exiled them for their greed and self-interest.

In the work of the Old Testament prophets, we once again find descriptions of a better world than that of the kings. We see the prophets looking forward to the New Covenant. But we also see the prophets focusing on social sins more than individual sins. Of course both are there, but one cannot escape noting how "Marxist" in flavor the prophets sound to Cold War, American ears. The prophets, like all of scripture, saw the world as a clash between God and Mammon, and this gave a certain priority to community sins. It's almost the opposite way the many modern Christians looks at fixing society. After the Enlightenment, we tend to say that if you fix individuals first, then the social will be solved. But the prophets (and Jesus) weighed heavily in the other direction: if you fix communal relationships, then individual sins will diminish. The prophets clearly took aim at economic sins, over and over again. Sharing is central.

But even folks who recognize the overwhelming attention the prophets gave to economic sins will often grant that economic sins take second place in the prophets to idolatry. Idolatry first, oppression of the poor second. Those are the two biggies, we're told. By this point, though, even that dichotomy should seem a bit unnatural and forced. Greed and idolatry are not two different kinds of sin, one to do with money and one to do with divine loyalty. If we continue to think in terms of God and Mammon, then it's easy to see that greed is idolatry. In fact, the apostle Paul says exactly that twice.

In the midst of two long lists of sins, Paul marks an important difference between greed or covetousness and other kinds of sin.

"Therefore put to death your members which are on the earth: fornication, uncleanness, passion, evil desire, and covetousness, which is idolatry" (Col 3:5).

"For this you know, that no fornicator, unclean person, nor covetous man, who is an idolater, has any inheritance in the kingdom of Christ and God" (Eph 5:5).

For Paul, greed is idolatry—a very strange connection to modern ears. We might be willing to grant that all sins are idolatry since they all betray God. But Paul doesn't say that. He emphasizes that greed—in distinction from sexual sins in particular—is idolatry. Sexual sins are not idolatry in an important way that greed is. Brian Rosner suggests that this difference might stem from the symbolism that "greed is a sin that involves leaving God's temple altogether and worshiping elsewhere, . . . sexual immorality constitutes sin in God's temple."[1]

One way to understand this identity between greed and idolatry is to think of it within the ancient world's devotion to polytheism—the worship of many gods. Just as the desire for more gold and food than we need is greed, so is a desire to multiply gods. Humans should be satisfied with one God, Yahweh, but, no, they lust for many more. Another angle on the greed-idolatry grows out of the impersonalism of idolatry and greed. The Lord condemned his people who have fallen for the lack of personality, the lack of personhood of wooden and gold idols:

> They have mouths, but they do not speak;
>   Eyes they have, but they do not see;
> They have ears, but they do not hear;
>   Noses they have, but they do not smell;
> They have hands, but they do not handle;
>   Feet they have, but they do not walk;
> Nor do they mutter through their throat.
> Those who make them are like them;
>   So is everyone who trusts in them. (Ps 115:5–8)

The impersonalism of the idols becomes manifest in "everyone who trusts in them." Greed, the inordinate desire for wealth, does the same. It becomes a devotion to the safety and silence of gods of metal, rather than the God who questions and challenges us. Greed is idolatry. It is a rejection of sharing.

---

1. Rosner, *Greed*, 115.

Trinitarian life, again, gives us insight into the claim that greed is idolatry. As we've seen, the way of the Trinity is the way of sharing. Father, Son, and Spirit live in sacrifice and self-denial toward one another. The way of greed, the way of Mammon, focuses on the health of one part of a community, while letting others go without clothing and water. The way of greed is not the way of sharing. It is the way of self-interest, not self-denial. In that sense, then, the way of greed and self-interest depict the life of another god or gods. Greed is idolatry. God's people are supposed to image the life of the Trinity on earth, and when, instead, we say we follow the Trinity but actually build communities that politely neglect those in need, we actually image the worlds of polytheism. A social system grounded in self-interest is not a Trinitarian system.

Paul's identity of greed and idolatry, then, shows us that the prophets don't focus primarily on two sins—idolatry then oppression of the poor. It's all one sin. When the prophets indict the people for idolatry, they are indicting them for greed and vice versa. This also explains why the prophets got so angry at issues that most middle-class Christians don't see as central. When the prophets see God's people enslaving other believers or taking advantage of the labor of the poor, the prophets rightly see idolatry as a big as Egypt and Babylon and the Enlightenment. Greed is idolatry.

Instead of the usual flood of passages from the prophets proving their focus on caring for the poor, let me highlight just one, since it pulls together so many of the pieces I've been discussing. It is a passage from Isaiah that speaks to well-meaning, religious people, very much like middle-class Westerners. They were even better than many of us, they fasted, but they still didn't get God's way. They still missed the big picture like we do:

> "Why have we fasted," they say, "and You have not seen?
>   Why have we afflicted our souls, and You take no notice?"
> In fact, in the day of your fast you find pleasure,
>   And exploit all your laborers.
> Indeed you fast for strife and debate,
>   And to strike with the fist of wickedness.
> You will not fast as you do this day,
>   To make your voice heard on high.
> Is it a fast that I have chosen,
>   A day for a man to afflict his soul?
>   Is it to bow down his head like a bulrush,
>   And to spread out sackcloth and ashes?

> Would you call this a fast,
>> And an acceptable day to the LORD?
> Is this not the fast that I have chosen:
>> To loose the bonds of wickedness,
>> To undo the heavy burdens,
>> To let the oppressed go free,
>> And that you break every yoke?
> Is it not to share your bread with the hungry,
>> And that you bring to your house the poor who are cast out;
>> When you see the naked, that you cover him,
>> And not hide yourself from your own flesh?
> Then your light shall break forth like the morning,
>> Your healing shall spring forth speedily,
>> And your righteousness shall go before you;
>> The glory of the LORD shall be your rear guard.
> Then you shall call, and the LORD will answer;
>> You shall cry, and He will say, "Here I am." (Isa 58:3–9)

The Lord desires mercy, not sacrifice. The Lord desires self-denial, not middle-class niceness and fasting. The Lord desires us to share like the Trinity, not Mammon.

That is why Jesus was such an opponent of charity. The way of sharing is not the way of charity. It's no wonder that charity is so acceptable for middle-class Westerners. When Jesus stood in the Temple, he watched "the rich putting their gifts into the treasury" (Luke 21:1). That's great, isn't it? The rich work and supply money to the place that was supposed to care for the poor, the Temple. The rich were giving so that ministries could succeed. I hear that often in my circles.

But Jesus wasn't impressed. Wrong messiah. He complained of the rich that "all these out of their abundance have put in offerings for God." But that's what charity is, isn't it? It's when we rich donate some of our abundance to the poor. That's how the world turns. Charity is our way, but it isn't the way of sharing. It isn't the way of the cross. Instead of giving out of our abundance, Jesus praised the widow: "He saw also a certain poor widow putting in two mites. So He said, "Truly I say to you that this poor widow has put in more than all; for all these out of their abundance have put in offerings for God, but she out of her poverty put in all the livelihood that she had" (Luke 21:2, 3). "She put in all the livelihood that she had." She gave all, in the way the Rich Young Ruler had refused. We resist his words at that point. All? Isn't that irresponsible? We qualify by running to other passages. But at some point we have to let Jesus's words weigh on us, just hang there for a long time. Wouldn't it be better for us to give up our distorted Christian profession than to follow some figment of middle-class imagination? Would we be Christians if Jesus called us to a vow of poverty? Or is that too much to fathom? (Don't worry, God loves rich people, we insert quickly. Remember Abraham and Joseph of Arimathea. We're cool.)

In a similar way, we often distort the meaning of community and feasting. Many churches have members who live individualized lives, hardly ever meeting each other. Then sometimes, folks grow tired of that and stumble upon seemingly vibrant churches where members share more deeply in one another's lives. These members eat and fellowship with each other during the week and holidays. To the first group of individualized Christians, this second kind of church really seems to produce a true sense of community. And that's what people end up calling a good church community.

There's certainly a place for the same kind of people with the same kind of ideas sharing meals together. Jesus ate with his apostles, after all. But both groups above end up disobeying Jesus more explicit call to community, to the way of sharing. In fact, what we call a "good church community," Jesus told us not to do: "When you give a dinner or a supper, do not ask your friends, your brothers, your relatives, nor rich neighbors" (Luke 14:12). Don't do that, he said. Don't do what we normally do. "But when you give a feast, invite the poor, the maimed, the lame, the blind" (Luke 14:13). Jesus is not opposed to feasts, just the kind we normally give. The way of sharing is not the way of "good church community." It is much more difficult. Perhaps it is too hard. Then, again, we should always consider switching faiths. More on the practical features of this later.

Half. The measure of half seems to play a very important role in the way of sharing. John the Baptist highlighted half first. John knew how to resist the ways of Mammon. He rejected all the shine and credentials the reigning leadership required. He didn't teach as a member of the authorized Temple as any "credible" prophet should have. He hung out in the wilderness, a seeming regress and haunt of Satan. He certainly needed style advice. But he had a large, if paradoxical, following. We think of John in the shadow of Jesus, but before Jesus grew large, John was the main story. He was the one everyone feared and talked about, even the highest levels of society were threatened by him.

He was also not very good at being "seeker friendly." He began sermons with insults such as, "Brood of vipers! Who warned you to flee from the wrath to come?" (Luke 1:7). Not exactly the best public relations intro. Still, people were drawn to him.

And when they were convicted of their sin and asked how they should repent—"What should we do then?"—John answered by invoking the notion of half: "He who has two tunics, let him give to him who has none; and he who has food, let him do likewise" (Luke 3:11). It was the way of sharing. It was repentance that harkened back to the manna and the quail. It was Isaiah's exhortation about fasting. Share.

But it was interestingly specific. John didn't give a call for them to give up "everything," just half. Two cloaks, down to one. John the Baptist's instructions about halfness seem to be echoed in John the Apostle's command examined earlier: "But whoever has this world's goods, and sees his brother in need, and shuts up his heart from him, how does the love of God abide in him?" (1 John 3:17).

In a similar way, James explained, "If a brother or sister is naked and destitute of daily food, and one of you says to them, 'Depart in peace, be warmed and filled,' but you do not give them the things which are needed for the body, what does it profit? Thus also faith by itself, if it does not have works, is dead" (James 2:15, 16). This is the way of sharing. People are more important than property.

The issue of halfness came up explicitly with Jesus, too. As we've seen, Jesus gave the wealthy a very difficult time: "Woe to you who are rich, for you have received your consolation. Woe to you who are full, for you shall hunger" (Luke 6:24, 25). No qualifications, no hesitations. Just a blanket woe. In fact, Jesus rarely has anything encouraging or positive to say about the rich. He does praise the Roman centurion's faith, and we learn that Joseph of Arimathea provided a grave for him.

The main wealthy person Jesus truly and explicitly praised was Zacchaeus. Not all tax collectors were rich, but Zacchaeus was a chief collector. The text also gives us a hint that Jesus and Zacchaeus had met earlier. In Luke 19, Zacchaeus wanted to see Jesus again, and he climbed a tree to see him. Jesus saw him and called him down by name—"Zacchaeus, make haste and come down, for today I must stay at your house" (Luke 19:5). Then Zacchaeus said, "Look, Lord, I give half of my goods to the poor; and if I have taken anything from anyone by false accusation, I restore fourfold" (Luke 19:8). Halfness again. He did more than the other rich. He didn't just give to the poor out of his abundance. He gave half of all he owned. Then, on top of that he paid fourfold restitution to people he had defrauded.

Did Jesus insult him for not giving all? Did Jesus pronounce a woe on him? No, Jesus gave one of the most glorious benedictions possible: "And Jesus said to him, 'Today salvation has come to this house, because he also is a son of Abraham; for the Son of Man has come to seek and to save that which was lost'" (Luke 19:9, 10). Jesus spoke of deliverance or salvation. By heeding Jesus, Zacchaeus had broken the chains of Mammon and embraced the way of sharing.

As discussed earlier, the way of sharing finds its roots in the exodus travels through the wilderness. Then we find it institutionalized in the Levitical jubilee laws. The prophets call God's people back to it, during the regress of the kings, and Jesus explains it again. But finally God's new people catch on and place it right at the center of their life in the early chapters of Acts. There we hear, again, the echoes of need we first heard in Exodus 16:

> Now the multitude of those who believed were of one heart
> and one soul; neither did anyone say that any of the things he
> possessed was his own, but they had all things in common.
> And with great power the apostles gave witness to the resur-
> rection of the Lord Jesus. And great grace was upon them all.
> Nor was there anyone among them who lacked; for all who
> were possessors of lands or houses sold them, and brought
> the proceeds of the things that were sold, and laid them at the
> apostles' feet; and they distributed to each as anyone had need.
> (Acts 4:32–35)

Not only did the church distribute according to need, but no one claimed absolute private ownership of their goods. They shared in common. Another version of this becomes institutionalized in the diaconate introduced in Acts 6. And through many centuries, even today, Christian groups of various sorts have successfully lived this life. Throughout the millennia, some monasteries became so successful in common life living that they naturally became targets of plunder. The first-century Essenes also had quite a successful common life at the same time, and today, many groups have lived successfully and fruitfully even in a Western context for many decades.

Most of us are quick, again, to dismiss a common life of possessions. An infamous reading in my conservative circles is that Christians lived a common life and sold their property because they knew Jerusalem would be destroyed in AD 70, and this was a way of "plundering the Egyptians." Of course, that has to be read into the text. This seems particularly clumsy attempt to defend Mammon. The text itself speaks of fulfilling needs of the saints. It is person focused, not self-focused. It ties the common life to the preaching of the glory of the resurrection, a jubilee connection. Acts 2–4 shows us a wonderful culmination of all that God had long urged his people toward. The way of sharing had triumphed and shaped the church for many centuries to follow.

The exodus way of sharing also shows up in the letters of Paul. Paul had been organizing a international donation from various churches for the churches in Judea. In the midst of reminding the Corinthians about their commitment, Paul said, "for you know the grace of our Lord Jesus Christ, that though He was rich, yet for your sakes He became poor, that you through His poverty might become rich" (2 Cor 8:9). Jesus was rich, yet he became poor. And he did that to make others rich. This is another good summary of the way of sharing.

Then Paul argued in an interesting way in favor of the Corinthian donation. Paul invoked the notion of balance and halfness and equality we've seen earlier:

> For I do not mean that others should be eased and you
> burdened; but by an equality, that now at this time your abun-
> dance may supply their lack, that their abundance also may
> supply your lack—that there may be equality. As it is written,
> "He who gathered much had nothing left over, and he who
> gathered little had no lack." (2 Cor 8:13–15)

Paul expects the Corinthians to understand his appeal to the justice of equality. Of course, he didn't want anything coerced, needless to say. But he does suggest the Corinthians give to relieve a lack "that there may be equality." Then he cites Exodus 16 about the manna, explaining with that verse that in the way of sharing, everyone's needs should be cared for within the covenant, old or new.

Jesus, John the Baptist, Paul, James, John, Luke all explain and exhort us to a radical way of sharing, a way grounded in the exodus and the prophets. It is the way of making Trinity on earth.

The final vision of Matthew 25 captures the way of sharing, too. We saw previously how Matthew 25 included the ways of weakness, renunciation, and deliverance. The vision, more than anything else, is certainly the way of sharing. The community of Matthew 25 shares its food, drink, friendship: "I was naked and you clothed Me; I was sick and you visited Me; I was in prison and you came to Me" (Matt. 25:31ff).

6

The Way of Enemy Love

"A soldier of civil authority must be taught not to kill men and to refuse to do so if he is commanded. . . . If he is unwilling to comply, he must be rejected."

—HIPPOLYTUS, C. AD 236

"Very few who are instigators of war actually take the field of battle. . . . It is usually those who are rioting on the labors of the poor that fan up the flame of war."

—DAVID LOW DODGE, PRESBYTERIAN LEADER, 1815

Christians don't believe in love. We don't believe love is a serious and thick force in the cosmos, a power that actually topples things. Love can't move mountains, we assume. We deny love is lightning that can explode trees or a dense river that cuts through granite. We even believe soft-tissued humans are stronger than love. We prefer intimidation and punishment to change people. Even we Calvinists, who believe so much about God is irresistible, spend more pages discussing the legitimacy of the sword and the civil magistrate than expositions of love. To most Christians, love is thin and frail, shattering on everything it touches. We believe love is fleeting and giggly, like early romance. Love is a teenage crush, not something for hard-headed life.

Christians act, however, as though ideas are stronger than love. We spend much more time sharpening our concepts and arguments. We believe in institutions more than love, too. We show great zeal in developing institutional bylaws and policies. We also have utmost confidence in the power of gravity and natural energy. We insist our enemies-of-the-moment only understand force. We must use force. We are closet Newtonians. Only force is truly effective. All bow to Hobbesian cause and effect. Love doesn't even enter that equation.

Imagine the opposite. Imagine we really believed, as Dante said, in "the Love which moves the sun and the other stars." Imagine if the universe truly acted and reacted in terms of Trinitarian love. Imagine, as Paul, said, "the whole creation groans and labors with birth pangs together until now" (Rom 8:22). Ernesto Cardenal captures this picture well.

> The whole universe yearns for union with God, and has so ever since it came forth from God. All things are scattered away from God and long to join each other. The law of love is the one physical and biological law of the universe and the one moral law. . . . All our desires and hungers, for food, sex, friendship, are a single appetite, a single hunger, for union with one another and with the universe. It is a cosmic communion that finds fulfillment only in Christ.[1]

He continues in evocative detail.

> All things love one another. Everything in nature feels itself in accord with all the rest. All plants, animals, and things have family features and copy one another. There are insects that imitate flowers and flowers that imitate insects, animals that are like water, rocks, the sand of the desert, snow, trees or other animals. All living beings love one another (and eat one another). . . . All things in nature are mutation, transformation, and change, of the one into the other; they hug and caress and kiss. And like the laws governing inert nature (which is also alive with a life we cannot see) are all contained in the one law of love. All physical phenomena are the one phenomenon of love. . . . The laws of thermodynamics and electrodynamics, the laws of light and universal gravity are all one and the same law of love. Everything in nature is incomplete, offers itself

1. Cardenal, Love, 71.

to another and clasps the other to it. All beings in their most
secret self and deepest depth, hunger and thirst for love.[2]

Modern Christians shift uneasily with this sort of language. And that
unease helps reveal who we are. It might sound too soft or too mystical
or maybe pantheistic or too something not right. We shudder and move
on. But what if it's exactly right? What if the "prairie wolf howling in the
night howls for God, and the owl hoots for him"?[3] What if the calf moos
and the lion roars and the frogs croak for Father, Son, and Spirit?

Given that Father, Son, and Spirit, the most fundamental personal
reality of the universe are "love" (1 John 4:16), we should expect the created order to run by the dynamics of love. In a universe driven by love,
Christ's commandments about love would sound natural and normal and
strong. They would be organic, fitting, obvious, the only way that makes
sense. But we can't bring ourselves to believe in a world truly moved by
love, and that's one of the reasons we dismiss Jesus when he commands
us to love our enemies. It's too alien for us. We find it an unnatural command. It's just folly in our picture. Love is unrealistic. It can't have any
power in Newton's world. Loving our enemies would just produce a lot
of dead Christians. So Christians have conspired quietly for centuries to
set aside Jesus's craziness, taming him for modern sensibilities. We reduce loving one's enemies to a purely private thing, not public policy, and
spiritual, for the most part, for nice enemies, interior, yeah, and spiritual,
sometimes.

And yet few commands are so central in Jesus's teaching. Jesus
rarely pays attention to predestination or freewill, yet many Protestant
traditions dedicate whole chapters to those subjects in our confessions.
Jesus repeats his command to love our enemies, explicitly and implicitly,
multiple times throughout the gospels, and love of enemies is not even
mentioned once in the most prominent Reformation creeds. Are we even
on the same planet? Are we looking at the same Jesus? "Why do you call
Me 'Lord, Lord,' and not do the things which I say?" (Luke 6:46).

Augustine even went so far as to redefine love in terms of violence:
"there is a righteous persecution, which the Church of Christ inflicts
upon the impious. . . . She persecutes in the spirit of love. . . that she
may correct. . . . She persecutes her enemies and arrests them, until they
become weary in their vain opinions. . . . We take measures for their

2. Ibid., 1, 2.
3. Ibid., 4.

good, to secure their eternal salvation."[4] Augustine can do this because he regularly takes refuge in the privacy of the heart, explaining Jesus as speaking a "precept with regard to the preparation of the heart, and not with regard to the visible performance of the deed."[5] We can persecute and kill our enemies, he argues, if we do it with a good motive.

Jesus, however, spoke very much about an outward, visible loving of one's enemy. He explained his "love your enemies" in external terms as "do good and lend, hoping for nothing in return" like the Father who is "kind to the unthankful and evil." We are to "be merciful, just as your Father is merciful" (Luke 6:34–36). And the Father shows mercy by making the, "sun rise on the evil and on the good, and sends rain on the just and on the unjust" (Matt 5:35). It's positive kindness and mercy and goodness.

And Paul gave the same exhortation, writing, "If your enemy is hungry, feed him; If he is thirsty, give him a drink" (Rom 12:20). In all these, loving one's enemy means showing, outward, positive mercy—sunshine, rain, food, drink. To construe it so that Jesus actually meant to justify the opposite, public unkindness, outward mercilessness, killing, is the height of doublespeak. One might as well have scripture say, if your enemy is hungry, slit his throat; if thirsty, drown him. Augustine completely eviscerated the command to love one's enemies, and so do most of us. We're far more comfortable with Mars than Jesus.

The way of enemy love is the way of the cross. If we walk in the way of the cross, then we have to be willing to say, "Father forgive them"(Luke 23:34) in the midst of torturers, as Jesus said about the crowd, the Romans, and the Jewish leaders who nailed him to the cross. We're called to love them, not carpet bomb them and torture them in return, as in the American way. Jesus loved his enemies and even sought to deliver them through his death and resurrection. At least, that's how Paul explained it. Paul said, "Christ died for the ungodly" (Rom 5:6). "God demonstrates His own love toward us, in that while we were still sinners, Christ died for us" (Rom 5:7). And again, "when we were enemies we were reconciled to God through the death of His Son" (Rom 5:10). While enemies, we were reconciled. While ungodly, Christ died for us. This is love for enemies.

This way of enemy love becomes one of the most repeated commands in the New Testament, most repeated and most ignored. It is

4. Augustine in Parsons, *Fathers of the Church*, 4:152.

5. Augustine in Kavanaugh, *Fathers of the Church*, 11:85.

revolutionary and counter-cultural in the deepest of senses. It runs contrary to everything we learn from the world. Egypt, Babylon, Rome, and the modern West dismiss the way of enemy love, but Jesus puts it at the center of his new world, his kingdom.

The apostle Peter told Christians that we are a "royal priesthood, a holy nation" (1 Pet 2:9), but unlike other kingdoms, there were to be a political body, "not returning evil for evil or reviling for reviling, but on the contrary blessing" (1 Pet 3:9). That is our foreign policy, absorbing their evil and blessing our enemies.

The apostle Paul commanded repeatedly:

"Repay no one evil for evil" (Rom 12:17).

"Do not be overcome by evil, but overcome evil with good" (Rom 12:21).

"See that no one renders evil for evil to anyone" (1 Thess 5:15).

"Being reviled, we bless; being persecuted, we endure; being defamed, we entreat" (1 Cor 4:12).

And this theme of overcoming evil with good shows up in the Book of Revelation. Jesus praised the church at Thyatria for its works of "love, service, faith" (Rev 2:29) and then exhorted, "he who overcomes, and keeps My works until the end, to him I will give power over the nations" (Rev 2:26).

Later in Revelation, we see the saints overcame Satan by suffering and more:

> Now salvation, and strength, and the kingdom of our God,
> and the power of His Christ have come, for the accuser of our
> brethren, who accused them before our God day and night, has
> been cast down. And they overcame him by the blood of the
> Lamb and by the word of their testimony, and they did not love
> their lives to the death. (Rev 12:10, 11)

Notice, here, that Christ's followers have overthrown Satan, just as Jesus noted part of that work during his own ministry (Luke 10:18). What's key is that the saints here didn't make Satan fall by attempting to overthrow oppressive Rome, like first-century zealots or American colonists, and they didn't overthrow him by means of a carnal crusade. They did it by resisting and suffering and sacrificing.

"Overcome evil with good" is the common feature of all of these commands. It itself is a summary of Jesus's commands to "Love your enemies, do good to those who hate you, bless those who curse you, and pray for those who spitefully use you" (Luke 6:27, 28).

"Overcome evil with good" should be our first instinct, first interpersonally, first interculturally, and first internationally. The way of enemy love lies at the heart of the way of the cross.

But these commands to love our enemies prompt giant questions. If loving our enemies means we can't kill them, then how are we to understand the clear and divinely commanded violence of the Old Covenant? The way of enemy love seems to undermine the entire Old Testament, and yet Jesus said he hadn't come to abolish the old (Matt 5:17). What does enemy love make of just wars and self-defense? And if we're supposed to love our enemies, why does God seem to do that, given judgment and hell?

Consider the Old Testament questions first. The Old Covenant certainly involved direct commands from God for violent actions and warfare. No need to prove that. But what we often miss is the Old Covenant's constant and perhaps paradoxical condemnation of violence. Some of the best anti-violence statements come not from Jesus but from the Old Covenant. Not only that. The Old Covenant anticipates the coming shift away from the older way of violence. First, consider a few passages and watch how unqualified and general they are in their simplicity. Modern defenders of "good" violence will often insert language of motives and justifications, without giving blanket condemnations of violence. It's interesting that many of the following don't attempt such a distinction. They simply speak of violence in general, without dividing between good and bad violence:

"The earth also was corrupt before God, and the earth was filled with violence. . . . And God said to Noah, 'The end of all flesh has come before Me, for the earth is filled with violence through them; and behold, I will destroy them with the earth'" (Gen 6:11,13).

"The LORD tests the righteous, but the wicked and the one who loves violence His soul hates" (Ps 11:5).

"Deliver me to the will of my adversaries; for false witnesses have risen against me, and such as breathe out violence" (Ps 27:12).

"Destroy, O Lord, and divide their tongues, for I have seen violence and strife in the city" (Ps 55:9).

"He will redeem their life from oppression and violence" (Ps 72:14).

"Therefore pride serves as their necklace; violence covers them like a garment" (Ps 73:6).

"They eat the bread of wickedness, and drink the wine of violence" (Prov 4:17).

"The mouth of the righteous is a well of life, but violence covers the mouth of the wicked" (Prov 10:11).

"A man shall eat well by the fruit of his mouth, but the soul of the unfaithful feeds on violence" (Prov 13:2).

"The violence of the wicked will destroy them" (Prov 21:7).

"Their heart devises violence, and their lips talk of troublemaking" (Prov 24:2).

"Their works are works of iniquity, and the act of violence is in their hands" (Isa 59:6).

"Violence shall no longer be heard in your land" (Isa 60:18).

"Do no wrong and do no violence to the stranger, the fatherless, or the widow, nor shed innocent blood in this place" (Jer 22:3).

"Your eyes and your heart are for nothing but your covetousness, for shedding innocent blood, and practicing oppression and violence" (Jer 22:17).

"Is it a trivial thing to the house of Judah to commit the abominations which they commit here? For they have filled the land with violence" (Ezek 8:17).

"By the abundance of your trading you became filled with violence within" (Ezek 28:16).

"Enough, O princes of Israel! Remove violence and plundering" (Ezek 45:9).

"let everyone turn from his evil way and from the violence that is in his hands" (Jonah 3:8).

"Rich men are full of violence" (Mic 6:12).

"They all come for violence; their faces are set like the east wind" (Hab 1:9).

Typical defenders of violence don't speak in these simple categories. These broad, Old Covenant condemnations of violence, for example, don't distinguish carefully between "terrorists" and "freedom fighters." They don't seem to understand the line between muggers and military heroes. They just seem to present us with God's opposition to violence as a whole. "Remove violence." "The unfaithful feeds on violence." "The earth is filled with violence." "Violence shall no longer be heard in your land."

Yet, the Lord certainly had Israel use violence for his ends. One way to mesh these blanket condemnations of violence with the sanctioned violence would simply be to force a distinction between good and bad violence. For example, one could say that all the verses above speak only of the wicked, and so only the wicked do this thing called violence. The good don't do violence but "coercive defense" or something. That seems pretty contrived, though, a way of forcing the text to say what we want.

Instead of trying to flatten or force texts, it makes more sense to note multiple voices in scripture. The Old Covenant speaks to and of multiple ages at the same time. It has past, present, and future at work throughout. This past-future overlap comes out, for example, when the Lord prohibits David from building his Temple. God's reason for prohibiting David sounds strangely hypocritical at first. David had long been God's approved warrior.

> You are my King, O God;
> > Command victories for Jacob.
> Through You we will push down our enemies;
> > Through Your name we will trample those who rise up
> against us. (Ps 44:4, 5)

God himself sometimes gave detailed war instructions to David. Early on, when the Philistines heard that David had been anointed king over Israel, they hunted him. So David went out to fight them, but he first inquired of the Lord: "Shall I go up against the Philistines? Will You deliver them into my hand?" And the Lord said, "Go up, for I will deliver them into your hand." When David was victorious, he declared, "God has broken through my enemies by my hand like a breakthrough of water" (1 Chr 14:10, 11).

It's not a little strange, then, that when David sought to build the Temple for the Lord that God issued this odd veto: "You shall not build a house for My name, because you have been a man of war and have shed blood" (1 Chr 28:3). He couldn't build it because he was a warrior? Because he shed blood the way God commanded him to? What could be going on with this divine reasoning? The strangeness only increases when we realize that God did in fact allow the idolater Solomon to build his Temple but not a military man. It is interesting that Solomon does declare, "Wisdom is better than weapons of war; but one sinner destroys much good" (Eccl 9:18).

Perhaps David had some special uncleanness as a man of violence that would pollute a new Temple. Perhaps creating so many corpses overwhelmed the holiness of the Temple. Or, most likely, David's way was the way of immaturity. Whatever the case, the divine prohibition against of "man of war" gives an interesting hint that something new is afoot. The Temple points to the future; it is a shadow of what is to come (Heb 8:5; 10:1). It points to the future New Covenant Temple, a purely personal Temple made up of human beings (1 Cor 3:16, 17; 2 Cor 6:16). In a sense, the tabernacle and Temple were always obsolete and never intended for adulthood. God had always planned to destroy them and create a Temple of people. And as the old Temple foreshadowed the new, a warrior didn't fit within its symbolism. For the new Temple would not fight with carnal weapons (2 Cor 10:4). The new Temple would live an entirely new way of life.

Isaiah pointed to this significant break between the old and new ways. Isaiah prophesied that in the "latter days," which the apostles understood as their own time, the very beginning of the New Covenant (1 Tim 4:1; 2 Pet 3:3):

> They shall beat their swords into plowshares,
> And their spears into pruning hooks;
> Nation shall not lift up sword against nation,
> Neither shall they learn war anymore. (Isa 2:4)

Like the veto of David, this is another past-future overlap. Isaiah prophesied during the era of the kings, full of armies and weapons and warfare legislation. War and violence were normal, accepted, and sanctioned. To speak of a world without weapons, a world without military academies, was to speak of a place radically different from the Old Covenant. The New Covenant kingdom would be distinct, with a radically different way of life. And that's exactly what Christ's kingdom, the church, became. It became a weaponless place. Pastors and seminaries don't teach carnal warfare. As an international body, the church is not a place in which nation lifts up sword against nation (except where the church has regressed into Old Covenant immaturity).

The lead for this shift away from the military way toward the way of enemy love is taken by Messiah himself. Isaiah prophesied that the future David, the "light to the gentiles," will not be characterized by violence, like the old David, but,

> Behold! My Servant whom I uphold,
> My Elect One in whom My soul delights!
> I have put My Spirit upon Him;
> He will bring forth justice to the Gentiles.

He will not cry out, nor raise His voice,
Nor cause His voice to be heard in the street.
A bruised reed He will not break,
And smoking flax He will not quench;
He will bring forth justice for truth. (Isa 42:1–4; cf. Matt,
12:15ff.)

The images of damaged reeds and burnt plants suggest prior judgment or military action. Something has already bruised and torched the land, but it wasn't messiah. Others have crushed and wounded but messiah will heal (Matt 12:15ff.), be gentle, and not fight like the old warriors. Isaiah 53 added that "he was led as a lamb to the slaughter" and "he opened not his mouth" (Isa 53:7). Then quite explicitly, "he had done no violence" (Isa 53:9). Messiah would not be a new man, not a man of the sword. He would have a kingdom without carnal weapons.

Isaiah pictured the time when "the gentiles shall come to your light" (Isa 60:3)—the New Covenant—as a time of foreign military surrender. "For the nation and kingdom which will not serve you shall perish" (Isa 60:12), and in language describing the surrender to the church in Revelation, "that men may bring to you the wealth of the gentiles, and their kings in procession" (Isa 60:11; cf. Rev 21:24). A key symbol of the New Covenant, then, becomes the surrender of warriors to Christ: "Also the sons of those who afflicted you shall come bowing to you" (Isa 60:14). This sign was so well known that it forms the important backdrop to Jesus's and the apostles' encounter with gentile centurions. In Luke 7, the Roman centurion comes to Jesus, via mediators "pleading with Him" for healing of his servant. In the apostolic parallel in Acts 10, another pagan centurion came to Peter and "fell down at his feet and worshiped him" (Acts 10:25), an even more direct fulfillment of Isaiah's "shall come bowing to you." The submission of the pagan centurions in the New Testament revealed that the new world had come. So would Cornelius now continue violating the enemies of Rome in Christ's name? After all, so the defenders of violence argue, no one tells these centurions to do otherwise. (That argument from silence also fails because no one condemned the prostitute Rahab either.) Isaiah 60, though, gives us some of the symbolic future of military converts like Cornelius: "I will also make your officers peace, and your magistrates righteousness. Violence shall no longer be heard in your land, neither wasting nor destruction within your borders" (Isa 60:17, 18). They're unemployed in the new kingdom. The church has no need of their services.

The Old Covenant pointed to the coming shift away from violence in other ways, too. Elijah and Elisha foreshadowed John the Baptist and Jesus. The parallels between Elisha and Jesus are well known and stunning. Both received the Spirit through their predecessor. Both transform water. Both show mercy to a widow. Both raise a child from the dead. Both cure leprosy. Both feed crowds in need.

Both Elisha and Jesus teach love of enemies. Jesus not only commanded love of enemies explicitly, he even dared to show mercy to an occupying enemy of Israel—the centurion (Luke 7). Elisha loved Israel's enemies in a way that stood out in stark contrast to the rest of the Old Covenant. At one point, Elisha helped foil the king of Syria, and so that king wanted to find him. The Syrian king sent a great army to surround Dothan, where Elisha stayed. Once surrounded, Elisha prayed that the Lord would blind the Syrian enemies, and the Lord did so. Then Elisha confronted the blinded enemies and offered to lead them where they wanted but took them to a seeming trap in Samaria:

> When they had come to Samaria, that Elisha said, "LORD,
> open the eyes of these men, that they may see." And the LORD
> opened their eyes, and they saw; and there they were, inside
> Samaria! Now when the king of Israel saw them, he said to
> Elisha, "My father, shall I kill them? Shall I kill them?" But he
> answered, "You shall not kill them. Would you kill those whom
> you have taken captive with your sword and your bow? Set
> food and water before them, that they may eat and drink and
> go to their master." Then he prepared a great feast for them;
> and after they ate and drank, he sent them away and they went
> to their master. So the bands of Syrian raiders came no more
> into the land of Israel. (2 Kgs 6:20–23)

The king of Israel wanted to execute them, but Elisha gave them food and water instead of death. In fact, they were given a feast, and then they were free to return to their master. This act of mercy to an enemy had the unexpected benefit that the raiders never returned to Israel.

The Old Testament itself, then, pointed to a shift away from violence. When Jesus came and started speaking about violence like a very different, a very un-Mammon king, it should have been expected. Jesus was the king of peace, bringing the way of enemy love.

Psalm 37 provides some of the background to Jesus' beatitudes. It is a Psalm that speaks of the way of weakness, "the poor and the needy"

(v. 14), and it highlights the way of deliverance. It contrasts the righteous with the violent wicked

> The wicked have drawn the sword
> And have bent their bow,
> To cast down the poor and needy,
> To slay those who are of upright conduct.
> Their sword shall enter their own heart,
> And their bows shall be broken. (Ps 37:14, 15)

The wicked and powerful slay the upright, but, in contrast to the violent, "the meek shall inherit the earth, and shall delight themselves in the abundance of peace" (Ps 37:11). Jesus began his ministry by invoking Psalm 37 as a description of those in his kingdom: "Blessed are the meek, for they shall inherit the earth" (Ps 5:5).

In the remainder of the Sermon on the Mount, Jesus echoed Moses in many ways. He was on a mountain, before a people, preaching a new kingdom, a deeper law, a law that filled out the shadow of the old. He was not ending the old law, but it was only a seed, limited and not full, and Jesus was the full-grown tree. In the sermon, Jesus pruned away many overgrown traditions, but he also went beyond surface readings of the old law.

Leviticus had said, "You shall not take vengeance, nor bear any grudge against the children of your people, but you shall love your neighbor as yourself: I am the LORD" (Lev 19:18). But Jesus took it further. He removed the tradition in favor of hating our neighbor, and then showed that God wanted more. He wanted us to love not just our friends and neighbors but also our enemies: "love your enemies, bless those who curse you, do good to those who hate you, and pray for those who spitefully use you and persecute you" (Matt 5:43,44). Elisha surpassed Moses.

In a similar way, the old law wonderfully aimed to curb ancient violence by restricting it to an equality, an eye for an eye, instead of a life for an eye. That mercy, too, headed in the right direction, but it didn't go as far as Elisha and Isaiah and Messiah. Jesus showed the deeper desire of God:

> You have heard that it was said, "An eye for an eye and a tooth
> for a tooth." But I tell you not to resist an evil person. But
> whoever slaps you on your right cheek, turn the other to him
> also. If anyone wants to sue you and take away your tunic, let
> him have your cloak also. And whoever compels you to go one

mile, go with him two. Give to him who asks you, and from
him who wants to borrow from you do not turn away. (Matt.
5:38–42)

Leaving aside the details of application for the moment, notice the larger
shift. Jesus wasn't afraid to move beyond the externalism of the old code.
The old code was good and holy, but it wasn't the whole story, just the
seed or a pointer that ends in Jesus—Christ is the goal of the law, what the
law aimed at (Rom 10:4). The law was an incomplete opening, and Jesus
explained the fuller kingdom. Most notably, however one interprets the
passages above, Jesus has made a significant shift away from the ways of
violence. Life was not to remain the same as in the Old Covenant. Jesus
carried on the way of Elisha rather than David.

In another context, Jesus again highlighted the limitations of the Old
Covenant in a way that prohibited a straight carry-over of the old code. In
correcting the Pharisees about their wooden understanding of the laws
of divorce, Jesus explained that divorce was much more restrained than
they understood. They asked why Moses allowed divorce, after all. "He
said to them, 'Moses, because of the hardness of your hearts, permitted
you to divorce your wives, but from the beginning it was not so'" (Matt
19:8). As many have noted, this is quite a significant revelation. It revealed divine motivation behind aspects of the law. It meant the Mosaic
code was a divine condescension. In a very important way, the Mosaic
law was Yahweh becoming "all things to all men" (1 Cor 9:22). To the
weak, he became weak. To the hard-hearted, he became hard-hearted. He
worked within their hard-heartedness. In other words, the Mosaic code
included prescriptions that even God wasn't pleased with. He wanted
something better, something different even as he gave and approved the
law to Moses.

The Lord was willing to work with immaturity. But the New Covenant shows us what he truly wanted: mercy, not sacrifice. And so in the
new, he curtails not only divorce, but polygamy, animal sacrifice, cleanliness laws, chattel slavery, and, quite importantly, war and violence. The
New Covenant would be a new age, a new world in which his people, the
peacemakers, would "beat their swords into plowshares."

The way of violence is the way of Mammon, after all. It lives by
surfaces and visible cause and effect. Satan tempted Jesus with all the
kingdoms of this world, with all their wealth and militaries and blind-
nesses. As Jesus and the apostles waited in the garden before the climax

of his ministry, we get to view a direct clash between the way of Mammon and the way of the cross. The Jewish leadership sent violence, "a great multitude with swords and clubs," to arrest Jesus. This was Mammon in action—power, deceit, glory, clubs, and swords. As the mob tried to grab Jesus, one of his disciples pulled out a sword to defend Jesus and struck off the ear of the high priest's servant. Jesus rebuked the disciple, "Put your sword in its place, for all who take the sword will perish by the sword" (Matt 26:52). (This rebuke also shows how badly the apostles had misunderstood Jesus's earlier eschatological language about bringing swords—Luke 22:35ff.)

The "die by the sword" rule is interesting. Defenders of violence dismiss it by explaining that this was a unique instance. Jesus knew he needed to atone for sin so to have resisted arrest violently at that point would have ruined his atonement. But in other circumstances, they argue, this sort of self-defense would have been quite acceptable and just. In other words, if it weren't for atonement, Jesus might have wielded the sword himself.

Several things work against this. Jesus's own words are quite universal and undermine the unique-moment response. He says "all who take the sword." That is a pretty wide scope. He's not arguing special circumstances. And the "it must happen thus" need not be a special circumstance of atonement either. The most obvious scripture he had in mind was one cited just a few chapters earlier and referenced multiple times in the New Testament: "The stone which the builders rejected has become the chief cornerstone" (Ps 118:22). And if this was the scripture he had in mind, then the circumstance was not unique. The Jewish leadership's rejection of Jesus was another instance of the universal struggle between God and Mammon. Mammon will always use violence against the way of Christ. It will regularly come with clubs and swords, but that is not the way of the cross. So Jesus gave a universal command against being a people of violence. The real clincher for universality, though, comes from the book of Revelation. Revelation 13 draws on the imagery of Daniel 7 to describe the terror of the Roman Empire. Rome was a beast who made war on the saints, and after describing this beast, the narrator concluded,

> If anyone has an ear, let him hear. He who leads into captivity
> shall go into captivity; he who kills with the sword must be
> killed with the sword. Here is the patience and the faith of the
> saints. (Rev 13:9, 10)

Here, then, long after the crucifixion, the Lord reiterated Jesus's command from the garden: "he who kills with the sword must be killed with the sword." In an interesting way, it is a reversal of the *lex talionis* applied broadly against violence itself. It is a new world. And in this new world, the people of God don't fight with carnal weapons, but "they overcame him by the blood of the Lamb and by the word of their testimony, and they did not love their lives to the death" (Rev 12:11). This is the world of Elisha and Jesus, not Moses and David. As the church father Tertullian (c. AD 160–225) noted, "the Lord, in disarming Peter, disarmed every soldier."[6]

The way of Mammon or its synonym "the world" runs counter to the way of the cross. That's why the interchange between Pontius Pilate and Jesus was so significant. Pontius Pilate represented the injustice and violence of Mammon, the world, and Jesus represented his new kingdom of plowshares. Pilate said Jesus's own people, the chief priests, had turned Jesus over to Rome. "What have you done?"

Jesus answered that if he were indeed a violent political rebel, like the many freedom-fighting zealots of Palestine, then his men would have taken up weapons to avoid his capture. But his kingdom was not a kingdom of Mammon. It was the beginning of the peace of heaven on earth. Or in Jesus's words: "My kingdom is not of this world. If My kingdom were of this world, My servants would fight, so that I should not be delivered to the Jews; but now My kingdom is not from here" (John 18:36). Notice, if his kingdom were worldly, his servants would use carnal weapons. You cannot serve Christ and Mammon—one loves his enemies and the other tortures them with bravado.

The apostles followed Christ's lead against violence. Not only did the apostles teach enemy love and the overcoming of evil by love, as noted earlier (Rom 12:17, 21; 1 Thess 5:15; 1 Cor 4:12; 1 Pet 3:9), they exhorted us explicitly to follow Christ's path:

> Christ also suffered for you, leaving you an example, that you
> should follow his steps: who did no sin, neither was guile
> found in his mouth: who, when he was reviled, reviled not
> again; when he suffered threatened not; but committed himself
> to him that judges righteously. (1 Pet 2:21ff)

The apostle Paul created special difficulties for defenders of violence. In order to get Paul on their side, Christian defenders of New Covenant

---

6. Tertullian in Roberts, *Ante-Nicene*, 3:73.

violence have to force a medieval and modern distinction into his teaching. They see Paul both defending the Old Covenant social order without change, as well as the modern distinction between church and state. But this creates painful contradictions in Paul.

Unlike most of us, Paul saw the church as a social order sufficient to itself, ultimately without the need of a civil realm. Consider the way Paul divided up society in his rebuke of the Corinthians: "For what have I to do with judging those also who are outside? Do you not judge those who are inside? But those who are outside God judges" (1 Cor 5:12, 13). Here, Paul marks the boundaries of Christian society in terms of those inside and outside the church. For him, those outside the church don't fall under the jurisdiction of a conceivable Christian state or civil magistrate. They don't fall under Christian jurisdiction at all: "what have I to do with judging those who are outside?" That's God's job, not the church's.

Paul expanded the significance of this even more in his subsequent point. The Corinthians had given legitimacy to pagan civil magistrates outside the church, and Paul found this scandalous. The realm outside of the church was virtually nothing. It had no serious relevance or say over Christ's kingdom, the church. He rebuked the Corinthians for not being a whole kingdom, able to resolve civil matters within itself:

> Dare any of you, having a matter against another, go to law
> before the unrighteous, and not before the saints? Do you not
> know that the saints will judge the world? And if the world
> will be judged by you, are you unworthy to judge the smallest
> matters? Do you not know that we shall judge angels? How
> much more, things that pertain to this life? If then you have
> judgments concerning things pertaining to this life, do you
> appoint those who are least esteemed by the church to judge?
> I say this to your shame. Is it so, that there is not a wise man
> among you, not even one, who will be able to judge between
> his brethren? But brother goes to law against brother, and that
> before unbelievers! (1 Cor 6:1–6)

Paul insisted that the saints had greater authority in judging issues the Corinthians used to take to the unbelieving courts. After all, the church will judge the world and angels. So how much more should the church be able to judge and order issues of this life? Again, Paul divided between two social realms, two kingdoms, but not the way some Reformation traditions do. It is not a divide between the church and a neutral state. The church is supposed to be able to do it all. The church has no need of an unbelieving or a so-called neutral state. The church is a kingdom to itself. Like Christ, Paul divided between God and Mammon, the church and Mammon, not Christian church-state vs. non-Christian church-state. The church is to be a fully functioning city, a "holy city, a New Jerusalem, coming down out of heaven from God." That's the picture in Jesus and Paul's mind. But Christ's city does not rule like Mammon's. It does not rule with violence.

If we don't see Paul speaking in terms of two, distinct social realms—Christ vs. Mammon—then Paul becomes self-contradictory, urging Christians toward and against violence at the same time. For Paul, the "we" is always the church, not the Mammon state. Consider Paul's famous exhortation against the way of violence: "For though we walk in the flesh, we do not war according to the flesh. For the weapons of our warfare are not carnal but mighty in God for pulling down strongholds" (2 Cor 10:3, 4; cf. Eph 6:12). Who is the "we" here? In the immediate context, it's explicitly the apostles, rulers of the church. The implied "they" is the realm of Mammon, Rome, Herodians, Babylon, Egypt, and the whole domination gang. On this divide, "we" the Christians of Christ's kingdom, the church, do not use carnal weapons, while the world does. But defenders of violence have to clip Paul's words here. They want to insert the possibility of a Christian state and military. And so they insist that Paul has to mean that Christians don't use carnal weapons unless they are part of this other realm within Christ's kingdom where they are politicians and warriors who can in fact use carnal weapons with God's approval. Christians do and don't fight with carnal weapons.

The same contradiction appears with Romans 13, the presumed hang-out for defenders of state violence. Defenders of Christian violence read Romans 13 as Paul laying out a doctrine for the legitimacy of a Christian state: "For there is no authority except from God, and the authorities that exist are appointed by God. Therefore whoever resists the authority resists the ordinance of God" (Rom 13:1, 2). They conclude, then, that both Christian and non-Christians states may legitimately slay, invade, bomb, and fight with carnal weapons. So, again, this reading has Paul teaching that Christians do and do not wield carnal weapons. In essence, such advocates argue for a realm within Christ's kingdom that does not fall under the commands against carnal weapons or enemy love. In some parts of the church, Christians are obligated to love their enemies but in other parts they can be obligated to kill those same enemies.

This ethical schizophrenia becomes particularly acute around Romans 13 because Paul's whole discussion about the civil magistrate is framed by the contrasting way of the church. Again, Paul's "we" is the church—"I beseech you brethren"—and just prior to arguing for a divine function for the state, he urged Christians to the way of enemy love: "Repay no one evil for evil" and did not add, "unless you hold civil or military office." He then exhorted, "Beloved, do not avenge yourselves," again not qualifying, "unless you do it as an agent of a Christian emperor." Finally, Paul explained "for it is written, 'Vengeance is mine, I will repay,' says the Lord" unless "you have Christian warriors, then vengeance is right back in your hands." These absurd qualifications don't stop. Every exhortation of Paul just before Romans 13 has to be twisted or disobeyed in order to make room for the defenders of violence: "If your enemy is hungry" continue the blockade. "If he is thirty" destroy his infrastructure with smart bombs. "Overcome evil with good," unless you have signed a contract with the Pentagon, then go ahead and do whatever Mars commands.

Paul makes much more sense if we remember his distinction between those inside the church and those outside. "We" don't use carnal weapons at all. We are the place where swords are transformed into farm tools. The same "we" operates in understanding Romans 13. Paul doesn't give anything like a constructive view of the state, there. He merely tells Christians not to use violence against the state, like the zealots. Since the beginning, God has used various Babylons and now uses Rome to accomplish his purposes in history. But that doesn't mean that God wants the church to fight with those same weapons. Romans 12 is the "we" of the church, and Romans 13 is the "them" of Mammon and Rome and the world. Yes, God will use them, even calling Cyrus his servant (Isa 45:1). But that's not grounds for establishing a Christian state that can disobey the entire framework of the New Covenant shift away from violence. "We" overcome evil with good; Mammon overcomes evil with evil.

The New Covenant brings deliverance in the church from the shallow machinations of violence. Humans are no longer captive to the reductionistic world of cause and effect. Jesus opened a new path and a new world. As the early church father, Justin Martyr (c. AD 100–165), recognized,

> We who were filled with war, and mutual slaughter, and every
> wickedness, have each through the whole earth changed our

warlike weapons—our swords into ploughshares, and our spears into implements of tillage.[7]

Similarly, Irenaeus (c. AD 130–202), declared,

The new covenant that brings back peace and the law that gives life have gone forth over the whole earth. . . . These people [Christians] formed their swords and war-lances into plowshares, . . . that is, into instruments used for peaceful purposes. So now, they are unaccustomed to fighting. When they are struck, they offer also the other cheek.[8]

Clement of Alexandria (c. AD 150–215) joined in, too:

In their wars, therefore, the Etruscans use the trumpet, the Arcadians the pipe, the Sicilians the pectides, the Cretans the lyre, the Lacedaemonians the flute, the Thracians the horn, the Egyptians the drum, and the Arabians the cymbal. The one instrument of peace, the Word alone by which we honor God, is what we employ.[9]

Origen (c. AD 184–254) described Isaiah's prophecy this way:

We are come, agreeably to the counsels of Jesus, to cut down our hostile and insolent wordy swords into ploughshares, and to convert into pruning-hooks the spears formerly employed in war. For we no longer take up sword against nation, nor do we learn war any more, having become children of peace, for the sake of Jesus, who is our leader.[10]

Athanasius (c. AD 296–373) described the effects of the gospel of peace in this way:

But when they [the Greeks and Barbarians] have come over to the school of Christ, then, strangely enough, as men truly pricked in conscience, they have laid aside the savagery of their murders and no longer mind the things of war; but all is at peace with them, and from henceforth what makes for friendship is to their liking.

Who then is He that has done this, or who is He that has united in peace men that hated one another, save the Beloved

---

7. Justin Martyr in Roberts, *Ante-Nicene*, 1:254.

8. Irenaeus in Roberts, *Ante-Nicene*, 1:512.

9. Clement of Alexandria in Roberts, *Ante-Nicene*, 2:249.

10. Origen of Alexandria in Roberts, *Ante-Nicene*, 4:558.

Son of the Father, the common Saviour of all, even Jesus Christ, Who, by His own love underwent all things for our salvation? For even from of old it was prophesied of the peace He was to usher in, where Scripture says: "They shall beat their swords into ploughshares, and their pikes into sickles, and nation shall not take the sword against nation, neither shall they learn war anymore."

And this is at least not incredible, inasmuch as even now those barbarians who have an innate savagery of manner, while thy still sacrifice to the idols of their country, are mad against one another, and cannot endure to be a single hour without weapons: but when they hear the teaching of Christ, straightway instead of fighting they turn to husbandry, and instead of arming their hands with weapons they raise them in prayer, and in a word, in place of fighting among themselves, henceforth they arm against the devil and against evil spirits, subduing these by self-restraint and virtue of the soul.[11]

Over and over again many church fathers recognized the centrality and power of the way of enemy love. They sang the glories of the New Covenant as a kingdom of plowshares that had already been established.

But still, what was the divine explanation for the shift from the old ways of violence to the new way of Jesus? We've already seen that the Old Covenant itself was hinting and moving toward Jesus's kingdom. We saw the generic condemnations of violence, the rejection of David's way, and the prophetic promises of a new nonviolent world of the messiah. But why? Why didn't the Lord just start off with Jesus's way of enemy love?

Part of the answer certainly turns on the notion of human maturity. We saw above how Jesus characterized part of the divine motive for the Mosaic code as a condescension to human hard-heartedness, a spiritual immaturity. The apostle Paul explicitly categorizes the Old Covenant as a form of immaturity when he speaks of the Mosaic law as "our tutor to bring us to Christ" but that with Christ "we are no longer under a tutor" (Gal 3:24, 25). Many more things are going on in Galatians, but Paul's categories at that point are highly instructive. Like Jesus, the apostle understood both the justice and the limits of the old ways.

In a very important sense, then, just as individuals cannot have instant maturity so it is with God's people. Just as individuals move from an important and necessary world of external rules and spankings to the maturity of virtues driving us from within, so the same with God's people.

11. Athanasius, *Incarnation*, 91.

We moved from an external code designed to prepare us for virtues of New Covenant adulthood. Maturity is largely the shift from external rules to a genuine morality ingrained in the heart. Even in the New Covenant, children pass through a childhood of external rules and codes until they begin to internalize God's ways and make them their own. In that time of immaturity, too, play-violence of war games and sports serves an important function in growing up. We all pass through the Old Covenant to get to the New. But at every point of childhood, parents long for the Spirit to write himself on the hearts of our children. We aim to move beyond the external chastisements of spankings and threats in order to see them win maturity. We want them to grow out of the immaturity of war.

That external-internal move is exactly what Scripture itself promised about the New Covenant: "I will put My law in their minds, and write it on their hearts" (Jer 31:31). The New Covenant would bring a new maturity, adulthood. As Paul explained the external-internal divide of the Old and New Covenants, the new is "Christ, ministered by us, written not with ink but by the Spirit of the living God, not on tablets of stone but on tablets of flesh, that is, of the heart. . . . for the letter kills, but the Spirit gives life" (2 Cor 3:3, 6).

The coming of the fullness of the Trinity—the coming of the Son and the Spirit—mark the move away from the way of Mosaic immaturity. In a very important sense, the Old Covenant lacked the full revelation of God, the Father, Son, and Holy Spirit. The fullness of the Triune life had not been revealed to them. That is one of the glories of the New Covenant: we received both the Son and the Spirit in a way radically unlike God's people in the Old Covenant. They had hints, but since they lacked the fullness of Yahweh, they could not be expected to be a people of maturity. They were bound to fail because, as a people, they could not fully obey from the heart the way the new people with Christ and the Spirit could. This yearning for the Spirit and the power to obey is found in the prophets. Ezekiel prophesied, "I will give you a new heart and put a new spirit within you; I will take the heart of stone out of your flesh and give you a heart of flesh. I will put My Spirit within you and cause you to walk in My statutes" (Ezek 36:26, 27; cf. Ezek 37:14), and the Lord also promised Christ, "David My servant shall be king over them, and they shall all have one shepherd; they shall also walk in My judgments and observe My statutes, and do them" (Ezek 37:24). The Son and the Spirit were the keys to the coming maturity.

PART ONE: What Is the Way of the Cross?

In the Old Covenant, God led Israel by the hand, with direct revelation about violence grounded in his omniscience, to wipe out people whose hearts and ends he could see clearly. He gave specific names—"the Hittite and the Amorite and the Canaanite and the Perizzite and the Hivite and the Jebusite, just as the LORD your God has commanded you" (Deut 20:17). Their goodness had turned to stone, and God knew exactly and justly how to wipe them out.

Deathly violence assumes omniscience. Just violence requires a knowledge of all the facts of a situation. It must weigh hearts, motives, reactions, material factors, and the coming blowback. It can succeed with direct, divine revelation from the mind of God. For example, he knows exactly when "for the iniquity of the Amorites is not yet complete" (Gen 15:16). He can read hearts and can know when individuals and whole peoples are so hardened as to be beyond rescue. He knows when they have shifted from humans to beasts and cannot be won by love.[12] The precise execution of violence by God is good and holy because of omniscience.

Omniscience also explains why vengeance belongs to the Lord (Rom 12:19; Ps 94:1; Deut 32:35). The Lord knows perfectly how to wield justice in a way that no human mind can fathom or anticipate. The Lord is a warrior (Exod 15:3), and, on our own, we cannot be.

But part of the fuller revelation of the Godhead in the transition from Old to New Covenants involved God no longer holding us by the hand with direct revelation. For all the glories of Moses and Isaiah, prophecy itself needed to come to an end. Jesus was the fullest and final revelation of God. But he ascended and delegated his work to us. He ascended and made us his body on earth to serve and overcome and suffer, extending his kingdom as spiritual adults. Trinitarian love is the greatest maturity:

> Love never fails. But whether there are prophecies, they will fail; whether there are tongues, they will cease; whether there is knowledge, it will vanish away. For we know in part and we prophesy in part. But when that which is perfect has come, then that which is in part will be done away. When I was a child, I spoke as a child, I understood as a child, I thought as a child; but when I became a man, I put away childish things. For now we see in a mirror, dimly, but then face to face. Now I know in part, but then I shall know just as I also am known.

12. My thanks to Liz Smith for this observation about beasts.

96

> And now abide faith, hope, love, these three; but the greatest of
> these is love. (1 Cor 13:8–13)

The ways of immaturity will pass away, but maturity is faith, hope, and love, with the greatest, love.

New Covenant maturity means the passing away of the hand holding that made violence and warfare normal. New Covenant maturity means that we are dedicated to the very hard work of enemy love. Vengeance still belongs to the Lord, but it is not ours. Our weapons are no longer carnal. Violence is now the way of great arrogance. Violence is the way of great immaturity. Does this mean pacifism or an absolute rejection of all violence? Some think so. I don't think so. One can despise the way of violence and still not be a pacifist.

Of course, this way of enemy love is terrifying to those devoted to Mars. It is terrifying because it seems to unrealistic, so contrary to the way of the world. Indeed, it is foolishness. Just as Paul explained: "For the message of the cross is foolishness" (1 Cor 1:18).

The final vision of Matthew 25 captures the way of enemy love, too. We saw previously how Matthew 25 included the ways of weakness, renunciation, deliverance, and sharing. The vision of Matthew 25 focuses on supplying food and drink for others, and Elisha's act for his enemies stands at the center of that kind of service. The community of Matthew 25 goes out of its way to serve the unlovely, the marginal, the shamed, the imprisoned: "I was naked and you clothed Me; I was sick and you visited Me; I was in prison and you came to Me" (Matt 25:31ff).

7

The Way of Foolishness

"Here God gave us only riddles. . . . Too many riddles oppress man on earth."
—DMITRI KARAMAZOV

"Why, sometimes I've believed as many as six impossible things before breakfast."
—RED QUEEN

"The world is an exam. Our eyesight is here as a test to see if we can see beyond it."
—TIMOTHY SPEED LEVITCH

The way of the cross looks very wrong. It runs contrary to reason and common sense. It is counter-intuitive. A gross waste of time and resources. It looks ridiculous, extreme, inefficient, overdone, shrill, outdated, inglorious, and especially—foolish. "The message of the cross is foolishness to those who are perishing" (1 Cor 1:18). Foolishness—the trait of acting stupidly or rashly or immoderately. The cross is silly. Jesus's way is rash. That's the reaction a healthy Christian community will provoke from the world.

Certainly, for example, the way of enemy love prompts rolled eyes. It is ridiculous in a world of steel weapons. That's why Christians generally avoid it. Mars means business. He isn't silly. He turns heads. He makes people want to salute. The way of weakness, too, looks limp and pathetic. It doesn't place the moneyed and powerful at the center of the church.

Generally when modern Christians acknowledge the language of the "foolishness of the cross," we think of it in purely intellectual terms—it involves the supernatural, and secularists find the supernatural silly. So we think we're living the way of the cross if nonbelievers make fun of our supernatural ideas about the cross. We like that kind of persecution. It's air-conditioned. We conservatives think we're more than pleasing God when we can stand firm by crazy ideas when lesser Christians, liberals, cave into contemporary intellectual fads (we're immune from that, by the way). Let God be true, though every liberal a coward. As long as we, ourselves, don't fall into any hint of intellectual idolatry then we're sure God cheers us on. First-century Pharisees fell into the same trap. Conservatives regularly stare at the scriptures, forever fine-tuning our systematic ideas of mint, anise, and cummin, knowing that in the perfection of doctrine is eternal life. More and more Bible studies. More and more Christian colleges that stare at ideas for years, testing conjugations. Throw in some short-term charity work. Long sermon lectures. God is so happy with us.

It's this intellectual focus, a gift of the Reformation, thank you, that diverts us from some of the interesting angles about foolishness and faith in the gospel. The way of the cross involves the way of foolishness, a way of living and special perception in history in the midst of God's silence and Mammon's shouting. It's a foolish way of intuition and insight contrary-to-appearances. Its foolishness repudiates the rule-following that characterizes most Christian lives, in favor of creative virtue. Its foolishness is inherently unpopular and marginal. Most Christians simply will not get it, Jesus said. This foolishness is the way of the Spirit, and it is the "just shall live by faith," with Habakkuk's meaning, not the Reformation's.

Part of "the broad way that leads to destruction" throughout church history has been to assume that the Christian gospel is mainly about using this mental thing called faith, i.e., intellectual assent to certain truths, as the key to getting individuals into heaven, one by one. This is the majority view in Reformation traditions. It's the view that Bonhoeffer complained about as "cheap grace." We got to this notion largely by a simplistic, reductionistic reading of the apostle Paul's contrast between faith and works. If "works" means doing things, and that's bad, then "faith" must mean thinking things, and that's what Paul wanted. Just believe your way into heaven. (Strangely, "believing" has always avoided being counted as a work of human effort, though it clearly is. Most Protestant creeds, then, teach salvation by human effort, even while denying it. We just insist the distinction is Paul's not ours, so belief just can't be a work, by definition. Paul, though, was talking about another subject entirely.)

We must have failed to hear Peter's claim that Paul's letters contain "some things hard to understand, which untaught and unstable people twist to their own destruction" (2 Pet 3:16). Peter's comment is a part of scripture itself, and so it's part of the teaching of scripture that Paul is hard to understand. We're required to believe that. Perhaps one example of Peter's complaint is that Paul often used something like shorthand or technical jargon, even when using a simple word like "faith." We often assume he wasn't, and that gets us into trouble. Like Jesus, Paul spoke in poetic, parabolic ways, though we insist he was the straight talker of the two.

Consider, briefly, Paul's strange use of "faith" at one moment in Galatians. Several times earlier in the epistle, Paul had explained that Abraham had faith (Gal 3:6ff.), then, speaking of hundreds of years after Abraham, he says "before faith came" and "after faith has come" (Gal 3:23, 25), as if Abraham couldn't have had faith. Even more interesting, "faith" is something, according to Paul, that showed up at a particular point in history, like a special event. It was an event parallel to the whole Mosaic system. Faith was a whole, new way of life—and a person. Faith was Christ who "was revealed" (Gal 3:23). Faith = Jesus. And, yet, in the same verses, faith is different from Christ and connects us to him and is, also, another way of saying baptism (Gal 3:26, 27). Paul is a poet, an exciting poet. His language is full of passion and enthusiasm and awe. His meanings overlap, substitute, expand. His language is full of play. And we bureaucrats want him to knock it off and just let "faith" mean one thing, belief or trust. But Paul is a prophet of the narrow path, and he has a different agenda than our systematic clarity.

Faith is Jesus. It is a new era, and it is a whole way of life. And it's in faith's nature as a whole way of life that its foolishness stands out. The easiest way to recognize the foolishness of faith and the cross is to set it next to Mammon or the world. Mammon says the world operates according to the laws of power and quantifiable exchange. It is predictable. You can watch cause and effect and draw inferences. According to Mammon, you can read the working of the world right off the surface. Just watch it and learn its mechanisms.

But the way of faith doesn't see so simplistically. The way of faith is a special kind of perception, a special insight into the deeper movements of life. Faith is not simply belief in the supernatural. It is more like x-ray vision. Faith sees through the surfaces of the world. It sees through appearances, through all sorts of conflicting obstacles, through the mechanisms of Mammon, right into the surprising ways of divine action. Faith refuses to stop at the surface of life. Faith is the special and regular intuition that grasps God's ways even when the visible surfaces indicate the opposite, "though every man a liar." We are saved by insight. We are saved by seeing past the lies of Mammon. Saved by penetrating vision. Saved by contrariness. Saved by counter-intuition.

"For we walk by faith, not by sight" (2 Cor 5:7). The contrast in this famous line isn't faith vs. works. Faith is opposed to seeing. Paul had just been speaking of persecution and the hope of resurrection. He could see through the tribulations to the glories to come. He saw past Mammon's condemnation of God's way. He perceived counter-intuitively.

In the prior chapter, Paul was more elaborate in describing this special perception: "We do not look at the things which are seen, but at the things which are not seen" (2 Cor 4:18). Here the contrast shows that both faith and seeing are kinds of perception. Faith "looks" at unseen things, but worldliness looks at seen things. Two kinds of seeing. Faith sees through the visible into the realm of the invisible. Paul adds, "for the things which are seen are temporary, but the things which are not seen are eternal" (2 Cor 4:18). Again, his topic is persecution. In the context of persecution, all the severe and credible and respectable people declare you to be dead wrong. The Temple authorities and Caesar's governor denounce you as a fool, with all their purple regalia and marble pillars. But faith sees past the propaganda and puppets of empire. Those powers are temporary, and, in fact, Paul noted that, already, the "rulers of this age, who are coming to nothing" (1 Cor 2:6). Christians see past the triumphal arches of Mammon to the victory of the Lamb of God.

In Romans, too, Paul carefully described hope in terms identical to faith: "For we were saved in this hope, but hope that is seen is not hope; for why does one still hope for what he sees? But if we hope for what we do not see, we eagerly wait for it with perseverance" (Rom 8:24, 25). Faith and hope are all about a certain kind of contrary sight. These distinctions are very important to Paul, and we ignore them because we force him into talking about assent vs. human effort. But here hope sees the invisible. We were delivered from the bondage of sin, looking to a better future, even if it has no signs in history at all. Faith and hope see contrary to the dominant facts.

Isaiah described Messiah himself as having this special perception (note the accompanying ways of weakness and deliverance):

> The Spirit of the LORD shall rest upon Him,
> The Spirit of wisdom and understanding,
> The Spirit of counsel and might,
> The Spirit of knowledge and of the fear of the LORD.
> His delight is in the fear of the LORD,
> And He shall not judge by the sight of His eyes,
> Nor decide by the hearing of His ears;
> But with righteousness He shall judge the poor,
> And decide with equity for the meek of the earth. (Isa 11:2–4)

God's man will "not judge by the sight of His eyes." He is a man of faith and a man of politics. He sees through the political lies and grasps the target of God's concern, the poor. Faith sees the remnant. Faith sees the powerless. Faith sees justice. Faith is political.

The book of Hebrews famously continued to explain faith as a special penetrating vision:

> Now faith is the substance of things hoped for, the evidence of
> things not seen. For by it the elders obtained a good testimony.
> By faith we understand that the worlds were framed by the
> word of God, so that the things which are seen were not made
> of things which are visible. (Heb 11:2, 3)

This passage seeks to turn worldly sight inside out. It speaks counter-intuitively of "faith" as a substance, as something solid and heavy. Faith grasps the thick and real. That seems so wrong. Faith is courtroom evidence. It convinces and receives the judge's approval. This reversal makes everything visible secondary and thin. Worldly sight only captures frail surfaces and misses what's really going on. To speak this way is insane. It goes contrary to all seriousness and good sense. It is so unrealistic. It is the way of foolishness. So says Mammon, with all its metal gauges, triplicate forms, and double-entry accounting.

The famous Hall of Faith in the rest of Hebrews 11 is often mistaken for a list of mere belief. We see loyal intellects. This is strange in itself, since every case is about action, a work, not just belief. The deeds assume belief, but that alone flattens the issue and misses faith as perception contrary to sight.

Noah "warned of things not yet seen." Abraham left, "not knowing where he was going." Abraham "waited for the city which has foundations." Sarah "judged Him faithful who had promised." These died "not having received the promises, but having seen them afar off." Abraham perceived God so well, he was willing to kill his son at God's bidding, "concluding that God was able to raise him up, even from the dead."

Moses had amazing, anti-Mammon perception. By penetrating insight, Moses,

> refused to be called the son of Pharaoh's daughter, choosing rather to suffer affliction with the people of God than to enjoy the passing pleasures of sin, esteeming the reproach of Christ greater riches than the treasures in Egypt; for he looked to the reward. (Heb 11:24–26)

"He looked." He looked through the visible, the sufferings, as well as the pleasures of Mammon, and saw the eternal, the reproach of Christ as greater than the wealth and privileges of Egypt. Moses "endured as seeing Him who is invisible" (Heb 11:27).

After reviewing the greats "of whom the world was not worthy," the author exhorted his readers to foolishness, to see through the obstacles of the world and grasp reality. "Let us run the race" with Jesus's ability to perceive in this strange way: "who for the joy that was set before Him endured the cross, despising the shame, and has sat down at the right hand of the throne of God" (Heb 12:2). He saw through Mammon's violence and reproach to the new kingdom.

The faith Hebrews spoke of did amazing works: "subdued kingdoms, worked righteousness, obtained promises, stopped the mouths of lions, quenched the violence of fire, escaped the edge of the sword, out of weakness were made strong, became valiant in battle" (Heb 11:33). Our modern, anemic understanding of faith as a mere intellectual, rather commonsensical act produces the following sort of paltry language: "By this faith, a Christian believeth to be true whatsoever is revealed in the Word."[1] That's it? Faith helps us believe ideas in scripture? No, this

---

1. Westminster Confession of Faith, XIV, 2.

Confession also says it enables us to act differently, tremble, embrace promises, and accept Christ. Intellectual assent can't really be expected to do much more than that. Faith is no deep perception, contrary-to-sight grasp of God's ways, strong enough to "subdue kingdoms." It's just flat. It didn't hear Hebrews. All it hears is the presumed difference between faith and works and stops. (Notice, the Confession above is so fearful of acknowledging even this believing is an actual work that it tries to cover it with numerous passive verbs and participles—"accepting, receiving, and resting." Why is Hebrews not constrained by that sort of fear? Again, confused subjects. I'll come back to it).

In the end, biblical faith is an act of adulthood. It requires maturity to see the invisible. The immature can't do it. They need tutors to show them how. Faith is liberation from the purely visible. Faith grasps the Father even if the Father doesn't hold your hand. And that's why Paul uses "faith" as a catch-all, technical term for the New Covenant way of life. For him, "faith" is the new kingdom of maturity established by Christ and the Holy Spirit. Faith is what has surpassed the Mosaic era. "Before faith came, we were kept under guard by the law, kept for the faith which would afterward be revealed" (Gal 3:23).

By contrast, the Old Covenant was the way of sight and immaturity. It was surface life. Grade school. It explained God's ways, step by step, sacrifice by sacrifice, law by law. The tabernacle and temple were giant, elementary-school dioramas. God had big displays of miraculous shock and awe that the kids loved, and he even spoke directly through leaders and prophets. "The law was our tutor to bring us to Christ. . . . But after faith has come, we are no longer under a tutor" (Gal 3:24, 25). "When we were children, [we] were in bondage" to Old Covenant ways (Gal 4:3; cf. 4:9, 10). Because of this regular hand-holding, the Old Covenant cannot be characterized as a whole by the term "faith." In general, the Old Covenant people lacked the ability to see through surfaces. They wanted to return to Egypt. They wanted a king like other nations. They executed the prophets. This general feature doesn't negate the deep, contrary-to-sight perception of some of Israel's leaders—Moses, David, and the prophets, and especially Abraham. Still, it is summarized as the era of immaturity.

It's because of this immature/mature contrast that Paul frames his entire letter of Romans with the book of Habakkuk. A long tradition has greatly distorted the book of Romans by forcing it to be something it isn't. We have long tried to make Romans into a tract about how to get into heaven. But imagine we're wrong about that. Try reading Romans as if it's about life in history on earth. In other words, read its use of words like "salvation," "justification," "adoption," and others like they are used in the Old Covenant. The Old Covenant cares very little about getting into heaven. It's primarily interested in saving people from earthly enemies and creating a holy community here. (Now this might seem a strange constraint after I just described the Old Covenant as immaturity but bear with me. The Old constantly pointed toward the new, too.)

The book of Habakkuk is central to New Testament thinking. It's cited three times—Romans 1:17, Galatians 3:11, and Hebrews 10:38. It's not too much to say that if we don't have a good grasp of Habakkuk, we can't really understand the foolishness of faith and the New Testament as a whole, certainly not Romans. Habakkuk prophesied before Babylon destroyed the first Temple, and that makes it significant to play so heavy a role in Paul's letter to Rome, another Babylon who will destroy another Temple.

The book of Habakkuk, like most Old Covenant texts, isn't interested in heaven at all (that doesn't mean there isn't a heaven, just that it's not a divine priority). Habakkuk is a complaint against God. It's a complaint that God appears to be unjust in not rescuing the righteous remnant from Israel's wicked leaders. It's a political complaint. (Notice, in each chapter, Habakkuk, like all the prophets doesn't believe everyone is depraved, just the leadership. The remnant he wants "saved" is poor and humble.)

> O LORD, how long shall I cry,
> And You will not hear?
> Even cry out to You, "Violence!"
> And You will not save.
> Why do You show me iniquity,
> And cause me to see trouble?
> For plundering and violence are before me;
> There is strife, and contention arises.
> Therefore the law is powerless,
> And justice never goes forth. (Hab 1:1–4)

The prophet can't see reality. He can't see past the surfaces. Then the Lord makes the visible even worse. He says he's going to bring the imperial power, Babylon, to crush the wicked leadership of Israel. The prophet still can't see the invisible, still lacks faith.

Habakkuk complains to God that he's supposed to be just and holy, so why is he allowing all this violence and then making it worse by bringing Babylon? The Lord is supposed to be so pure that he can't allow evil to the innocent. What's the Lord going to do about the righteous remnant? Let them die?

> You are of purer eyes than to behold evil,
> And cannot look on wickedness.
> Why do You look on those who deal treacherously,
> And hold Your tongue when the wicked devours
> A person more righteous than he? (Hab 1:13)

Then Habakkuk uses the later language of faith and says he'll "watch to see" how the Lord answers for his injustice. And the Lord answers by calling Habakkuk to faith, by calling him to look deeper into reality, to see beyond the apparently insurmountable evil leadership and even the coming devastation of Babylon.

The Lord explains that the "proud" will not be able to see what God is doing. But the holy person will grasp what the Lord is doing. The righteous person will be like Abraham and see resurrection. Or as the Lord famous tells Habakkuk, "the just shall live by faith" (Hab 2:4).

The Lord even explains faith that way we later hear it from Paul, a way of seeing the invisible:

> the vision is yet for an appointed time;
> But at the end it will speak, and it will not lie.
> Though it tarries, wait for it;
> Because it will surely come,
> It will not tarry. (Hab 2:3)

Faith sees past corrupt Israel and Babylon and sees the goal down the road. Faith waits because its sees the good end that "will surely come." In other words, the Lord tells Habakkuk he must live in a counter-intuitive way. He cannot be overwhelmed that the leadership is so corrupt and unfixable. He can't even be overwhelmed by Babylon's military might. He has to see through them to the joy to come.

Habakkuk's expression of faith became doubly relevant for the apostle Paul because both he and Habakkuk wrote prior to the two destructions of the Temple. Both were soon to live in a world without even the ability for Mosaic ceremonies. Faith will have to suffice in both eras, since the rituals will be gone.

After all this came to pass, Habakkuk admitted that God was vindicated and that "his ways are everlasting" (Hab 3:6). Habakkuk summed up God's saving work as, "You went forth for the salvation of Your people,

for salvation with Your Anointed. You struck the head from the house of
the wicked" (Hab 3:13).

Then Habakkuk returned with his own summary of faith as counter-
intuition. He gave several normally negative signs—crop failures, dead
farm animals—but then still sees God's contrary-to-sight hand:

> Though the fig tree may not blossom,
> Nor fruit be on the vines;
> Though the labor of the olive may fail,
> And the fields yield no food;
> Though the flock may be cut off from the fold,
> And there be no herd in the stalls—
> Yet I will rejoice in the LORD,
> I will joy in the God of my salvation. (Hab 3:17, 18)

We walk by faith, not sight. The just shall live by faith. In other words,
Habakkuk exhorted the righteous remnant to look past appearances and
persevere through tribulation and persecution, and God will be proven
just in the end.

And that is the main message of Romans, too. Paul explained to
the Roman Christians that even though everything looked bad, with
depraved Roman rulers, persecuting Jewish leaders, and especially the
more immense power of death and Mammon behind them all, God was
still on the side of the righteous remnant, even this time adopting the
gentiles, in history, through the death and resurrection of Christ—"If
God is for us, who can be against us?" "The God of peace will crush Satan
under your feet shortly." The righteous remnant will, again, persevere
through counter-intuition, and God will have been vindicated, contrary
to all sight.

In the midst of Paul's general treatment of counter-intuitive faith
in Romans, he then took the argument deeper by contrasting the way
of Abraham with the way of Moses. Paul moved from faith as counter-
intuition to faith as maturity. Paul's main encouragement here for gentiles
was that, though the current defenders of Moses had all the power, they
were not ever God's main plan. Moses was a temporary sidetrack from
Abraham. God's main plan was the way of Abraham, and Abraham started as an uncircumcised gentile, and now, in Christ, God was fulfilling the
original promise to "gentile" Abraham. In other words, adding gentiles
like Abraham was God's intention from the very start.

On the surface of Romans, Paul often appeared to be contrasting
intellectual assent to human effort, "faith" vs. "works." That's what most

of the Reformation tradition says. If we step back, though, and take in all of biblical history, that debate looks very strange and out of place. Where do Moses and the prophets spend so much time debating the mechanics of getting into heaven?

But if we let Habakkuk and the rest of the New Testament frame Romans, instead of marginal Augustinian polemics, we can see that Paul is talking of blessings in history not heaven. He's simply repeating the decision of the Council of Jerusalem (Acts 15), with some poetic, technical terms. At the Jerusalem Council, Peter started the discussion with a contrast of the way of faith with the way of the law:

> Men and brethren, you know that a good while ago God chose
> among us, that by my mouth the Gentiles should hear the
> word of the gospel and believe. So God, who knows the heart,
> acknowledged them by giving them the Holy Spirit, just as He
> did to us, and made no distinction between us and them, puri-
> fying their hearts by faith. Now therefore, why do you test God
> by putting a yoke on the neck of the disciples which neither
> our fathers nor we were able to bear? (Acts 15:7–10)

Here is the contrast between faith and works. Faith doesn't primarily mean intellectual assent or even trust. Faith, in Paul's shorthand, primarily means *without the Mosaic rituals*, without the old yoke. The way of faith was the way of Abraham before circumcision and the Mosaic works. Both are ways of obedience. Both are actions and life. Abraham acted and so did the followers of Moses. It's not assent vs. actions. Faith vs. works is simply the way of Abraham vs. the way of Moses, non-Mosaic-rituals vs. Mosaic rituals. "Works" is Paul's normal shorthand for Mosaic rituals or "works of the law" (Rom 9:32; Gal 2:16; 3:2, 5, 10). Because Paul was contrasting the way of Abraham and the way of Moses, he can speak of the "obedience of faith" (Rom 1:5; 16:26) without falling into later worries about Pelagianism (which can be addressed elsewhere). He was comparing two ways of life, the obedience of faith (Abraham) with the obedience of Mosaic rituals. Our much later debate about assent vs. human effort simply wasn't on Paul's horizon. He was trying to assure Christian gentiles that, contrary to all appearances, God was truly on their side from the beginning, like Abraham—"a man is justified by faith apart from the deeds of the law" (Gal 3:28). Or, God is on the side of gentiles like he was on the side of Abraham, quite apart from Moses. This explanation of faith as the lack of Mosaic ceremonies was right on Habakkuk's horizon.

Babylon would destroy the Temple, and faith would have to prevail in this time, too, just as it would shortly have to in the first century.

God sided with Abraham not because Abraham performed the deeds of the law ("faith which he had while still uncircumcised"—Rom 4:11) but because Abraham followed, believed, and obeyed Yahweh *before and outside* the rituals of Moses, that is by "faith." And that obedience that Abraham showed was counter-intuitive. It saw through appearances to God's surprising ways of acting: "contrary to hope, in hope believed" (Rom 4:18). Abraham looked past his and Sarah's aged bodies—"he did not consider his own body, already dead (since he was about a hundred years old), and the deadness of Sarah's womb" (Rom 4:19). And Abraham's counter-intuitive seeing, imitated God's own perception, the God who contrary to human expectations, "gives life to the dead and calls those things which do not exist as though they did" (Rom 4:17).

"Contrary to hope, in hope believed." That is the way of foolishness. The way of faith. And what more could mark Abraham as *the* epitome of faith than his willingness to sacrifice Isaac. Abraham saw through God's request for him to sacrifice his only son. It was a test not only of Abraham's love but also of his future. Abraham "gave up all" for the Lord, first by cutting off his inheritance and then by cutting off his future, Isaac. But Abraham saw through God's seemingly insane and pagan command for child sacrifice. Abraham knew God had promised Isaac would be the future, and so he perceived through appearances and concluded "that God was able to raise him up, even from the dead" (Heb 11:19) to accomplish his goals. That is the person God wants, someone not locked to surfaces, a whole people like Abraham and Jesus.

Most first-century Jews, however, couldn't perceive Jesus. They couldn't see his way was God's way. His way of the cross violated every predictable, safe, orderly way of life. He was an embarrassing and scandalous failure. The Jewish leadership had already confessed having no king but Mammon (John 19:14), and that killed their ability to see counter-intuitively. In fact, that inability to see became a significant summary of the problem. The passage the early Christians used to capture the Jews' situation focused on the inability to see past appearances—Psalm 18:

> The stone which the builders rejected
>> Has become the chief cornerstone.
> This was the LORD's doing;
>> It is marvelous in our eyes. (Ps 118:22, 23)

Psalm 118 is the most quoted psalm in the New Testament. This portion helped early Christians overcome the hostility of the Jewish leadership because it predicted a failure of sight. The expert builders failed to see the quality inherent in a rock. The stone failed to meet their expectations. They judged it as unworthy and flawed. But, in fact, it was the most important stone, the cornerstone. The onlookers are amazed at both the failure of the experts and the unpredictability of the Lord's ways. "It is marvelous in our eyes."

Jesus challenges the Jewish leadership with this psalm. "Have you never read in the Scriptures?" (Matt 21:42). He quotes it and then concludes, "Therefore I say to you, the kingdom of God will be taken from you and given to a nation bearing the fruits of it" (Matt 21:43; cf. Mark 12; Luke 20). In Acts, Peter cites Psalm 118 to explain the Jewish leadership's rejection of Jesus. And in his first epistle, Peter gathers to Psalm 118 other passages that reinforce the failure to perceive the cornerstone (Isa 28:16; 8:14).

This failure to see counter-intuitively did not just grip the first-century Jewish or gentile leadership—"but we preach Christ crucified, to the Jews a stumbling block and to the Greeks foolishness" (1 Cor 1:23). The failure to walk by faith afflicts professing Christians, too. This failure forms the background of Jesus's warnings about the broad and narrow ways.

> Enter by the narrow gate; for wide is the gate and broad is the
> way that leads to destruction, and there are many who go in
> by it. Because narrow is the gate and difficult is the way which
> leads to life, and there are few who find it. (Matt 7:13, 14)

Walking the narrow path requires that one "finds" it. It requires special perception. It's not grasped by the majority but by the Abrahams. To most people, the way of foolishness and the broader way of the cross will be embarrassing and ridiculous. Jesus knew this. In referencing his way of weakness, Jesus added, "and blessed is he who is not offended because of me" (Matt 11:6).

Jesus's way was so counter-intuitive it easily tricked the people of the broad way. "Has not God made foolish the wisdom of this world?" (1 Cor 1:20). In explaining the foolishness of God's wisdom, Paul saw how contrary to sight the crucifixion itself was:

> But we speak the wisdom of God in a mystery, the hidden wis-
> dom which God ordained before the ages for our glory, which

none of the rulers of this age knew; for had they known, they
would not have crucified the Lord of glory." (1 Cor 2:7, 8)

If the principalities and powers had the insight to see what God was really
doing, they wouldn't have allowed Jesus to vindicate the way of the cross.
The powers of Mammon were tricked because they were short-sighted.
They lacked faith.

Jesus was at his most "embarrassing" in describing the sort of marginal and ridiculous people who would make up his kingdom on earth.
He describes the character of losers in his kingdom in his beatitudes. But
to grasp the counter-intuitive nature of the beatitudes, first consider what
the reasonable beatitudes of first-century Rome/Mammon would sound
like:

> Honorable are those who see like the strong,
>> for theirs is the Mediterranean.
> Glorious are those whose husbands and sons die in battle
>> for they shall be most praised.
> Honorable are the bold,
>> for they shall receive the glory of Rome.
> Glorious are those strive and conquer for power,
>> for they shall have slaves and land.
> Honorable are those who don't show mercy,
>> for they shall obtain respect.
> Glorious are the pure in blood,
>> for they shall carry Rome forever.
> Honorable are those who impose peace by an iron fist,
>> for they shall be called sons of Mars.
> Glorious are those who are serve the fatherland,
>> to them belongs the eternal city.

Christ's beatitudes are an inversion of all these. To the Romans, Christ's
beatitudes are utterly foolish:

> Blessed are the poor in spirit,
>> For theirs is the kingdom of heaven.
> Blessed are those who mourn,
>> For they shall be comforted.
> Blessed are the meek,
>> For they shall inherit the earth.
> Blessed are those who hunger and thirst for righteousness,
>> For they shall be filled.
> Blessed are the merciful,
>> For they shall obtain mercy.

> Blessed are the pure in heart,
>> For they shall see God.
> Blessed are the peacemakers,
>> For they shall be called sons of God.
> Blessed are those who are persecuted for righteousness' sake,
>> For theirs is the kingdom of heaven. (Matt 4:3–10)

The kingdom Jesus describes here is an upside-down Rome. Instead of the wealthy, powerful, violent, and unjust at the center, Jesus places the poor, the crushed, the nonviolent, and the just. These beatitudes are, first and foremost, autobiographical. As we saw earlier, Jesus is poor in spirit, being a rich man (2 Cor 8:9), he took on the perspective or spirit of the poor (Phil 2:5–7) and judged the world from that angle (Luke 6). He faced oppression, lived enemy-love, and thirsted for a new world, free of Mammon. He was the beatitudes, and he wants us to be them, too.

But the beatitudes are foolish. They show a community of foolishness. They go contrary to all the safe, respectable ways of the world. Without faith, without counter-intuitive sight, it is impossible to please God (Heb 11:6). The beatitudes show us a mature community, imitating God's insight into reality. This community knows how the world really works and that Mammon fights on the surfaces.

At the core of the beatitudes, at the core of Christian faith lies the most counter-intuitive way of all. Jesus's kingdom simply cannot function without it. Churches and programs, friendships and marriages have often crashed through the centuries without it. It is the biggest foolishness. It is Jesus's most repeated discipline and the most set aside. We pat its head. It is the requirement which makes Mammon look so commonsensical. It is the exceeding foolishness of self-denial. "If anyone desires to come after Me, let him deny himself" (Luke 9:23, 24). "For whoever desires to save his life will lose it, but whoever loses his life for My sake will find it" (Matt 16:25). As Thomas a Kempis (1380–1471) explained in his famous treatise on the way of the cross, "To carry the cross, to love the cross, to chastise the body and bring it to subjection, to flee honors, to endure contempt gladly, to despise self and wish to be despised, to suffer any adversity and loss, to desire no prosperous days on earth—that is not man's way."[2]

What could be more counter-intuitive to those captivated by the world of Mammon? Conservative Christians regularly leap to defend

2. Thomas, *Imitation*, 42.

the legitimacy and importance of self-interest, drawing big thick lines between it and some very, very different and evil thing called selfishness. The world has to run on self-interest, we're told. It's the only way to avoid the tyranny of communism and the dictatorship of long lines and empty shelves.

Jesus called for something different. From his foolish faith, selfishness and self-interest stand together over against self-denial. Jesus introduced a vision of a whole city on a hill growing out of self-denial. But the craziness of genuine self-denial, the giddy giving up of power, wealth, and prestige, to serve one another wasn't new. It was just the Trinity, again. It was making Trinity on earth. Since all eternity, Father, Son, and Spirit have denied their interests to raise up each other. They have each denied themselves to ensure the mission of the other. The Trinity has always been foolish in this way. The Trinity has always lived the way of faith.

The final vision of Matthew 25 captures the way of foolishness, too. We saw previously how Matthew 25 included the ways of weakness, renunciation, deliverance, sharing, and enemy-love. That vision is certainly foolish. It is grounded in self-denial. Matthew 25 cleverly captures the spirit of self-denial in that the blessed are surprised to learn about their actions—"the righteous will answer Him, saying, 'Lord, when did we see You hungry and feed You, or thirsty and give You drink?" (Matt 25:37). They're pictured as so other-focused that they meet Jesus command about sincerity and focus—"do not let your left hand know what your right hand is doing" (Matt 6:3).

8

The Way of Community

"Sooner or later, we enjoy only souls."

—LUC DE CLAPIERS

"I think what revolts me about Christianity is the self-interest involved. You make yourself do this or not do that to get to heaven."

—EMMANUELLE RIVA IN *LEON MORIN, PRIEST* (1961)

Certainly one of the most misleading classics of the modern period was Bunyan's *Pilgrim's Progress*. Its influence seeped deep into Protestant culture, so deep that recovery from it will take centuries. The book's message wasn't new in itself. It gathered all the worst emphases of the Reformation in one place and soaked our consciousness thoroughly.

Pilgrim's Progress presents a deeply selfish vision of salvation. It pretends to be about self-denial all while forcing a radical self-focus. Selfish salvation assumes that each Christian stars as the main character in the gospel story. Selfish salvation believes that the gospel is primarily about getting individuals into heaven and that self-interest is the primary motivation that gets us there. Selfish salvation focuses on an individual's struggle with personal sins over and above the community.

Bunyan's main character is the personality-deprived, Christian, a morbidly introspective Gnostic, who is intent only on getting himself into heaven by means of fine-tuned theological ideas. Bunyan notes at one place, "Christian was walking solitary by himself."[1] That redundancy is telling. One modern reprinting of this allegory gives an accurate subtitle: "One Man's Search for Eternal Life."

Like most modern Christians, Bunyan's protagonist focuses obsessively on his personal sins, and when asked about his wife and children, he replies, "I am so laden with this Burden, that I cannot take pleasure in them as formerly: methinks, I am as if I had none."[2] He had, in fact, run away from them, literally blocking his ears to their cries and taunts.

Christian's burden of sin is, of course, only his personal sin. Communal sins rarely if ever entered his (or our) consideration. Accordingly, Bunyan's cross is also focused on removing individual sins: "just as Christian came up with the Cross, his Burden loosed from off his shoulders, and fell from off his back, and began to tumble, and so continued to do. . . . Then was Christian glad and lightsome."[3] Phew. Lucky for him.

Christian repeatedly described his selfish journey to heaven in this form: "If I go back to mine own country, that is prepared for Fire and Brimstone, and I shall certainly perish there: If I can get to the Celestial City, I am sure to be in safety there."[4] Heaven is all about self-interest.

On his way to heaven, Christian and his various travel companions had no concern to live Christ's petition that the kingdom be "done on earth as it is in heaven." Christian himself did not aim to create a City on a Hill on earth, and even defenders of Bunyan have been embarrassed by the howling absence of the church in it. Christian was on a journey, after all, and he had no time for living in communion. Even when Christian came close to a communal expression of the kingdom, he couldn't take the actual step. When he taunted Talkative for being a "dead carcass" of mere "saying," Christian actually dared to cite James on pure and undefiled religion as visiting "orphans and widows in their trouble." Christian himself, though, didn't have time for that sort of focus on others. He needed heaven first, after all. In reality, Christian was nothing but another Talkative. Ironically, he even noted, "at the day of Doom, men

1. Bunyan, *Pilgrim's*, 11.
2. Ibid., 11.
3. Ibid., 35,36.
4. Ibid., 42.

shall be judged according to their Fruit: It will not be said then, Did you believe? But were you Doers or Talkers only?"[5] Amen. But watch that 2 x 4 in your eye, Christian.

In the end, Christian and his friend, Hopeful, successfully got into heaven because they correctly believe a highly-nuanced and precisely-qualified definition of "Justifying Faith," which their fellow-traveler Ignorance failed to grasp. The idiot. Ignorance came right up to the Gates of Heaven, but Christian discovered, "that there was a Way to Hell, even from the Gates of Heaven."[6] Too bad for Ignorance. Who knew that Heaven was only for theology engineers?

Selfish salvation sees the gospel primarily as a means of satisfying that individual's desires and prayers. It has little to no sense that the gospel as a kingdom of self-denial or really even contains others, and it certainly doesn't "seek first the kingdom of God" (Matt 6:33). Salvation is all about me, me, me. My needs. My heart. My purpose. My prayers. My goals. My personal sins. My place in heaven. It's an exhausting and redundant autobiography. And yet, selfish salvation is the most common expression of Christian faith in our time. Thanks, Bunyan.

It's not fair to blame Bunyan alone, though. For example, in my tradition, as wonderful as the Heidelberg Catechism (1563) is, it too begins from a selfish angle. What is "your only comfort in life and death?" Not a question about God's kingdom. Not a question about God's people as a whole. Not even a question about the gift of the Trinity. No otherness. It's about *your* individual spiritual comfort. The famous answer continues that narrow focus: "That I with body and soul . . . my faithful savior . . . my sins . . . delivered me . . . preserves me . . . my head . . . all things must be subservient to my salvation . . . assures me of eternal life." Ironically, this answer starts off with the claim that I "am not my own" but then does the opposite. Did Jesus talk like this? The second question of the Heidelberg Catechism doesn't improve things. It asks what things are "necessary for you to know, that you enjoying this comfort, may live and die happily?" Ugh. Knowing is king. More of me, me, me. More *Pilgrim's Progress* before its time. More morbid focus on personal sins to the exclusion of the social: "how great my sins and miseries are." More selfish salvation.

In contrast, the way of the cross is inherently the way of community in several respects. It recognizes the importance of communal sin,

5. Ibid., 87, 88.
6. Ibid., 189.

communal salvation, communal discipleship, communal living, and more. It doesn't deny the individual, but it takes second place. Community and individuality are both important, but moderns exclude the communal. And like the Trinity, the way of the cross cannot be lived individualistically, though it's often been tried. It seems designed to fail on an individual level, designed to crush the lone ranger.

Jesus privileged the social over the individual in the Sermon on the Mount, when he commanded us to "seek first the kingdom of God" (Matt 6:33). First. Before other things. The Lord of heaven and earth exhorted us to consider the social before the individual. Seek first the community, then the individual will be taken care of. He raises this command in the middle of common individual worries of the poor: "What shall we eat? What shall we drink? What shall we wear?" (Matt 6:31). Individual needs are important. The Father knows we have these needs. But Jesus directed us to the way of counter-intuition: don't start with the individual, start with the communal, the kingdom. "Seek first the kingdom of God, and all these things shall be added to you." Communal first, individual second. Sure, that looks wrong, especially to radically individualistic Westerners. But the way of the cross never looks right at first.

Jesus's command should reshape not only our individual material needs but also our spiritual needs. Unlike *Pilgrim's Progress*, instead of only asking "What about my personal sins?" or "How do *I* get into heaven?" we should first look more broadly. Seek first the kingdom. What are the sins of my people? What sins have bound my nation for centuries? How has my community failed in the way of the cross? Failed the weak? To deliver? To share? To love enemies? And why does the New Testament speak of sin as social and communal, like some massive, objective, living, tyrannical beast ruling over the whole human race? "Death reigned" "Death no longer has dominion." "Sin shall not have dominion over you." "Slaves of sin." "Power of death." "Power of Darkness."

The apostle Paul was very concerned with social sin, "principalities" and "powers" that tried to "separate us from the love of God" (Rom 8:38, 39). Paul said, even after the cross, we fight deep communal sin:

> For we do not wrestle against flesh and blood, but against
> principalities, against powers, against the rulers of the darkness
> of this age, against spiritual hosts of wickedness in the heavenly
> places. (Eph 6:12)

Seek first the kingdom. The divine response to this oppressive rule of sin was (and is) also social first, individual second. The Exodus from Egypt, and its repetitions in the later tyrannies and exile is supposed to stand out as the main model for what salvation looks like (in other words, it's no accident that Jesus's death and resurrection took place during the celebration of the Exodus—Passover).

But what happened in the Exodus? It had both individual and communal aspects, but the social came first. Let my people go. It gave us the pattern for salvation: election, promise, sin, grace, blood, deliverance, discipleship, promised land. God had initially called Abraham by grace alone and promised to bless all peoples of the world through him. Later, the Israelites found themselves oppressed by very public and social powers of sin and death. Egypt was a kingdom of idols, a Mammon. By grace and God's action alone, God had first chosen Israel and then intervened miraculously and with great power to overthrow the tyrant of sin—Pharaoh and all his principalities. The people did not free themselves by human effort or good works. They did not earn the removal of Pharaoh by being good. They did not even entice God's initial calling and election of Abraham. It was grace alone that did all that. God's love and mercy alone moved him to deliver a sinful people whom he loved.

Then the Lord gave them a community code explaining how to live as a good and just nation, and the people gratefully embraced this new, non-Mammon way of discipleship—"All the words which the LORD has said we will do" (Exod 24:3). On top of the gracious gifts of deliverance and discipleship, the Lord promised them a paradise of milk and honey, if they faithfully followed him and didn't go after other gods. He would be their God by grace and continue to sanctify them and train them up into maturity. Though the Lord overthrew Pharaoh once, his people were still called to struggle against other Mammons all their lives and continually overthrow them. And if God's people didn't reject their God and embrace idolatrous ways of discipleship, then they would retain the gift of promised land. But if they rejected God, then he would cut them off from paradise, everyone except a faithful remnant, and he would later include others, gentiles, into his people as well. Overall, then, they were saved/delivered by grace and judged by works.

Within this Exodus picture, *Pilgrim's Progress* would be very out of place. Imagine blending the stories. Christian would be a Hebrew desperately trying to get rid of his personal guilt, while God and Moses kept calling on Pharaoh to stop oppressing the people. Christian would tell

Moses that God needed to look after the good of each Hebrew's soul first and not worry about outward trappings. If the people's hearts were right, then that's all that mattered. Then, at some point, Christian would say that he himself had confessed his sins and entreated God on his knees for forgiveness, and now he was going to head off, solitary by himself, toward the promised land. After all, he'd say to Moses, God had given him the promised land. Wave bye. Moses might have explained to Christian that he was still an Egyptian slave, and he couldn't just walk out of Pharaoh's realm. He'd be imprisoned. Christian would explain that the important promised land wasn't truly on earth. He could enter paradise in his prison cell. The big issue was that Christian's own sins had fallen away, and he was light and ecstatic, regardless of that Pharaoh character or the whining of the Hebrews. Sheesh, Moses needed to get his priorities right. Then Christian would walk away to go read his Bible and figure it all out on his own. Who needed pontifical Moses, anyway?

Selfish salvation doesn't just look odd side-by-side with the Exodus. It looks odd in contrast with the entire Old Testament. The mission of the Old Covenant was always about creating a new and unique community. God wanted a special community that would serve and bless the entire world. The apostle Paul used the word "gospel" to describe this mission. He said that this "gospel" was preached to Abraham long before New Testament preaching of the gospel. What was this gospel preached to Abraham?

> And the Scripture, foreseeing that God would justify the Gentiles by faith, preached the gospel to Abraham beforehand, saying, "In you all the nations shall be blessed." So then those who are of faith are blessed with believing Abraham. (Gal 3:8, 9)

"In you all the nations shall be blessed." This gospel was not focused on getting into heaven. It was not even focused on forgiveness of sins or atonement, though they would later play into it. It focused on people, on a worldwide community tied into the way of Abraham, the obedience of faith. God himself would side with this community. He would be their God, and they would be his people (Genesis 17; 22).

The Lord gave this community a code that marked it out as unique and different from the surrounding nations. God's people were not permitted to follow in the way of the surrounding nations and gods. Instead they were supposed to be a model of social wisdom to every other nation:

> Surely I have taught you statutes and judgments, just as the
> LORD my God commanded me, that you should act accord-
> ing to them in the land which you go to possess. Therefore
> be careful to observe them; for this is your wisdom and your
> understanding in the sight of the peoples who will hear all
> these statutes, and say, "Surely this great nation is a wise and
> understanding people." For what great nation is there that has
> God so near to it, as the LORD our God is to us, for whatever
> reason we may call upon Him? And what great nation is there
> that has such statutes and righteous judgments as are in all this
> law which I set before you this day? (Deut 4:5–7)

The remainder of the Old Testament followed the path of this community.
The focus remained constant throughout—social and communal. How
to live as a just and merciful people. That's what God was most interested
in. The Old Covenant rarely talked about the afterlife, and even less about
heaven. It is an earthly focus, yet it is divine and spiritual concern for a
just community in history.

This same social focus continued throughout all the prophets. The
prophets never sounded like Bunyan and always sounded like the Exodus
and Moses. They repeatedly called God's people back to a just society.
That's what God had forever sought, and God's people weren't living it,
having turned to the ways of Mammon instead.

And their great vision of the servant of the future didn't speak of a
Son of Man to come and encourage selfish salvation. He wasn't described
as a messiah to guarantee us a place in heaven if individual souls just believed the right ideas about him. Messiah's focus would be on building a
unique and just community: "He will bring forth justice for truth. He will
not fail nor be discouraged, till He has established justice in the earth"
(Isa 42:1, 3, 4). Justice to the gentiles. Justice on the earth. That's what
God aimed for since the beginning. Mary recognized this communal
focus (Lukek 1:51ff), as did Jesus, announcing he had come "To set at liberty those who are oppressed." We spiritualize Jesus's claims, though. We
limit them to freeing individual hearts, completely severing the claims
about establishing "justice in the earth."

So how did we get from this communal gospel to modern Christian
selfish salvation? Did the New Covenant introduce some radical shift
from God's mission of creating a unique community? Did the Lord give
up on creating a just society and opt for getting individual souls into
heaven? This would have been an enormous change in plan. It would

have thrown out everything Moses, Isaiah, and the rest preached in God's name. Yet modern Christians have to believe that some such crazy chasm like this happened. We say things like Jesus "just needed to get up on that cross." "His teaching wasn't important." (I actually heard a pastor preach that once.) And for centuries, we've believed, for example, that the Book of Romans had nothing to do with the communal agenda of Isaiah and Habakkuk and the Psalms, even though Paul cited them repeatedly as if his message matched theirs.

One way of spotting the continuation of the communal, earthly interests from the Old to New Covenant is to jump to the end of scripture, the book of Revelation. Here the grand communal themes come to the fore clearly.

Revelation begins with a communal description of Christ's people as a "kingdom of priests" (Rev 1:6), an international political realm from "every tribe and tongue and people and nation" (Rev 5:9), which "shall reign on earth" (Rev 5:10). The saints are supposed to reign. They are a political body, but they are the opposite of a Mammon politics. The saints do not follow the way of the beasts (Rome) or the harlot (i.e., Jerusalem who loves the ways of Rome). God's people introduce a unique politics that doesn't wield the sword (Rev 13:10) and doesn't live for money, like Tyre and Jerusalem (Revelation 18). Notably, the community in Revelation fights like Jesus, by swallowing up death in victory. It absorbs the evil of the world by eating it at a great supper (Revelation 19).

At the same time, Revelation tells the tale of these two cities as two women, the harlot and the bride in white, the faithless old Jerusalem and Christ's people, the new Jerusalem, the bride (Revelation 21). This bride community is not just a group of individuals. It is not just a community of like-minded people. The bride is the *church*, the beginning of a new politics. The way of the cross is the way of community, and the way of community is most significantly the way of the church.

Jesus's earlier antithesis between God and Mammon still stands out strongly in Revelation. You cannot serve Christ and the Beast: "If anyone worships the beast and his image, and receives his mark on his forehead or on his hand, he himself shall also drink of the wine of the wrath of God" (Rev 14:9, 10; cf. Rev 13:15–17; 16:2; 19:20; 20:4). Rome's economy was not to be the economy of the church. Romanized Jerusalem lived in luxury, glorifying itself (Rev 18:7), basking in everything from "gold and silver," "cinnamon and incense," and "horses and chariots" to slaves, "bodies and souls of men" (Rev 18:12–14). The struggle between the church and Mammon is political and economic.

The church *is* the kingdom. The Westminster Confession (a central Reformed confession of 1646) recognized this: "The visible church . . . is the kingdom of the Lord Jesus Christ, the house of the family of God" (25.2). This confession also marked a thick line between the church as the kingdom and the state outside of that kingdom: "The civil magistrate may not assume to himself the administration of the Word and sacraments, or the power of the keys of the kingdom of heaven" (23.3).

This claim that the church is the kingdom grew increasingly less popular and commonly rejected in later Reformed traditions, especially under Dutch influence. Later Reformed thinkers broadened the kingdom to include the state and military and all of life within it. But the Westminster Confession had it right to limit the kingdom to the church.

As seen above, the book of Revelation limited the kingdom to the church. There, the "kingdom of priests" that reigns on earth had been redeemed by Christ's blood (Rev 5:9). Christ and the church fought with the spiritual weapons (Revelation 19; cf. 1 Cor 10:4), in contrast to worldly warriors (Rev 19:18, 19). Finally, Christ's kingdom in Revelation was a bride married to Christ, just as Paul had taught earlier (Eph 6:22f). The New Jerusalem is the institution of the church. Unlike the state, the church was specifically identified with "twelve foundations, and on them were the names of the twelve apostles of the Lamb" (Rev 21:14). And unlike some "Christian state" where Christians rule over believers *and* unbelievers, the New Jerusalem, as the church is characterized as a place of holiness: "But there shall by no means enter it anything that defiles, or causes an abomination or a lie, but only those who are written in the Lamb's Book of Life" (Rev 21:27).

This identification of the kingdom with the church matches the earlier language of Jesus in the Gospels. There, too, Jesus did not describe the kingdom as some church-state hybrid (and it certainly wasn't a purely future or purely spiritual construct). Jesus introduced his kingdom in space and time in the first century (Matt 12:28; 16:19; Luke 11:20). He taught us to pray "Your kingdom come. Your will be done on earth as it is in heaven" (Matt 6:10). And that kingdom was not even merely the reign of God over church and state alike. Christ described his kingdom in terms that applied only to the church, namely, a source of evangelism, redemption, and spiritual regeneration (Matt 13:38, 47; Luke 6:20; Col 1:13).

Christ's church-kingdom has authority that does not belong to the state: "I will give you the keys of the kingdom of heaven, and whatever you bind on earth will be bound in heaven, and whatever you loose on earth will be loosed in heaven" (Matt 16:19). Christ's kingdom requires the Holy Spirit for its citizens, quite unlike a mere civil realm: "unless one is born of water and the Spirit, he cannot enter the kingdom of God" (John 3:5). And as in the book of Revelation, Christ's kingdom fights like the church, not like a carnal empire: "My kingdom is not of this world. If My kingdom were of this world, My servants would fight, so that I should not be delivered to the Jews; but now My kingdom is not from here" (John 18:36). Jesus delegated this kingdom, this church, to his apostles so that they could develop, train, and expand this city and politics at odds with the world:

> But you are those who have continued with Me in My trials.
> And I bestow upon you a kingdom, just as My Father bestowed
> one upon Me, that you may eat and drink at My table in My
> kingdom, and sit on thrones judging the twelve tribes of Israel.
> (Luke 22:28, 29)

The church is indeed Christ's kingdom. It is a city on a hill, descended from heaven itself. We are to seek first the church and its way of community. It renounces the way of Rome and Mammon. It lives an entirely different life from the world. And because of this it aims to be more and more complete and whole and self-sufficient to itself, a real city, not dependent on or mixed the world, though not out of the world. "Come out of her, my people, lest you share in her sins" (Rev 18:4).

Because of this antithesis between the church and Mammon, their conflict continues through the ages. They are two different and opposed ways of organizing life. They each seek the surrender of the other. In the book of Acts, the people of Mammon recognized this. They complained concerning Christians that "these who have turned the world upside down have come here too. Jason has harbored them, and these are all acting contrary to the decrees of Caesar, saying there is another king—Jesus" (Acts 17:6). Their complaint was correctly political. The church proclaimed a competing king, a competing system that threatened the economics of Mammon.

This is why Jesus promised persecution to the church. "A servant is not greater than his master. If they persecuted Me, they will also persecute you" (John 15:20). Guaranteed. Jesus repeated this promise so many times in various ways it's surprising it hasn't been more widely accepted as one of the key marks of the church. Most churches today, especially those of us in the Western world, don't face the sort of persecution Jesus faced. (Sure, some Christians like to play the victim of secularist taunting and the "liberal media," but they aren't suffering for taking up the way of the cross, just for typical conservative surliness. Both are still partners in the big system.)

So why don't Christian churches face the persecution Jesus promised? At least two options come to mind: (a) either our presence has so transformed modern society that Mammon has been largely abandoned or (b) we have become so blind that, like the Pharisees' adultery with Rome, we can't even see how far we've embraced Mammon's ways. Obviously, I think the latter is clearly the case. We do not provoke the powers of Mammon in the West because we have joined those powers. We are not a threat because Mammon has tamed us to play by his rules, and we even wave flags for him.

The way of the church is the way of persecution. The way of the church does seek to turn the world upside down. "If the world hates you, you know that it hated Me before it hated you. If you were of the world, the world would love its own" (John 15:18).

The way of the church includes all the other ways of the cross we've looked at. The way of community or the church finds its best expression in the ways of weakness, renunciation, deliverance, sharing, enemy-love, and foolishness. All of these should mark out the church, and they have done so, at least for the most mature, through narrow-way expressions of the church throughout the centuries.

And the church has always kept at least the testimony of the way of the cross in its most central rituals—the Lord's Supper and baptism. The apostles guarded the way of weakness in the Supper when "breaking bread from house to house," they ensured that no one was in need (Acts 2:45ff.). The Supper marks the way of renunciation by being restricted to those in the new covenant, excluding the world. The Supper reenacts deliverance by having Christ's body feed those who hunger. It shows the way of sharing by being the new manna in the wilderness. The Supper brings former enemies together under the mantle of love and fellowship. The Supper demonstrates foolishness by seeing in it the invisible Christ. And, the Supper is a meal for the community, not for loners.

In the end, the way of community, the way of the church finds its chief summary, its constitution of virtues in the Sermon on the Mount.

As noted earlier, the Sermon on the Mount prodded Bonhoeffer and others back to the way of the cross. It is Jesus's central and communal expression. It shows us all the ways of the cross in one place.

The beatitudes reveal the way of weakness, deliverance, and sharing. Central to the sermon is the antithesis between God and Mammon. In it, Jesus explicitly calls for enemy-love, and the whole teaching is so counter-intuitive to the world's ways that it shows us true faith. "The Sermon is not primarily as list of rules. Something bigger—and indeed more startling—is at work. The Sermon on the Mount offers a vision of an alternative world. It is an odd world that runs counter to the presuppositions, rationalities, and myths of Jesus' day—and of our own."[7] It is a foolish sermon. Then each of these ways of the cross finds expression, again, in even more condensed form in the Lord's Prayer—weakness, renunciation, deliverance, manna sharing, etc.

Like Paul, Jesus defends the glory of the Old Covenant laws, but he also shows how they pointed beyond themselves. They were merely seeds. The whole sermon captures Jeremiah and Ezekiel's promises of the move from the external to virtues. Jesus gives a series of contrasts that touch on each of the Ten Commandments and the old path traditions that grew up around them. In each of these contrasts, Jesus moves from merely external obedience to genuine, heart obedience. From impersonalism to personalism. From rules to virtues. From the way of Moses to the way of the Spirit, the obedience of faith.

Jesus's Sermon on the Mount is the ancient but new constitution for Christ's kingdom. Jesus stands as the new Moses, drawing out the depths of the old law, laying down not a new external code to be obeyed impersonally but the new realm of the Spirit and virtue, directly from the lips of the deliverer, the Son. It is not an external constitution; it is triune personality opened up for us to take in and live out. It is the kingdom. It is the way of the church. "If there had been a law given which could have given life, truly righteousness would have been by the law" (Gal 3:21).

Followers of the Sermon on the Mount have long noted how anti-individualistic it is. People who finally stumble or are dragged to the way of the cross often attempt to live this Sermon on their own. They might repudiate Mammon and begin trying to deliver the homeless. They might give up on savings and live simply by themselves. They might refuse violence and give more charity to the poor. But in a very important way,

---

7. Campbell, "Folly," 62.

this misses Christ's teaching. This sermon is not a code for individual behavior. It is given to the church, and the church has to take the lead in living it in community. People who try it on their own quickly burn out. It is made to crush the individual but give life to the church. One person cannot live the life of the Trinity. The church is the Trinity on earth, and all the gifts and body parts are crucial to sustaining the way of the cross.

And yet, with all this, Christ's Sermon seems to end on a sour or realistic note. The way of the cross captured in the Sermon on the Mount might be impossible for an individual, but it's still very difficult for a single congregation. For all the revelation of the Son and the outpouring of the Spirit, the way of the cross is still intentionally difficult: "narrow is the gate and difficult is the way which leads to life, and there are few who find it" (Matt 7:14). He knows the way of the cross is humiliating. He knows it takes great courage to go against the gods of the day. He knows self-denial in community takes great patience and practice. He knows facing execution in the absence of God's voice is overwhelming. But that is Jesus's way. It is better we abandon it than pretend it is something else, some moralistic code or a mere worldview.

Even the final judgment takes place within the context of community. Certainly individual aspects will be dealt with, but it's intriguing that Jesus speaks of us being judged for what we did as a community. Imagine we were judged only for our communal acts. That's what Matthew 25 by itself suggests. Only King Jesus appears there as an individual. The rest of us are we. The faithful community moves into the future version of the kingdom: "Then the King will say to those on His right hand, 'Come, you blessed of My Father, inherit the kingdom prepared for you from the foundation of the world'" (Matt 25:34). Why? Because they, as a community, delivered and shared with Jesus in his weakness. They thumbed their noses at Mammon and clothed their enemies. What could be more contrary to sight than the way of the cross?

The seven themes or ways that I've surveyed in this opening portion of the book are one way of summarizing the historic and, hopefully, biblical practice of the way of the cross—the ways of weakness, renunciation, deliverance, sharing, enemy-love, foolishness, and community. When Jesus called on his followers to take up their crosses and follow him, these are what was built into that call. These ways blend together and overlap in real life situations to gives us the New Testament's "narrow way." They make up the kingdom that Jesus promised and preached. Most importantly, they are the way he lived. Jesus himself is the way of the cross, even before the crucifixion. Now, in the middle portion of this book, I want to turn to popular assumptions and trends that keep us from seeing the way of the cross. If we could jettison these treasured fictions, then we would have a much easier time even grasping Jesus's mission. But these assumptions go deep, and we don't want to give them up. In fact, we too often mistake them for Jesus's gospel itself.

PART TWO

Special Blinders to
the Way of the Cross

9

Superficial Providence

In many ways, Thomas Watson's *All Things for Good* is a good and holy Puritan classic, worthy of meditation. I share its traditional Reformed assumptions about providence, predestination, and election. But it's also a book that has bothered me for years now. It seems to have a dark underside, not in the simple doctrine of providence, but in Watson's peculiar *application* of providence that has become common in Reformed piety, as well as many other traditions by default. More importantly, this peculiar application of providence often blocks the way of the cross. Our take on providence can easily cement us in the worst sort of self-righteousness.

At some point it struck me how we Reformed (and many non-Reformed) greatly overuse the doctrine of providence, applying it promiscuously to so many different questions, problems, and situations, all in a way scripture never does. Scripture simply doesn't invoke providence as the answer to every question. In our regular parlance and counseling, though, we tend to view scripture as if every chapter ended in Romans 8:28. And yet, if we applied this sort of Watsonian providence to many of the voices of scripture, then most of them—the prophets, psalmists, apostles—would be told to be quiet and calm down. So many complaining biblical voices clearly violate our standard understanding of providence.

Watson's application of providence is forever concerned to remove distress, bring calm, and instill peace. God is always on our side, smiling. Watson exhorts us, "the most dark, cloudy providences of God have some sunshine in them."[1] If God is always smiling at us from behind the clouds, then it's fundamentally wrong to raise righteous complaints against him. In other words, if Watson's version of providence is correct, then the psalmist was clearly out of line to complain, "LORD, how long will the wicked, how long will the wicked triumph?" (Ps 94:3). The complainer should have known that God had good and holy reasons for his delay and should not be accused of delinquency. Calm down. The psalmist should instead have said, "Lord, we are at peace with your timing concerning the wicked. We're calm about their triumph. It is well with my soul."

Or, when Habakkuk seemed to completely forget Watsonian providence and declared, "O LORD, how long shall I cry, and You will not hear? Even cry out to You, 'Violence!' and You will not save" (Hab 1:2), he should have heard Watson's exhortation: "Learn to love providence,"[2] and "how little cause we have then to be discontented at outward trials and emergencies."[3]

Or when the martyred saints quite inappropriately "cried with a loud voice, saying, 'How long, O Lord, holy and true, until You judge and avenge our blood on those who dwell on the earth?'" (Rev 6:10), they should have just understood Watson's rebuke, "There are no sins God's people are more subject to than unbelief and impatience."[4] What could be more annoying than sinning martyrs?

Clearly, part of our problem is a confusion of biblical providence with Stoicism. Stoicism is that ancient Greek and Roman philosophy that can be summarized as "living in agreement with nature," as Cleanthes described it. Or as Marcus Aurelius put it, "Nothing happens to any man which he is not framed by nature to bear." And because of this, Stoics seek to suppress complaints, passions, laments, anger, disquietude, and frustration as quite inappropriate for the virtuous person. Watson even quotes the famous Stoic Seneca with approval at one point.[5]

It seems that Watson and many others, at times, side with the Stoics over against the often shrill psalmists and prophets. It's certainly often hard to tell the difference between Stoics and Watson. Here's a quick quiz to see if you can (answers below):

1. Watson, *Things*, 56.
2. Ibid.
3. Ibid., 61.
4. Ibid.
5. Ibid., 58.

1. Who said the following—a Stoic or Thomas Watson?

   "Everywhere and at all times it is in your power to accept reverently your present condition."

2. Who said the following—a Stoic or Thomas Watson?

   "Wherever I go, it will be well with me."

3. Who said the following—a Stoic or Thomas Watson?

   "Providence is the queen and governess of the world."

4. Who said the following—a Stoic or Thomas Watson?

   "He brings order out of confusion, harmony out of discord."

5. Who said the following—a Stoic or Thomas Watson?

   "It is one heart-quieting consideration in all the afflictions that befall us that God has a special hand in them."

6. Who said the following—a Stoic or Thomas Watson?

   "Let us be cheerful and brave in the face of everything."

Even if you got all the answers correct, these parallels should make us a little uncomfortable. Why are the expressions so close, while scripture sounds so different?[6]

Now wait a minute, some will object. The apostle Paul talked that Stoic way, too. You can't complain against the Puritans without also faulting Paul. "Rejoice in the Lord always. Again I will say, rejoice!" (Phil 4:4). "Rejoice always" (1 Thess 5:16). "Be anxious for nothing" (Phil 4:6). Wouldn't those exhortations count as Stoicism, too?

No. If Paul taught Puritan Stoicism, then he was really bad at it. He would have contradicted himself quite regularly. The same Paul who said "Rejoice always" also taught, "Rejoice with those who rejoice, and weep with those who weep" (Rom 12:15). The same Paul who said "Do all things without complaining" complained against those "whose god is their belly" (Phil 2:19) and shouted, "Beware of dogs, beware of evil workers, beware of the mutilation!" (Phil 3:2). The same Paul who said, "Be anxious for nothing" spoke in the same letter of "my distress" (Phil 4:14) and hoped to "be less sorrowful" (Phil 2:28) and even encouraged

6. Quiz Answers: 1. Marcus Aurelius; 2. Epictetus; 3. Thomas Watson; 4. Thomas Watson; 5. Thomas Watson; 6. Seneca.

"fear and trembling" (Phil 2:12). Paul wasn't a Stoic and not a Stoic in the same letter.

The answer is fairly simple. Paul didn't decontextualize "Rejoice always" the way the Puritans did and do. He wasn't concerned with modern, middle-class anxieties—jobs, cars, marriage, bills. Paul was speaking to Philippians facing violent persecution. The Philippians were "terrified" (Phil 1:28) and physically suffering for Christ's sake (Phil 1:29). Paul exhorted them in the way of the cross, the way of the poor in spirit—Christ "made Himself of no reputation, taking the form of a bondservant" (Phil 2:7). Paul himself was "being conformed to His death" (Phil 3:10), and he explained joy and peace within a conditional: "The things which you learned and received and heard and saw in me, these do, and the God of peace will be with you" (Phil 4:9). In other words, we can rejoice in all things if we are suffering like Christ, if we are in the way of the cross.

Providence didn't even enter in to Paul's discussion. Paul didn't have to read or interpret providence especially for him. He simply repeated Jesus's exhortation about rejoicing from the beatitudes: "Blessed are you when they revile and persecute you, and say all kinds of evil against you falsely for My sake. Rejoice and be exceedingly glad" (Matt 5:11, 12; Luke 6:23). Peter made the same connection between rejoicing and persecution—"greatly rejoice, though now for a little while, if need be, you have been grieved by various trials" (1 Pet 1:6; cf. 2 Cor 4:7–18). Neither Peter, nor Paul, nor Jesus invokes providence the way we so often do. They exhorted us to faith, to see counterintuitively in the face of suffering. They didn't universalize the comfort of providence to every situation.

In contrast, the Watsonian approach to providence encourages us to live by sight, not faith. It leads us to read every event as a revelation of God's direct will. If a person loses his or her job, then, we infer, clearly God opposed it. If the car crashes, then that's what God wanted. If Job is humiliated, then God was angry with him.

Though charismatic and Reformed theologies often seem at odds, Puritan providence reveals an interesting handshake between the two. We Reformed tend to look down on charismatic claims that God is directly doing and revealing such-and-such in individual, personal lives, e.g., giving advice on cars, mates, jobs, etc. But Watsonian providence turns out being just as charismatic. Because "God works all things for us," we tea-read every open and closed door, every success, every failure, as if it's the direct, simple revelation of God's will. Like charismatics, we too believe that God speaks directly to us individually through providence.

We both would instinctively read disaster of "the tower of Siloam" (Luke 13:4) simplistically and want to know "who sinned, this man or his parents, that he was born blind?" (John 9:2). Charismatic-Puritan providence encourages the sort of thinking that Jesus resists.

A Puritan reading of providence encourages believers to study the things seen—providential ups and downs—and then infer God's will. It's true, for example, that success and wealth come from faithfulness (Deut 28–30), but it's also true that many times success and wealth are curses (Ezek 26–28). And, yes, God sometimes curses the wicked with judgment and death, but, on the surface, the same happens to his people (Rev 6:10). A superficial reading of providence can mislead us greatly.

But why try to read providence anyway? Is it really crucial to following Christ? We're called to walk by faith, not sight—to live contrary to appearances. Discerning providence just isn't that important to the life of faith. God's hidden ways belong to God and are rather irrelevant to our day-to-day living—"The secret things belong to the LORD our God, but those things which are revealed belong to us and to our children forever, that we may do all the words of this law" (Deut 29:29). Why can't we live like that? Why must we resist the way of faith in the name of Puritan piety?

The biggest obstacle setup by a Puritan reading of God's "secret things" is a thick, protective barrier that blocks hearing the obvious things of God. Reading providence can be a way of quenching the Spirit. Consider how we regularly assume that a nice, middle class life is a sign of God's approval. We work hard, pay our bills, have a nice house, a good car. Maybe some minor trials, darn transmission. But overall, God is pleased with us. No doubts. Think about it. If we read God's providence as God directly opening and closing doors for us individually, if we see him "blessing" our lifestyles, then surely he can't be displeased with us at the same time? If God got me this job and this house, then he can't want me to be living any differently. He wouldn't want me to give them up. If God blessed me with all this food and technology, then he must want me to continue down this path. Visible blessing proves God's approval, doesn't it? As the popular conservative pundit Sean Hannity noted,

> Why do I believe passionately in the power of the American
> dream? It's simple: I'm living it. . . . I've worked hard to achieve
> my dreams. I've seized opportunities as they've arisen. . . .
> I've tried to be true to my faith in God and my faith in others.
> I've been blessed with a wonderful wife and two beautiful

> children. . . . So when people call me up and tell me you can't
> make it in America. . . I tell them they're crazy. Of course you
> can make it.[7]

Who can argue with a good marriage, good kids, and a good job? All is well. God is pleased and blesses. He wants us to keep going. Don't change a thing, Sean.

This reading of visible success as God's positive endorsement expands beyond individuals and families. Americans often make the same inference about the United States and all of Western civilization. We say, the West has experienced positive growth and improved health and technology for centuries. This must be the blessings of faithfulness Moses spoke of. God gave us wealth because of our discipline and benevolence. Hannity again: "As Americans, we've inherited our traditions from men and women who made sacrifices to acquire and preserve freedoms—the freedoms we enjoy today. They laid the path for us. Let's not whine and complain about the hard work it will take to maximize our potential. Let's be grateful for the opportunities."[8] Ancient Tyre could have said the same. We say, God is on our side, unlike those undisciplined people in the Third World. In fact, we rebuke people who question that equation. We tell them they ought to be grateful for all God has done for America and the West. Ingrates. Pessimists. America-haters.

See the self-protection? Blessings are unfalsifiable within that thick sphere of superficial providence. Nothing can get through. If America's wealth and freedom are proof of God's favor, then what contrary evidence could ever break through? If providence proves that my nice, middle-class way of life has God's direct approval, confirmed through daily charismatic providence, then every note of disapproval gets dismissed quickly. My ears can hear no criticisms. All is well with my way of life.

That was the same problem the Old Testament prophets faced. "I spoke to you in your prosperity, but you said, 'I will not hear'" (Jer 22:21) "How can you say, 'We are wise, and the law of the Lord is with us'?" (Jer 8:8). It was the same problem Jesus had in getting through to the Pharisees. "Abraham is our father." Washington is our father.

Israel under the kings had many material blessings—"I will build myself a wide house with spacious chambers, and cut out windows for it, paneling it with cedar, and painting it with vermilion" (Jer 22:14). "I will

7. Hannity, *Freedom*, 282.
8. Ibid., 284.

destroy the winter house along with the summer house; the houses of ivory shall perish, and the great houses shall have an end" (Amos 3:15). Why should the people hear God? God's providence had given them beds of ivory, couches, excellent meat, cool music, good wine, and the best creams, perfumes, and shampoos (Amos 6:3–6). Weren't they reading providence correctly? Material blessing proves God's pleasure.

When the prophets condemned the Israelites' injustice, the accused should have replied "I don't know what you're talking about. God blessed me with these fields, house, wife, and kids. You're preaching ingratitude and envy. Be off with you." Or, as they said in silencing Jeremiah, "this man does not seek the welfare of this people, but their harm" (Jer 38:4).

"Woe to you," the Lord said to protected ears, over and over. Woe. But no one could hear it. "Let not the mighty man glory in his might, nor let the rich man glory in his riches" (Jer 9:23). Such blindness continued in the New Covenant: "Because you say, 'I am rich, have become wealthy, and have need of nothing'—and do not know that you are wretched, miserable, poor, blind, and naked" (Rev 3:17). It doesn't matter. Superficial providence helps blind us to the way of the cross.

10

Unconquerable Sin

What difference would it make to our understanding of Christ's gospel if many humans were genuinely good and virtuous without Christ and the Spirit? If all people weren't desperately wicked in their hearts would we have anything at all to preach? The apostle Peter ran into this situation with the Roman centurion Cornelius. Our later tradition says that people without Christ and the Spirit are completely trapped in depravity, but scripture described a representative pagan, a man without Christ or the Spirit this way: "There was a certain man in Caesarea called Cornelius, a centurion of what was called the Italian Regiment, a devout man and one who feared God with all his household, who gave alms generously to the people, and prayed to God always" (Acts 10:1, 2).

Cornelius was a good and virtuous and praiseworthy pagan who explicitly lacked both Christ and the Holy Spirit. I don't think we'd know what to say to him. We have a different view of the gospel. Cornelius wasn't a gross sinner, wringing his hands over his sin. He still needed Christ and the "remission of sins" (Acts 10:43), but it wasn't because he was depraved. Peter himself recognized Cornelius's genuine inner and outer goodness: "Peter opened his mouth and said: 'In truth I perceive that God shows no partiality. But in every nation whoever fears Him and works righteousness is accepted by Him'" (Acts 10:34, 35). God accepts those who fear him and work righteousness. Why don't those kind of words show up in our evangelism? Cornelius was a "non-Christian" who feared God and did good works. It's possible. It's right there. The way we usually get around Cornelius is to say well, he was special, the Spirit really was already at work in him, even though the passage makes the explicit point that the Spirit hadn't fallen on him. So we hem and haw. I've heard some even suggest Cornelius was a hypocrite, nice only on the outside. In other words, we let a more abstract systematic theology about the universal depravity of man force our exegesis. Why not let such texts speak for themselves?

Our exaggerated view of sin is simply another way of evading the way of the cross. Christian tradition has found very holy ways to avoid imitating Christ. The holiest and most humble-sounding misdirection has been a very lopsided obsession with personal sin. Waves of this have shown up in both Reformation and Roman Catholic traditions.

The way this misdirection works is this: we begin by assuming that the key thing God is most obsessed about in all of history is our individual and personal sin. We say, since the Fall, we are thoroughly sinful, and so sinful in fact that the God directed all the forces of the universe and carefully orchestrated the death of his Son just to take care of this overwhelming problem—individualized sin. We see this problem as so overwhelming that it acts like a whirlpool, sucking the entire gospel and even God's character into its demands. Because of private sins, we excuse ourselves from taking public and collective sins seriously. After all, we say, if we could just fix individual sins, then corporate sin would take care of itself; it all has to do with the individual first, we insist.

And because of God's apparent focus on punishing or atoning for individual sin, we not only minimize corporate sin or have no clue how to handle it, we give up on serious maturity and sanctification. Even though, we say Jesus died to cancel sin and take our punishment, we think personal sin is still so bad we never escape its domination. We assume, even after Jesus's sacrifice, Christians are still pretty much bound by sin. We still say that even after Christ and the Spirit and sanctification, our righteousness is as filthy rags (stripping Isaiah 64 out of context). We resign. We give up overcoming. We end up agreeing with Enlightenment egoists on the permanence of sin. We're forever driven by self-interest, says Adam Smith, ho hum, what can we do but surrender to vice? Let it reign and shape an entire politics of resignation to self-interest because neither Christ nor the Spirit can overcome our personal sin. We lock ourselves into perpetual immaturity. Why try to grow up? Let us just confess and confess, obsess and obsess about our overwhelming private sin. In the end, real transformation of individuals and communities is impossible, a self-fulfilling prophecy.

The Lutheran and Reformed traditions have been leading contributors in this. We have been experts in making personal sin the axis around which the gospel turns. The influential Reformed thinker Lorraine Boettner captured this view somewhat ironically. He begins by assuring us that "total depravity" doesn't mean that "all men are equally bad" or that "any man is as bad as he could be," nor even "that any one is entirely destitute of virtue," but then he undoes all these nice qualifications:

> He possesses a fixed bias of the will against God, and instinc-
> tively and willingly turns to evil. He is an alien by birth, and a
> sinner by choice. The inability under which he labors is not an
> inability to exercise volitions, but an inability to be willing to
> exercise holy volitions. And it is this phase of it which led Lu-
> ther to declare that "Free-will is an empty term, whose reality is
> lost. And a lost liberty, according to my grammar, is no liberty
> at all." In matters pertaining to his salvation, the unregenerate
> man is not at liberty to choose between good and evil, but only
> to choose between greater and lesser evil.[1]

It's hard to see how an unbeliever can have some virtue on the one hand, as Boettner grants, but also have "a fixed bias against God" and "an inability to be willing to exercise holy volitions." Why didn't Peter talk this way about Cornelius?

The Westminster Confession and Heidelberg Catechism shaped this sort of focus on individual sin in pretty morose ways. Heidelberg Question 5 has children confess "I am prone by nature to hate God and my neighbor." (That wasn't true of Cornelius.) A series of questions deepens this focus, and in the middle of them, Question 10 says, God "is terribly displeased" with "our original as well as actual sins; and will punish them in his just judgment temporally and eternally." The Westminster Confession raises the stake even more: "we are utterly indisposed, disabled, and made opposite to all good, and wholly inclined to all evil" (VI, 4), and, as noted above, this deep sin never really leaves us after conversion: "This corruption of nature, during this life, does remain in those that are regenerated" (VI, 5), even though it's pardoned. We're just as trapped by sin before as after conversion? Wow. Why even try? It's rather hopeless. We just have to trudge on under this weight of sin forever. Maybe someone

---

1. Boettner, *Reformed*, 40.

should update Peter. No wonder we won't see the way of the cross. It assumes real growth and real overcoming. It says Christ and the Spirit actually overcome sin. It assumes we do live in a genuinely new heaven and earth of Christ's kingdom. It says that divine love is actually stronger than sin and violence.

My main complaint is not against the existence or seriousness of individual sin. I'm not at all denying the real and tragic place of personal sin. But part of my complaint is against the grossly lopsided nature of this view. Why does individual sin get to veto corporate sin? Why does it get all the attention? Perhaps we've got it all backward. Perhaps we need to deal with communal sin first, or at least at the same time. Instead, everything else in our theology and practice has to bend around our obsession with personal sin and exaggerated depravity.

Sometimes I wonder if we can even see communal and corporate sin anymore. When you ask American conservative evangelicals about social sins the only examples we keep coming back to time and again are abortion and homosexuality. Those are huge and serious issues. But we should wonder just a bit about why we so easily default to those sins. To be honest, one reason we "confess" those national sins is because they don't poke conservative Christians themselves in the eye. We talk about lamenting those national sins and even sometimes use language that has "us" take responsibility for them, but, in fact, they are quite safe targets because they are not generally our sins but belong to other groups. So on those rare occasions when evangelicals dare to speak about national sins and immediately mention abortion and homosexuality, it's hard not to worry about them as convenient, self-righteous examples that leave us comfortable in our devotion to Mammon.

Even more, though, it's not accidental that we can see only those two sins. Like our view of life and sin, they are decidedly individualistic actions. They are not sins of social structure or whole communities. These acts are largely individual, and those involved are individuals. Again, the question is the lopsidedness. Jesus, too, was surrounded by cultures of abortion and homosexuality, yet he never mentioned them. Why did he seemingly "ignore" these issues and focus instead on the powers of Mammon? It doesn't have to be an either-or issue, but that's my point. Why can we only care or see individualistic acts? It makes perfect sense if we have rejected genuine corporate and communal sins. It makes perfect sense if Protestantism has privileged medieval nominalism and individualism from the start. But we can still correct our way.

An obsession with personal sin shapes not only our understanding of politics and cultural transformation but also God himself. I regularly ask young, middle class teen students which is it that fundamentally drives God—justice or love? Class after class I continue to get the same initial reactions: justice. Students almost always launch into stories about the depravity of man (even those from non-Reformed backgrounds). We're so sinful, they say, that God is furious and has to punish someone. He can't just forgive it. His justice demands punishment. Some try to be smarter and suggest that God is driven equally by justice and love, but then they quickly come to the point that God had to punish his Son to exact justice. No matter how they try to qualify, justice always beats love.

In the middle of one of these discussions, I asked some students to consider Christ's parable of the prodigal son. They read through it, and I asked where it landed on the ordering of God's justice vs. love. Slowly their answers came out. They're very honest as young teens. I love them. But to stick with the primacy of justice, they actually started criticizing the prodigal's father. They defended the older brother. They suggested the father was a bit too easy on the prodigal. He was soft. The prodigal's father, they said, lacked a healthy sense of justice, on and on. My jaw drops every time. Where do they learn this stuff? Finally, I asked them to stand back and see what was strange about their criticisms of the prodigal father. Then it hit them who had spoken the parable.

Jesus—who knew the Father intimately. Sometimes the lights come on. Then we look at the parable of the forgiven servant who receives plenty of mercy and softness and then goes and punishes his debtor cruelly. Students hesitate a bit, but they're still more comfortable with the servant who exacts justice than the one who forgives the debt. It's hard when it's deep in us. Interestingly, when I ask them what sort of father or leader in the parables they would want or want to be, they all choose the examples of love over justice.

Certainly the centrality of personal depravity didn't just pop out the sky. It's got to have heavy grounding in scripture. Yes, and usually that view starts from the first chapters of Romans. That's where Augustine and the Reformers camped out. But it's early Romans where we can get a feel for how easy it is to let our individualism run rampant and ignore the text and context. In Romans 3, Paul gives his famous litany of sin that begins almost every discussion of depravity:

There is none righteous, no, not one;
There is none who understands;
There is none who seeks after God.
They have all turned aside;
They have together become unprofitable;
There is none who does good, no, not one. . . .

There is no fear of God before their eyes. (Rom 3:10ff)

That seems like an insurmountable list, at first. It seems to be a clear and universal indictment of the depravity of everyone. But you have to look at what Paul was citing. Those passages he cites actually speak contrary to the way we use Paul's words.

Paul quotes mainly from the Psalms, some prophets, and in each of those Psalms, we don't find the claim that every last person is totally depraved or that we are each "wholly inclined to all evil." We find contrary points. We find some are depraved, and some are innocent and righteous. In each of the Psalms Paul quotes, the psalmist speaks of the righteous weak remnant in contrast to the powerful depraved:

"There is none who does good." (Ps 14:1)
   but also:
"For God is with the generation of the righteous. You shame the counsel of the poor, but the LORD is his refuge." (Ps 14:5, 6)

"For there is no faithfulness in their mouth; Their inward part is destruction; Their throat is an open tomb." (Ps 5:9)
but also:
"But let all those rejoice who put their trust in You; . . . For You, O LORD, will bless the righteous." (Ps 5:11, 12)

"Deliver me, O LORD, from evil men; . . . The poison of asps is under their lips." (Ps 140:1, 3)
but also:
"I know that the LORD will maintain the cause of the afflicted, and justice for the poor. Surely the righteous shall give thanks to Your name." (Ps 140:12, 13).

"The wicked in his pride persecutes the poor; . . . The wicked in his proud countenance does not seek God; God is in none of his thoughts. . . . Under his tongue is trouble and iniquity." (Ps 10:1, 4, 7)

but also:
"You have heard the desire of the humble; You will prepare
their heart; To do justice to the fatherless and the oppressed."
(Ps 10:17, 18)

And so on. Contrary to appearances, the Psalms themselves spoke of
the injustice and oppression, a situation that the Roman Christians then
found themselves in. That would be encouraging to Paul's audience. The
psalmist and Paul spoke of the wicked, then the upright, the powerful
then the righteous and humble poor. Neither indicts every human being
universally as individually depraved. That would have directly contradicted the point of each of these quotes, as well as Paul's encouragement
of the Roman Christians.

In other words, like the Psalms (and Habakkuk), Paul wasn't speaking of all people as depraved sinners. Paul was comparing wicked leaders
and representatives with the holy kingship of Christ—"the seed of David,
declared to be the Son of God" (Rom 1:3). Paul described the sick Roman
leadership of the time, especially the Roman nobles and Caesars (Romans
1), as well as the hypocritical Jewish leadership (Romans 2). These both
stood in contrast to Christ's new representation, new priesthood. This fits
in perfectly with Paul's overall encouragement from Habakkuk. Paul was
teaching the Roman gentiles how to see counterintuitively, how to look
past surface blessedness. Though Roman leadership looked triumphant
and vindicated by all its wealth, and though the synagogues had authority, wealth, credentials, and the Temple, God was not on the side of either.
God had rescued an alien remnant through Christ, vindicating Christ,
and, all united to him, in his resurrection.

With this sort of understanding of early Romans, we also remove a
budding contradiction in Paul himself that the personal depravity tradition has had to ignore. Just prior to the litany in Romans 3, Paul himself
spoke quite positively of many unbelievers: "when Gentiles, who do not
have the law, by nature do the things in the law, these, although not having the law, are a law to themselves, who show the work of the law written
in their hearts" (Rom 2:14, 15). The law written in their hearts? Usually, we just let Paul in Romans 3 negate Paul in Romans 2. But we don't
have to do that, now. Paul, like the Old Testament, wasn't ever teaching
personal, universal depravity. He believed in people like Cornelius, too.
In fact, we find in later world history that we would stumble upon entire
tribes and regions of the world that were much like Cornelius. Again,
Paul anticipated this, when preaching in Athens: "He has made from one

blood every nation of men to dwell on all the face of the earth. . . . so that they should seek the Lord, in the hope that they might grope for Him and find Him, though He is not far from each one of us" (Acts 17:27). Unbelievers who desire God? Why didn't Paul speak like the Heidelberg Catechism?—"I am prone by nature to hate God and my neighbor." Mix this depravity view with Western imperialism, and you have the formula for Western expansion into the southern hemisphere that was happy to spread lies about rampant cannibalism and savagery, all while we were being the true genocidal savages. The belief that every unbeliever was utterly twisted and depraved made it easier for Western plundering and genocide, far beyond anything else in world history, hundreds of millions killed. Forcing total depravity into our reading of alien cultures made it easier to brutalize, enslave, and butcher the "beastly savages."

Objections about scripture's view of sin remain, of course. Doesn't Paul himself universalize these texts? "For all have sinned and fall short of the glory of God" (Rom 3:23), so that "all the world may become guilty before God" (Rom 3:19). Actually, this sort of conclusion fits very well within the kind of argument I've suggested Paul actually makes. They only become problematic if we continue reading them individualistically. Certainly Paul indicted all kinds of wicked rulers, gentile and Jewish, but he also described the whole world as "under sin."

Romans 5 explains how Sin and Death enslaved the whole world. The key is that a person can be trapped under the corporate domination of sin without each person needing to be utterly depraved. One can be under the domination of the spiritual principalities and powers, under the curse and judgment of God culturally, without being a wicked sinner. Cornelius was a virtuous and normal sinner. But more importantly, he had been trapped by spiritual Pharaohs, as was every gentile. He needed deliverance, "remission," from his normal failings as well as from the powers of darkness that kept him away from direct communion with God. The good gentiles that Paul spoke of in Romans 2 needed deliverance more from the principalities and powers than from any innate wickedness in themselves. Yes, Death reigned over them, but that didn't rule them out as genuinely decent people, just as Paul and Peter said.

So what's the big deal then? All still need Christ. All are under sin. Is it really that big a difference? Yes, it's the difference between two worlds. It's the difference between perpetual immaturity and real transformation. It's the difference between default hopelessness and real hope.

Our modern focus on personal sin distracts us from seeking first the kingdom of God. We're so busy fussing with our interior morality, thinking the right thoughts, that we feel freed from doing what Jesus called us to do. (Of course, the interior work has a place, as I'll defend in the last chapter.) If we think Jesus was more fixated on our private morality, then we can legitimately neglect the weightier matters of the law, justice, and mercy. And it's so easy to spend decades focused on private morality and never truly grow spiritually. It's strange how an exaggerated view of sin hinders spiritual growth in millions of Christians.

If we're stuck and static, believing that Christ cannot truly overcome basic sins and habits, then the Sermon on the Mount becomes the counsel for the perfect alone, a kingdom not for this world at all. I can't tell you the countless times I've been in discussions about the Sermon on the Mount when others will click over to the impossibility of doing what Jesus says because we're all depraved sinners, we're not Jesus. These responses pop out especially in response to Jesus's rather fundamental commands about loving our enemies. Those are just impossible, apparently, in a world of sinners, as if Jesus didn't live in a world of sinners. Oh Lord, keep us from the excuses of depravity.

11

Automatic Heaven

Scripture says relatively little about heaven, especially in comparison to the topics it finds most important. It's there, of course, but it's not the obsession of Scripture the way it is with medieval, Reformation, and modern Christians. In the Old Covenant Scriptures, we hear virtually nothing about heaven at all, maybe a couple verses here and there. Moses and the prophets saw more pressing topics to address, and then the apostles themselves used the prophets to establish New Covenant priorities, which didn't differ all that much from what Isaiah was concerned about—not about heaven.

One of the premier passages we mistakenly believe is about heaven is the depiction of the New Jerusalem, the bride of Christ at the end of the book of Revelation (Revelation 21, 22).

> I saw a new heaven and a new earth, for the first heaven and the first earth had passed away. Also there was no more sea. Then I, John, saw the holy city, New Jerusalem, coming down out of heaven from God, prepared as a bride adorned for her husband. And I heard a loud voice from heaven saying, "Behold, the tabernacle of God is with men, and He will dwell with them, and they shall be His people. God Himself will be with them and be their God. And God will wipe away every tear from their eyes; there shall be no more death, nor sorrow, nor crying. There shall be no more pain, for the former things have passed away." (Rev 21:1–4)

Surely this has to be about heaven, if anything. Randy Alcorn's influential book, *Heaven*, agrees: "The city at the center of the future Heaven is called the New Jerusalem."[1] It will be a city "filled with natural wonders, magnificent architecture, thriving culture," and it will be huge, a metropolis that would, comparatively, "stretch from Canada to Mexico." Alcorn explains that this future city will have twelve gates, but they are merely ceremonial since "there will be no enemies outside the city's gates.... All enemies of the Kingdom will be forever cast into the lake of fire, far away from the New Earth. So the gates will remain open."[2]

Actually, we can see this is false from Revelation itself. John says in reference to the gates of this city, "outside are dogs and sorcerers and sexually immoral and murderers and idolaters, and whoever loves and practices a lie" (Rev 22:15 and compare 21:26, 27). That's quite a direct contrast to what Alcorn says—"there will be no enemies outside the city's gates." What's going on here? How could he miss a text that important? That's the blinding power of heaven in our thinking. Everything else must submit to our notions, regardless of what the texts actually teach.

In addition, Alcorn repeatedly insists on literalism to make his case in Revelation 21, but he doesn't live up to it. John described the New Jerusalem as a city and a *bride*. John sees "the bride, the Lamb's wife" (Rev 21:9).

The imagery of the New Heavens and New Earth in Revelation 21, 22 comes from Isaiah 65. Both John and Isaiah can't be speaking about heaven because both include death and sin. We've seen John mention the gross sin living outside the city, and Isaiah spoke of glorious health but also remaining death in the new heavens and earth: "No more shall an infant from there live but a few days, Nor an old man who has not fulfilled his days; for the child shall die one hundred years old, but the sinner being one hundred years old shall be accursed" (Isa 65:20).

Neither Isaiah nor John's "new heaven" is about a future place. They are statements about life on earth. They speak in the song of opera. Where opera aims to reveal the depths and realities of human subjectivity, the prophets speak in arias that reveal the hidden depths of life and spirit. The prophets see by glorious faith, not surfaces.

In Revelation's opera, John described something radically new, a glorious work of Christ and the Spirit, but to look around in the first

1. Alcorn, *Heaven*, 241.

2. Ibid., 243.

century, it was "just" the church on earth in the—trodden, mournful, poor, surrounded by immorality. But the opera said look deeper. In reality, the church is a glorious city centered around Christ. She is a spotless bride. She is founded on prophets and apostles. She is a place of refuge where tears are wiped away and thirst assuaged. The church descends out of heaven because her citizenship (Phil 3:20) and source (John 18:36) are from heaven.

Notice how blind we become, then, if we're looking off into the future, but Christ is trying to get us to see the church here and now. We become irrelevant. The way of the cross becomes irrelevant. Our goal becomes just to guarantee a spot in that far-off city. We are trapped in falsity and triviality like Christian in *Pilgrim's Progress*.

It's no surprise, then, that Randy Alcorn's book on heaven gives us that same, tiresome cheap grace that prevails in conservative evangelical churches. How does Alcorn assure us that we'll make it into heaven? He first warns us that "religious activities alone" will not get us into heaven. No, his preferred answer is purely intellectual: "Make the conscious decision to accept Christ's sacrificial death on your behalf."[3] Oooh. It's not mere belief, no. It's a special "conscious" decision. That captures so much of modern evangelicalism.

The modern Christian assumption that getting a guaranteed spot in heaven is the central concern of Christ's gospel has become a central in dismissing Jesus's main call to the way of the cross. In fact, when modern Christians read Paul talking about being "determined not to know anything among you except Jesus Christ and Him crucified" (1 Cor 2:2), they don't think about the ways of weakness, sharing, and enemy-love, they assume Paul is determined to think about nothing else except the need merely to belief Christ shed his blood so we can automatically get into heaven. Like one pastor said, Jesus just needed to "get up on that cross," nothing else. Automatic heaven is all that counts.

Dietrich Bonhoeffer complained about this pervasive notion of cheap grace back in World War II. We still haven't learned his basic lesson. We've now institutionalized cheap grace throughout many Christian traditions. Bonhoeffer lamented,

> Cheap grace is the deadly enemy of our Church. We are fighting today for costly grace. . . . Cheap grace means grace as a doctrine, a principle, a system. . . . An intellectual assent to

3. Ibid., 36.

> that idea is held to be of itself sufficient to secure remission
> of sins. . . . Cheap grace is grace without discipleship, grace
> without the cross.[4]

Bonhoeffer inspired many of us to try avoid cheap grace and search out the words of Christ more deeply. Many evangelicals heeded Bonhoeffer's criticism by making their belief thicker and heavier. They memorized a lot of scripture to assure themselves their belief was hard and not easy. That's what he must have meant. His famous phrase "cheap grace" also confuses. It cuts us, but when we start thinking about it, isn't grace a gift? Paul, himself, spoke of salvation as a "free gift" (Rom 5:15–18). After all is said and done, what is the big difference between free and cheap?

Perhaps Bonhoeffer is partly to blame for such confusions. His first chapter, from where these quotes come, is hard to grasp within the traditional context of a Protestant opposition to salvation by works. On the surface, it's hard not to think Bonhoeffer is calling for works-salvation. So many evangelicals can't make it past that first chapter.

Bonhoeffer was a good Lutheran, though, and he didn't give up on salvation by faith alone. How did Bonhoeffer, then, connect the free gift of salvation and the obedience of discipleship, the way of the cross? One way of understanding him is that the language of "cheap grace" was effectively startling and puzzling, but he wasn't speaking against free grace but against cheap discipleship. That fits his argumentation. And he certainly wasn't calling for any meritorious view of salvation, but he connected the gift of salvation, the gift of Christ with a duty, an obligation. To accept Christ was to accept an obligation, and that obligation was the way of the cross. In Bonhoeffer's words, "Luther had said that grace alone can save; his followers took up his doctrine and repeated it word for word. But they left out its invariable corollary, the obligation of discipleship."[5] On that reading, faith in Christ morally entails obedient discipleship, but it doesn't in any way merit that salvation.

Still, a problem lingers. What if we fail to live costly discipleship? Do we lose our salvation? Without discipleship are we not truly believers? If so, then it looks as if it is discipleship and not intellectual assent that gains salvation. So how does that differ from salvation by works? It's still confusing on the surface, and our dispute is not really with Bonhoeffer but with Christ. Bonhoeffer merely repeats Christ.

4. Bonhoeffer, *Cost*, 43.
5. Ibid., 50.

Let's complicate things even more. In the end, Protestants have been pretty shameful over the centuries in the way we ignore or diminish the many passages that clearly make judgment by works much more central than we're comfortable with. We may mention them, but we quickly insert our qualifications about justification by faith alone, even when the text doesn't even mention it. For us, everything turns around getting the mechanics of faith and works lined up. Everything else is subordinate to that. That's our identity, regardless of Jesus' calls to take up the cross.

Consider a small pile of such passages:

"For the Son of Man will come in the glory of His Father with His angels, and then He will reward each according to his works" (Matt 16:27).

"For the hour is coming in which all who are in the graves will hear His voice and come forth—those who have done good, to the resurrection of life, and those who have done evil, to the resurrection of condemnation" (John 5:28).

"You are treasuring up for yourself wrath in the day of wrath and revelation of the righteous judgment of God, who 'will render to each one according to his deeds': eternal life to those who by patient continuance in doing good seek for glory, honor, and immortality" (Rom 2:5–7).

"For we must all appear before the judgment seat of Christ, that each one may receive the things done in the body, according to what he has done, whether good or bad" (2 Cor 5:10).

"God is not mocked; for whatever a man sows, that he will also reap. For he who sows to his flesh will of the flesh reap corruption, but he who sows to the Spirit will of the Spirit reap everlasting life" (Gal 6:7, 8).

"I saw the dead, small and great, standing before God, and books were opened. And another book was opened, which is the Book of Life. And the dead were judged according to their works, by the things which were written in the books. The sea gave up the dead who were in it, and Death and Hades delivered up the dead who were in them. And they were judged, each one according to his works" (Rev 20:12, 13).

Can we be honest with these texts? Or do we have to let our traditions set them aside? Can we hear the Spirit speaking in them? Why don't they mention anything from the Reformation? Why don't they mention faith? Why don't they mention believing hard in Jesus sacrifice? Why don't they even mention union with Christ? It's all mixed up. Yet this is Jesus and Paul and John. Why don't they talk like we do? They are relentless—works, works, works. Why did Peter preach, "But in every nation whoever fears Him and works righteousness is accepted by Him" (Acts 10:35). Fear and works? No faith?

We all know the usual way of dismissing the full force of these verses. We insert and qualify and rearrange. Because we've misconstrued Paul's advocacy of the way of Abraham vs. the way of Moses as a struggle between faith and merit in the abstract, we force that discussion into judgment day passages to protect mere belief as our key into heaven.

Still, regardless of our traditions, scripture never taught salvation by merit. Again, think of it in terms of salvation in the Exodus. Did Israel merit God's election of Abraham? Did they force God by their goodness and merit to pour out his wrath on Pharaoh? Did their good works merit their deliverance from Egypt? Did they merit God's promises? Did they merit the promise land? No, of course, not. God's love and mercy and empathy did all that. Even while they were sinners God did that, just as for us (Rom 5:8). God's enemy-love delivered us. We had no part in it, not even the back-handed pelagianism of Protestant faith-that-some-how-we-agree-is-not-really-human-effort. What odd corners we paint ourselves into.

Neither faith nor works entered into God's deliverance of Israel from Egypt. They couldn't do anything to save themselves from slavery. Liberation was a gift. So where did faith and works enter in, then? As Bonhoeffer said, God's work of deliverance created an obligation of thanks. Moses explained this obligation this way:

> Beware, lest you forget the LORD who brought you out of the land of Egypt, from the house of bondage. You shall fear the LORD your God and serve Him, and shall take oaths in His name. You shall not go after other gods, the gods of the peoples who are all around you. . . . You shall diligently keep the commandments of the LORD your God, His testimonies, and His statutes which He has commanded you. And you shall do what is right and good in the sight of the LORD, that it may be well with you, and that you may go in and possess the good land of which the LORD swore to your fathers. (Deut 6:12–18)

Exodus entailed obedience. Deliverance requires loyalty. Christ delivered, and we owe faith, like Abraham, without the rituals of the old Temple.

The key problem is that faith is invisible. Abraham's faith was invisible. Not even God could see it (however one works out the details about omniscience; perhaps it's divine a refusal to see it; not important). God tells Abraham to sacrifice Isaac, a great act of counterintuition. Yet, somehow, God could not see Abraham's faith, even though God can read the heart. Something mysterious goes on here, and in every act of faith. Whatever the case, Abraham lines Isaac up on the make-shift altar and prepares to do what looks like utter horror to those without faith. Abraham raises his knife, and we hear: "Do not lay your hand on the lad, or do anything to him; for now I know that you fear God, since you have not withheld your son, your only son, from Me" (Gen 22:12). *Now I know. Now I know.* Abraham's faith was invisible before the raising of the knife. Faith has to be incarnated to be seen by God. Without that incarnation, God cannot see it. It is nothing.

If faith alone is invisible, then we can see that, though the Westminster Confession (and almost all other Protestant/evangelical expressions) is on the right track, it unnecessarily complicates things. Listen to this confession with Abraham's sacrifice and the later Exodus in mind:

> Faith, thus receiving and resting on Christ and his righteous-
> ness, is the alone instrument of justification; yet is it not alone
> in the person justified, but is ever accompanied with all other
> saving graces, and is no dead faith, but worketh by love.[6]

First, this would be like saying God delivered or vindicated the Israelites because of the instrument of invisible faith in their hearts. Nothing of the sort happened. He justified/delivered Israel from Pharaoh on his own. No need to go toward soft Pelagianism. Second, even once they were delivered and then obligated to follow his way, it seems to suggest that God looked into their hearts and saw faith and works, and though faith was side by side with works, God only saw faith, somehow a nonwork. The larger point is that scripture teaches that such faith is invisible. God can not or will not see it. If he couldn't see Abraham's faith, he certainly can't spot ours.

The Confession seems to get closer to the truth when it explains under the chapter on good works that, "These good works, done in obedience to God's commandments, are the fruits and evidences of a true and lively faith."[7] Protestants often take the path of tree-and-fruit to help reconcile the passages on faith and works. The usual argument runs that God can be said to judge us by works because these works grew out of true faith, and God is really looking past the good works to the sapling of true faith. The works themselves are unimportant.

6. Westminster Confession of Faith, XI, 2.
7. Ibid., XVI, 2.

Apart from still misplacing the whole faith-works discussion into the Exodus itself, instead of the promised land, this version of the story still assumes that faith could be visible by itself. The relationship of tree-and-fruit is still too far apart. It doesn't fit the passages on works above. It's a way to fudge the passage a bit to force our understanding.

We can get closer to the biblical language on faith and works if we remember that works are the *incarnation* of faith. They are not two different things, though they are distinct. Faith is not a tree and then this other thing comes out, the fruit, the good works. Works are faith made visible (keep in mind the distinction between Exodus and promised land). Neither faith nor works got the Israelites out of Egypt, but both kept them in the promised land.

So why does scripture call for faith, and yet pile up passages that we'll be judged by works? We're the same as Abraham. He had faith, but it was invisible. When he raised his knife, God could then see Abraham's faith. In the same way, if Abraham hadn't acted against Isaac, then God would have known and judged that no true faith existed. Note it's not just a quiet faith. It would be nonexistent. Good works are the only acceptable proof of faith available to humans and God. "I will show you my faith by my works" (Jas 2:18). On the last day, we will not be judged by some hidden faith. There is no such thing that counts. We will be judged by our incarnations. Saved by the Incarnation, judged by our incarnations.

The Reformed tradition rightly likes to add that even such faith is a gift, and it is. Even in the wilderness and promised land, faith was a gift of God. But if it was invisible, it wasn't there at all. "For as the body without the spirit is dead, so faith without works is dead also" (Jas 2:26).

All this means, though, that we don't have a guaranteed spot in heaven just because we assure ourselves that we have invisible faith in our heart and heads. Invisible faith is not faith. God refuses to count it until we lift the knife. Alcorn and the rest of us get it terribly wrong to suggest that all we need to do is "Make the conscious decision to accept Christ's sacrificial death on your behalf." Abraham could have made a thousand conscious decisions, and they wouldn't have counted as faith. God will only judge incarnations.

If we're to be judged only by the incarnations of true faith, then we had better pay attention to the sort of incarnations Christ wants. What might those be? Here we falter again, fearful of giving any serious place to works. As an example, again, the Westminster Confession describes the works or actions of saving faith, that is the really good faith as:

yielding obedience to the commands, trembling at the threat-
enings, and embracing the promises of God for this life, and
that which is to come. But the principal acts of saving faith are,
accepting, receiving, and resting upon Christ alone for justification, sanctification, and eternal life, by virtue of the covenant
of grace.[8]

Yielding, trembling, embracing, accepting, receiving, resting. Are those
the really the principal sorts of actions Jesus required?

We know typical good deeds won't suffice, let alone mere belief.
After explaining the way of the cross through the Sermon on the Mount,
Jesus marked out the sort of obedience that would not go well.

> Not everyone who says to Me, "Lord, Lord," shall enter the
> kingdom of heaven, but he who does the will of My Father in
> heaven. Many will say to Me in that day, "Lord, Lord, have we
> not prophesied in Your name, cast out demons in Your name,
> and done many wonders in Your name?" And then I will
> declare to them, "I never knew you; depart from Me, you who
> practice lawlessness!" (Matt 7:21–23)

These are above average works. These are what pastors and church leaders do. But Jesus rejected that approach to life. Because Jesus places these
words at the end of the Sermon on the Mount, he has marked off these
works from those of the Sermon on the Mount. The faith he wanted,
then, involved those ways elaborated in the sermon: the way of weakness, renunciation, deliverance, sharing, enemy-love, foolishness, and
communion.

Could it really be that we'll be judged on the way of the cross? That
the faith incarnated would be taking up our crosses in those specific
ways? Will our faith be judged by how we shared, delivered, loved our
enemies, and showed mercy to the poor? How can we miss it?

That's exactly the point of the final judgment in Matthew 25, which
we've seen as the summary of the way of the cross. Note, Matthew 25
is a judgment like Abraham's, a judgment on incarnated faith. And the
incarnations are all expressions of the way of the cross: "I was thirsty and
you gave Me drink; I was a stranger and you took Me in; I was naked and
you clothed Me; I was sick and you visited Me; I was in prison and you
came to Me.'" (Matt 25:35, 36). James also thought in this groove. In the

---

8. Ibid., XIV, 2.

midst of explaining how faith becomes visible through works, he thinks not of middle class diligence but mercy for the poor:

> What does it profit, my brethren, if someone says he has faith but does not have works? Can faith save him? If a brother or sister is naked and destitute of daily food, and one of you says to them, "Depart in peace, be warmed and filled," but you do not give them the things which are needed for the body, what does it profit? (Jas 2:14–16)

The apostle John captured all of this, the invisibility of faith, incarnational obedience, and *walking the same path of Jesus*, the way of the cross:

> Now by this we know that we know Him, if we keep His commandments. He who says, "I know Him," and does not keep His commandments, is a liar, and the truth is not in him. But whoever keeps His word, truly the love of God is perfected in him. By this we know that we are in Him. He who says he abides in Him ought himself also to walk just as He walked. (1 John 2:3–6)

To walk just as he walked. And how did Jesus walk? What way did he live his life on earth? The way of the cross. Jesus explained his mercy work this way in conveying his life to a worried John the baptist:

> Jesus answered and said to them, "Go and tell John the things you have seen and heard: that the blind see, the lame walk, the lepers are cleansed, the deaf hear, the dead are raised, the poor have the gospel preached to them. And blessed is he who is not offended because of Me." (Luke 7:21–23)

Peter described the same way of Jesus's walk: "God anointed Jesus of Nazareth with the Holy Spirit and with power, who went about doing good and healing all who were oppressed by the devil" (Acts 10:38). Jesus walked the path of a deliverer of the poor, and that's the path we're called to walk, and those are the incarnations of faith we'll have to show.

Faith is a gracious gift from God, but, in the end, if he can't see it, then it's not there. Without the way of the cross, we remain outside the kingdom of heaven.

12

God the Accuser

"The prophecy of old is come to completion, that my father spoke, when he said Poseidon would be angry with us. . . . We must dedicate to Poseidon twelve bulls, chosen out of our herds. Then he might take pity on us, and not pile up a high mountain over our city."

– KING ALKINOOS, *THE ODYSSEY*

"Die he [Adam] or Justice must; unless for him
Some other able, and as willing, pay
The rigid satisfaction, death for death. . . .
'Behold me [Christ] then, me for him, life for life
I offer, on me let thine anger fall.'"

—*PARADISE LOST*, JOHN MILTON

E ven our view of the cross can keep us from the cross. That seems to be what has happened historically, especially in the last few centuries. How might a "high" view of Christ's work on the cross actually undermine the way of the cross, Jesus's way of discipleship? This could and has happened in several ways. Imagine, for example, if you thought, as in the previous chapter, that Christ's work on the cross automatically guaranteed you a place in heaven. Then you'd have no reason to imitate Jesus's way of life. Imitation wouldn't be central. Discipleship would be unimportant. We might even suspect it as a way of "works righteousness" to be avoided.

Or imagine you thought that Christ's work on the cross was so unique and unrepeatable and complete that it would be blasphemous to talk about imitating it. Then, certainly, you'd have to minimize all Jesus's instructions about taking up a cross. He alone needed to do that, not us depraved sinners. The cross was a once-and-done event, we say, between Christ and the Father alone, and any talk of duplicating that work would be seen as grossly undermining the special glory of Christ's shed blood.

Or, imagine you believe that the whole point of Christ's death on the cross was so that sinners wouldn't have to die. He died, after all, *instead* of us. You might say, for example, as the Westminster Confession says, that Christ's "obedience and satisfaction [was] accepted in their stead,"[1] or as the Puritan John Owen said, that Christ "underwent the punishment due them, and that in our stead,"[2] or as the influential J. I. Packer said, that "Substitution is, in fact, a broad idea that applies whenever one person acts to supply another's need, or to discharge his obligation, so that the other no longer has to carry the load himself."[3] Notice, the other *will not* have to carry the load.

And yet, the New Testament teaches, "We died with Christ" (Rom 6:8). "I have been crucified with Christ" (Gal 2:20). "We have been buried with him" (Rom 6:4). The apostle Peter says we are to imitate Christ's suffering on the cross: "Christ also suffered for us, leaving us an example, that you should follow His steps" (1 Pet 2:21). But how can the apostles call on us to identify with Christ's crucifixion if he was supposed to die as the perfect sacrifice in our place to satisfy the Father's anger? If Christ was the perfect sacrifice to placate the Father, then it makes no sense for us to join him on the cross. How would sinners appease the Father? That was Jesus's job, not ours. Was Jesus an exclusive or inclusive substitute? Did he do it alone or do we participate with him? Something isn't connecting between our language and the New Testament's. That should make us suspicious.

1. Westminster Confession, XI, 3.
2. Owen, *Death*, 167, 168.
3. Packer, "Logic," 98.

These are a few of the many questions and tensions that have developed over the centuries between the two main pictures of Christ's work on the cross, two views of the atonement: the penal substitution and restorative substitution[4] (Christus Victor) views. The topic is vast and the literature thick.[5] The discussion between the two views will be a central and important debate over the next twenty years. The consequences are huge. I won't pretend to make any dent in that larger discussion in this short space. I'm only interested in the narrower slice of the question of how a view of the atonement can hinder us from the way of the cross. Mine is a question about implications and consequences. Certainly it's got to be an interesting side question if a major view of the atonement actually distracts us from following Jesus. That's what the penal atonement view appears to do, block us from the way of the cross, perhaps more than any other issue. In my own discussions, I was surprised to find people so often trying to resist the way of the cross by taking refuge in some form of penal atonement. This caught me off guard, at first, but pretty soon, the pattern developed.

In brief, what are these two main views of atonement? The penal substitution view is the view that "God gave himself in the person of his Son to suffer instead of us the death, punishment, and curse due to fallen humanity as the penalty for sin."[6] It is the view that "the Lord Jesus Christ died for us—a shameful death, bearing our curse, enduring our pain, suffering the wrath of his own Father in our place."[7] The wrath of the Father. That's key.

In contrast, the restorative substitution (or Christus Victor) view is the story that "God deals decisively with sin by dealing death a final defeat through the life, death, and resurrection of Jesus Christ—thereby making a way for us to participate in God's victory over death."[8] N. T. Wright summarizes it this way: "Jesus, anointed with God's Spirit to fight the real battle against the real enemy, to take the full power of evil and accusation upon himself, to let it do its worst to him, so that it would thereby be

4. Derek Flood uses this helpful contrast—penal vs. restorative substitutions in Derek Flood, "Substitutionary Atonement," 142–159.

5. The best, current defenses of the two views are: penal atonement—Steve Jeffery, et al, *Pierced for Our Transgressions* and restorative atonement—Darrin W. Snyder Belousek, *Atonement, Justice, and Peace.*

6. Jeffery, *Pierced*, 21.

7. Ibid.

8. Belousek, *Atonement*, 380.

exhausted, its main force spent. He would be the David for this ultimate Goliath. . . . [though] this David would win the battle by losing his life."[9] For Wright, the cross was not about "a God who wanted to punish people was content to punish the innocent Jesus instead."[10] Rather, Jesus went ahead of his people, "to meet the powers of destruction in person, to take their full weight on himself, so as to make a way through, a way in which God's people could be renewed. . . . could be rescued from their continuing slavery and exile."[11]

The two main views have many variations, and they sometimes overlap in interesting ways. But, fundamentally, they face different directions and seem to produce two different faiths. Penal atonement seeks to solve the problem of the Father, and restorative substitution finds the problem in Death and Satan. Penal substitution focuses on placating the Father's wrath and often draws all the rest of the faith into that singular task. Restorative substitution focuses on how the Father and Son together conquer Death and free people from Satanic domination. Restorative substitution is the story of the Exodus for the entire cosmos.

One question that captures the deep difference between the two views is: in the Christian story, *are we saved from the Father or Satan?* Do we need deliverance from God or Satan? Sometimes Christians hesitate even to concede that we're delivered from Satan. They say Christians focus too much on Satan. But they back off this line when they're reminded of the New Testament's repeated focus on overthrowing Satan—"For this purpose the Son of God was manifested, that He might destroy the works of the devil" (1 John 3:8; cf. Matt 12:27–28; John 12:31; Acts 10:38; 26:18; Heb 2:14; Col 1:13; 2:15).

Most Christians I raise the question with tend to say we're saved from *both* the Father and Satan. They recognize the tension of putting those two side by side, so usually, they're quick to add that we're really saved from the *wrath* of God and also a bit from Satan. But that doesn't really soften the question. The Father still has a problem. His holy character needs placating before he can be friends with us. His wrath isn't something distinct in his pocket. He is his wrath, in some sense.

In fact, we can refocus the same question and ask, who, for us, is the "Accuser," the Father or Satan? Those who know the scriptural answer

9. Wright, *Simply*, 188.

10. Ibid., 184.

11. Ibid., 178.

can see that this is a loaded question. Scripture consistently reserves the title "Accuser" for Satan alone. But the question highlights one of the most worrying features of the penal atonement view, namely, that in that view the Father also appears to function as the accuser. This should be very disturbing, and it marks a deep difference between the two views of atonement. Sophisticated defenders of penal atonement will rightly reject the claim that the Father is the Accuser, but it's hard to avoid the characterization. They'll reject the label but still have the Father fill all the functions of that office under a different name.

I've used these two questions to help us grasp the deep difference between the penal and restorative views of Christ's work on the cross, but my purpose here is to highlight the implications, specifically to point out how the penal atonement view can obstruct the way of the cross. I'll focus on just three key, objectionable aspects of the penal atonement view, namely, the feature just raised above, (a) that the Father functions as the Accuser, followed by (b) the claim that God's justice and holiness won't allow him to be in the presence of sin, and (c) that God needs blood to be shed before he can forgive or be reconciled.

(a) *God is an Accuser*: In scripture, as is commonly known, the personal name of the devil is Satan, which means the adversary or the accuser, and so Satan bears that name and fulfills that role against the saints (Job 2:1–7; Zech 3:1–2; Rev 12:10). Does this mean that God never accuses? No (Ps 103:9; Isa 57:16). But accusation is not God's basic orientation. Unlike Satan, God is "compassionate and gracious, slow to anger, abounding in love. He will not always accuse, nor will he harbor his anger for ever" (Ps 103:8, 9). God isn't characterized by accusation and wrath. That's Satan's basic trait. In contrast to Satan's perfectionistic justice, God "does not treat us as our sins deserve or repay us according to our iniquities" (Ps 103:10). Instead of being an accuser, the Lord is an advocate and defender (Ps 68:5; Prov 23:11; Isa 19:20), our comforter, counselor (John 14:26). The whole Trinity is serves as a defender, and when Christ comes, his mission is to overthrow and disarm the Accuser:

> Then I heard a loud voice saying in heaven, "Now salvation, and strength, and the kingdom of our God, and the power of His Christ have come, for the accuser of our brethren, who accused them before our God day and night, has been cast down. And they overcame him by the blood of the Lamb and by the word of their testimony, and they did not love their lives to the death." (Rev 12:10)

Notice that it's Satan who accuses the saints "before our God day and night." Not the wrath of the Father. Revelation doesn't give us a picture of Christ taking the wrath of the Father. They're on the same side. In this passage, the Father isn't doing the accusing. Satan condemns us constantly, not the Father. "For God did not send his Son into the world to condemn the world, but to save the world through him" (John 3:17). We're delivered from the condemnations of the Accuser, the slavery of Sin. And, later, when Satan, Death, Sin, and the Law are out of the way, Paul can declare, "there is now no condemnation for those who are in Christ Jesus, because through Christ Jesus the law of the Spirit who gives life has set you free from the law of sin and death" (Rom 8:1, 2).

And yet, penal atonement largely switches this story. God plays the part of the Accuser. He is the one who can't overlook any little offense. He is the one whose holiness keeps us at arm's length. As J. I. Packer says, "Penal substitution, as an idea, presupposes a penalty (*poena*) due to us from God the Judge for wrong done and failure to meet his claims."[12] The Heidelberg Catechism does the same: "God is terribly displeased with our original as well as actual sins; and will punish them in his just judgment temporally and eternally" (Q. 10). The subsequent question raises the stakes even more: "Is not God then also merciful?" The Catechism answers: "God is indeed merciful, (a) but also just; (b) therefore his justice requires, that sin which is committed against the most high majesty of God, be also punished with extreme, that is, with everlasting punishment of body and soul" (Q. 11). Punished with extreme. We have transformed God into the giant Pharisee in the sky. He cannot allow any failure. He not only disapproves but must punish severely, extremely. This God is far beyond a mere fussy librarian, petty and scolding. He points out every failure. What kind of a father is this? We seem to have confused the Father and Satan. How is this not a great theological crime? How is this not blaspheming God's character in our most cherished teachings?

It's no surprise, then, that penal atonement has hindered us from seeing the way of the cross. If God is the Accuser, then the kingdom of Christ has to take second place. If appeasing the accusations of the Father with the execution of the Son "is the very heart of the Christian gospel,"[13] all concern for weakness, earthly deliverance, sharing, and community largely miss the supposed heart of the issue. Divine accusation will always

12. Packer, "Logic," 108.

13. Ibid., 85.

beat talk of weakness. Weakness and failure are always suspect, since the Father is first and foremost angry with the weak. They have failed in countless ways, and our message must first take care of their offenses against God before we should give them food or clothing. Priorities. And if God is the Accuser, then delivering people from the oppression of poverty and Satan can't ever be as important as delivering them from the wrath of the Father. And if God is the Accuser, then we can't press too hard on the renunciation of Satan's system of Mammon because the Father's fundamental concern doesn't differ all that much from Satan's. Both Accusers are obsessed with external codes and punishments.

And especially interesting, if God is the Accuser, then the individual always outweighs the community. Penal atonement is normally framed in a highly individualistic manner: Christ's righteousness is imputed to a single person, and that person's sin is imputed to him, case by case, one by one, faith by faith—"accounting and accepting their persons as righteous."[14] Though they could, penal atonement advocates don't normally speak of an exchange of communal sin for Christ's righteousness. I suspect this is because the tool or "instrument of justification" is individualistic faith. Penal atonement, itself, then appears to have been a contributing cause of the later, Enlightenment individualism that so many Christians have come to lament. And if we ponder atonement within an individualistic theology, the way of the cross has to appear confused and misdirected. Our view of the cross can keep us from the cross.

(b) *God is Too Holy for Sinners*: Habakkuk told the Lord "You are of purer eyes than to behold evil, and cannot look on wickedness" (Hab 1:13). This has become one of the key axioms for penal atonement. It seems to suggest that the Lord's holiness prevents him from being anywhere near sin. It suggests that his own character is so just and pure that he cannot bear to be in the presence of sin without burning with wrath. Sin makes him punish. The penal atonement view infers from this sort of claim about holiness that God must be placated with blood, ultimately perfect blood, before he can be close to sinners.

This claim about God's holiness is, of course, easily false. The Lord has no personal problem being near sin. How do we know this? Jesus. Jesus was fully God and fully man, and he was perfectly holy throughout his life. Yet, he regularly hung out with sinners. He touched dead people. He spoke to demons. He sat next to prostitutes and thieves. He communed

14. Westminster Confession, XI, 1.

with Pharisees and apostles and Judas. Never did they burn up in his presence. Never did he destroy them with his holy and divine wrath. Belousek broadens this argument to encompass the whole Incarnation: if God is too holy, "one wonders how the Incarnation—the union of God and creation in the divine-human person, Jesus—was possible in the first place." But God "did unite with the creation through the Incarnation."[15] We alienate ourselves from God by our sin and hostility, but God has no personal limit to being involved with sin in order to overcome it. On top of this, Habakkuk's original claim about God's purity wasn't God's description of himself. It's the classic declaration of a frustrated and lamenting prophet. Habakkuk was complaining about God's silence in the face of gross injustice—"How long, Lord, must I call for help, but you do not listen?" (Hab 1:2). "Why do you tolerate the treacherous?" (Hab 1:13). It was a holy taunt to get the Lord to act, and God would indeed judge, but not on Habakkuk's schedule.

Sometimes penal atonement advocates see the Father's holiness keeping him away from even his Son on the cross—"My God, my God, why have you forsaken me?" (Matt 27:46). The penal story often understands this moment as that in which Christ "became sin" for us, and the Father had to forsake him and turn away because the Father could not stand to be in the presence of sin. Jonathan Edwards saw something like this in Christ's cry:

> God dealt with him as if he had been exceedingly angry with him, and as though he had been the object of his dreadful wrath. This made all the sufferings of Christ the more terrible to him, because they were from the hand of his Father, whom he infinitely loved, and whose infinite love he had had eternal experience of. Besides, it was an effect of God's wrath that he forsook Christ. This caused Christ to cry out. . . 'My God, my God, why hast thou forsaken me?'[16]

The problem with this line of argument from Psalm 22 is that the psalm actually teaches the opposite. The psalm expresses the humiliation Messiah faces. It acknowledges that the servant appears to be abandoned, appears to be humiliated by God. But rather than complaining about God's absence the speaker sees, contrary to fact, that God is actually present with him during his humiliation. He knows, in other words, that God has

15. Belousek, *Atonement*, 136.
16. Cited in Packer, "Logic," 119.

not in fact forsaken him. Christ's lament was a declaration of faith, not a cry of absence. Christ's full expression of the situation would include the latter part of Psalm 22, too.

> For he has not despised or scorned
> the suffering of the afflicted one;
> he has not hidden his face from him
> but has listened to his cry for help. (Ps 22:24)

The Father did not turn his face from the Son. He was right there indwelling the Son throughout the crisis. Psalm 22 declares the Son's solidarity with the Father, not his alienation. Christ and the Father are one.

This notion that God is too holy to be around sinners strikes right at the heart of the way of the cross. As we've seen, Jesus himself lived and breathed among sin and sinners. But even more, the too-holy assumption undermines the centrality of love in the way of the cross. In the supposed struggle between God's justice and love, it makes justice always win. On this view, God cannot truly love or be in true communion, until his justice has been done first. On this assumption we would really need to rewrite the Parables of the Prodigal Son and the Unforgiving Servant. The Prodigal's father seems to have no perfectionistic sense of purity and holiness. He just loves the wayward son. Similarly, we need to side with the Unforgiving Servant rather than the "softy" master who "took pity on him, cancelled the debt and let him go" (Matt 18:27). No sense of justice, there, again. What is wrong with these guys? But the Unforgiving Servant had a great sense of justice over love:

> But when that servant went out, he found one of his fellow
> servants who owed him a hundred silver coins. He grabbed
> him and began to choke him. "Pay back what you owe me!" he
> demanded. His fellow servant fell to his knees and begged him,
> "Be patient with me, and I will pay it back." But he refused.
> Instead, he went off and had the man thrown into prison until
> he could pay the debt. (Matt 18:28–30)

Now that's justice. Demand what was owed and imprison until the debt was paid. But that isn't Jesus's or the Father's way, even in the atonement. As James says, in God's way, "Mercy triumphs over judgment" (Jas 2:12). James's line is another way of stating that key thesis of all of Scripture: "I desire mercy, not sacrifice" (Hos 6:6; Matt 9:13).

The too-holy assumption of penal atonement view makes for some strange gymnastics when it comes to love and justice. This helps explain how the penal atonement view undermines Jesus's command to love our enemies, a key provision in the way of the cross. The strange gymnastics comes from penal atonement's view that God hates sin because he is holy, and yet he says he loves us. On the penal view, God simultaneously loves and hates. He loves us and is hostile to us at the same time. J. I. Packer recognizes this strange tension and follows Calvin in saying that God's simultaneous hatred and love are a deep mystery of God's character:

> So, for instance, faced with John's declaration in 1 John 4:8–10, "God is love. . . . Herein is love, not that we loved God, but that he loved us, and sent his Son to be the propitiation for our sins," Calvin can write without hesitation: "The word propitiation (*placatio*; Greek, hilasmos) has great weight: for God, in a way that cannot be put into words (*ineffabili quodam modo*), at the very time when he loved us, was hostile (*infensus*) to us till he was reconciled in Christ." Calvin's phrase "in a way that cannot be put into words" is his acknowledgement that the mystery of God is beyond our grasp. To Calvin, this duality of attitude, love and hostility, which in human psychological terms is inconceivable, is part of God's moral glory; a sentiment which might make rationalistic theologians shake their heads, but at which John certainly would have nodded his.[17]

But this is only a mystery because of the too-holy assumption in penal atonement. Other views don't have to go blank to try and make sense of God's alleged simultaneous hatred and love. On the restorative substitution view, God has pity for us in our sin. We're enslaved by Satan like the Israelites under Pharaoh—"they cried out; and their cry came up to God because of the bondage. So God heard their groaning" (Exod 2:23, 24). He loves us and wants to free us, but he's not personally prickly about getting involved with sin and sinners. On the restorative view, divine pity does most of the work. Yes, God's long-suffering sometimes comes to an end, especially for leaders, and he pours out his wrath. But for the most part, "mercy triumphs over judgment," and the Prodigal's father embraces the wayward son without any perfectionism or hostility. God pities us, lost in our sin, but he isn't normally hostile to sinners. No mystery needed.

Penal atonement's unnecessary invocation of mystery at this point also helps explain why the penal atonement tradition has never been very comfortable with that key provision of the way of the cross—loving one's enemies. Because penal atonement assumes that God loves and hates us

17. Ibid., 92.

at the same time, it either can't process enemy-love or leaves it on the curb as unimportant. After all, on the penal view, God both hates and loves, so we, too, don't really have to love our enemies or make sense out of the commandment. Surely, then, we can both love our enemies and kill them. We can love and bomb. It's another mystery that penal atonement generates, and we don't really have to obey. But Christ's enemy love wasn't so mysterious. It sounded like this: "Father, forgive them, for they do not know what they do" (Luke 23:34).

(c) *God Needs Blood Sacrifice*: Bloodshed lies at the heart of penal atonement. Without blood this view would have nothing to hold it together. The penal view usually places much weight on biblical claims such as, "without the shedding of blood there is no forgiveness" (Heb 9:22). That seems to settle it. Justice beats mercy. God does require sacrifice, after all. But Belousek and others have recognized that penal atonement advocates tend to treat this claim as a universal axiom for God, and they fail to notice some very important qualifications built into the passage. Just before the without-blood claim, the author qualifies it with "according to the law almost all things are purified with blood" (Heb 9:22). Two qualifications: in the law, and "almost all." The "almost all" would seem to include Old Testament sacrifices that didn't involve blood at all, for example, the law permitted the very poor to bring grain (Lev 12). The first qualification also suggests that forgiveness was possible without blood outside the law, throughout Genesis. Belousek concludes his careful survey with the observation, "All the evidence from Scripture demonstrates that God can and does act freely to forgive sin and cleanse iniquity 'apart from the law,' without requiring sacrificial bloodshed as a prior condition."[18] Obviously, this topic is huge, but the tabernacle and Temple need not be read in terms of penal atonement. If that's what the sacrifices were doing, then why were sacrifices required after childbirth (Leviticus 12) and for many other issues not dealing with sin? Was God offended by childbirth? Did mothers need to appease him? The point is that many more rich and interesting things were going on in Old Testament sacrifices than fit with penal atonement.

But we can address a simpler question about God's alleged need for blood. Was the Temple system for us or for God? In other words, did the Lord *need* the tabernacle/Temple? This is significant because pagan deities clearly needed their temples. They needed to be appeased and

18. Belousek, *Atonement*, 207.

manipulated by sacrifices. In contrast to pagan deities, several lines of biblical evidence suggest that God didn't need or truly want a Temple (but we did). First, the Lord seemed to complain about the Temple, even though he condoned it. When David expressed all his great plans for a new Temple and the prophet Nathan approved it as well, the Lord was less than enthusiastic: "Would you build a house for Me to dwell in?. . . Wherever I have moved about with all the children of Israel, have I ever spoken a word to anyone. . . saying, 'Why have you not built Me a house of cedar?'" (2 Sam 7:5ff.). This makes sense. The Lord wanted a Temple made up of people. Both tabernacle and Temple were mere placeholders that he would destroy, even as he gave instructions about how to build it. Second, the Lord's complaints carried on past David and Solomon: "Heaven is My throne, and earth is My footstool. Where is the house that you will build Me?" (Isa 66:1; Acts 7:49). Instead of a Temple, the Lord continued to look for "him who is poor and of a contrite spirit, and who trembles at My word" (Isa 66:2). Somehow the Temple system was in tension with this deeper goal. Third, the main biblical thesis—"I desire mercy, not sacrifice"—suggested that God's heart was not really in the Temple business all along. David recognized that God even wanted to work forgiveness outside of blood sacrifice. In Psalms 40 and 51, David explains that the Lord does not require blood sacrifice for forgiveness or communion with his people:

> Sacrifice and offering You did not desire;
> My ears You have opened.
> Burnt offering and sin offering You did not require.
> Then I said, "Behold, I come;
> In the scroll of the book it is written of me.
> I delight to do Your will, O my God,
> And Your law is within my heart." (Psalm 40:6–8).

Sacrifice not required. Notice, David doesn't even hint eschatologically that God really wanted a future, perfect sacrifice. "Offering you did not require." So God didn't need the Temple. Even more shocking is Psalm 51. This is David's great psalm of repentance, after his sin with Bethsheba and the horrific setup to kill her husband Uriah (2 Sam 11:14–17). The psalm begins with a plea for cleaning and forgiveness, "Blot out my transgressions. Wash me thoroughly from my iniquity, and cleanse me from my sin" (Ps 51:2, 3). Certainly, if any gross sins required blood sacrifice to appease the Lord, these sins did. Yet David recognized God's deeper ways:

> For You do not desire sacrifice, or else I would give it;
> You do not delight in burnt offering.
> The sacrifices of God are a broken spirit,
> A broken and a contrite heart—
> These, O God, You will not despise. (Ps 51:16, 17)

God did not desire sacrifice and burnt offering for these sins? But what about, "without the shedding of blood there is no forgiveness?" Instead, even with these heinous sins, astoundingly, "the sacrifices of God are a broken spirit." In other words, God can forgive without blood. God doesn't need a tabernacle, Temple, or any sacrificial system at all to appease him.

Is there any way to interpret the sacrificial system other than penal atonement? Instead of thinking of the sacrifices as appeasing God, many have suggested that we see the sacrifices pointed in the other direction—toward us. Instead of God needing blood, we can think of God mercifully using the sacrifices to clean us. God becomes the subject cleaning rather than the object appeased. On this view, the sacrifices don't calm God's burning anger; they act as God's gracious detergent to cleanse all our impurities, sinful and not. Overall, the sacrificial system seemed more concerned with controlling the pollution of death than sin. Sin seems more of a consequence of death but not the main issue in the sacrifices. The "life is in the blood" (Lev 17:11), and sacrifices release that blood-life to clean away all the death oppressing God's people. Jesus's blood would do this even more, at a cosmic level. As Belousek notes, "In atoning sacrifice, God is the primary actor, not humans; sacrifice atones, not because it 'satisfies' God, but because God acts through it to make atonement. . . . God acts to cleanse and forgive sinners by removing sin and pollution through sacrifice, thereby restoring covenant fellowship. Divine justice is done here, but it is restorative justice, not retributive justice."[19]

This picture stands in stark contrast to the ancient pagan system of divine pacification. The apostle Paul seemed to bring this contrast right before the god-appeasing Athenians with their necessary temples.

> God, who made the world and everything in it, since He is
> Lord of heaven and earth, does not dwell in temples made with

19. Ibid., 191.

hands. Nor is He worshiped with men's hands, as though He
needed anything. (Acts 17:24, 25)

Paul cuts right to the heart. The true God doesn't need a temple, never
did. And, more importantly, God does not "need anything." He doesn't
need our sacrifices to appease him. That's not his character. This is a lesson we should have learned even back in the time of the patriarchs. It
seems to be part of the lesson the Lord taught Abraham. The pagan gods
of Abraham's time needed human sacrifice, especially child sacrifice. But
the Lord stopped Abraham's hand and revealed himself as a God who
is not pacified by sacrifices. He is unlike pagan deities. Even back then,
"You do not desire sacrifice, or else I would give it; You do not delight
in burnt offering." We got it all terribly mixed up. Our Lord was never a
God needing penal sacrifice before he could love or forgive or commune.

In the end, the burden lies on the penal atonement view to distinguish itself from a pagan view of appeasement. How does penal atonement really differ from ancient pagan views of pacification? This is
an older worry about penal atonement, but it has stuck because penal
atonement advocates give such thin answers. So much is at stake in this
question. We, again, run the risk of attributing Satanic needs to the true
God. Weak answers won't suffice. John Stott famously tried his hand at
differentiating Christian vs. pagan views of penal atonement. He argued
that the two forms of penal atonement differ in three ways: (a) pagan
gods were unpredictable but the true God is "always predictable" in his
"steady, unrelenting, unremitting, uncompromising antagonism to evil in
all its forms;" (b) humans initiated pagan sacrifices but in Christian penal
atonement, God took "the initiative;" and (c) Christian penal atonement
"was neither an animal, nor a vegetable, or a mineral" but "a person. And
the person God offered was not someone else. . . . In giving his Son, he
was giving himself."[20]

But these differences don't match the stakes. They concede too
much to the critic of penal atonement. Surely, the penal atonement view
can do better than this. These replies grant all the worst assumptions of
the objection and give an answer largely in terms of degree: God is not as
unpredictable as pagan gods, but, yes, his anger still demands blood; God
took the initiative and that rarely happens in pagan appeasement; God
demanded an innocent human sacrifice, and, yes, pagans did that, too,
but the gods didn't sacrifice themselves, and neither did the Father, but

20. Stott, *Cross*, 171–2.

he got his child to do it. John Stott was a grand and important gentleman of evangelicalism. He even had a wonderfully radical view of the way of the cross and the Sermon on the Mount, but these replies are inadequate when so much is on the line.

As with the two prior aspects of penal atonement, this one, too, keeps us from the way of the cross. Think in terms of divine need. The objection here is that God does not need temples or blood sacrifice to appease his anger, but penal atonement advocates find this need very important to his character. But this need-claim seems to overturn every-thing Jesus taught about self-denial and sacrifice and service. For God to demand blood before he can love is not the talk of a servant. It is the talk of someone "lording it over" his subjects. It sounds like a despot who demands that his people first satisfy his need before he serve them. If we become what we worship, then, penal atonement encourages the same sort of self-focused demands in us. If the Father demands service first, then Jesus's talk of self-denial seems quaint and unserious. If the Father requires service to himself first, then Jesus seems wrong in saying "He who has seen Me has seen the Father" (John 14:9). Jesus revealed a foot-washing God.

As noted, this discussion about atonement is large, and these three objections aim to show how out of sync penal atonement is with Jesus's way. If we embrace penal atonement, it appears to move us in a direction opposite to Christ's way of life. So how might restorative substitution or Christus Victor fit better with the way of the cross? Obviously, defenders of restorative atonement explain things in different ways, as do advocates of penal atonement. I'd like to sketch just one angle on it, focusing par-ticularly on the biblical notion of "swallowing death."

What was Jesus's work on the cross if not pacifying the Father? Even on the restorative view, God's wrath has many roles to play. How did we become slaves of Satan, for example? Ultimately, God exiled us from the Garden of Eden. He let us go the way we wanted to go, and that's often how scripture describes God's wrath (cf. Ps 9:15,16; Obad 15; Isa 64:7). Similarly, the Prodigal's father showed his wrath in letting his son head off on his own. Many times, the Lord's wrath is direct punishment, but many times, too, God's wrath is simply God turning us over to what we want (Rom 1:24, 26, 28). All that is involved in the cross, even in restor-ative substitution. But restorative substitution leads us into the way of the cross, not away from it.

N. T. Wright uses the helpful language that on the cross, Jesus "has taken the accusations that were outstanding against the world and against the whole human race and has borne them in himself."[21] Jesus took the condemnation of the Accuser, not the Father. Wright uses the helpful language of Jesus "exhausting" all the Satanic forces of Death, Sin, and Darkness. This language of receiving, bearing, exhausting fits well the imagery that Paul celebrates in speaking of the "victory through our Lord Jesus Christ" (1 Cor 15:57), both in the first century and in the future. Paul understood Christ's work as fulfilling Isaiah's language that "Death is swallowed up in victory" (Isa 25:8). In speaking of swallowing death, Isaiah invoked some very interesting imagery. He was not an individualist, so he saw death and sin as a corporate entity, a "surface of the covering cast over all people, and the veil that is spread over all nations" (Isa 25:7). This is a helpful picture to frame Christ's work on the cross:

> And in this mountain
> The Lord of hosts will make for all people
> A feast of choice pieces,
> A feast of wines on the lees,
> Of fat things full of marrow,
> Of well-refined wines on the lees.
> And He will destroy on this mountain
> The surface of the covering cast over all people,
> And the veil that is spread over all nations.
> He will swallow up death forever,
> And the Lord God will wipe away tears from all faces;
> The rebuke of His people
> He will take away from all the earth;
> For the Lord has spoken. (Isa 25:6–8)

Isaiah saw that God would "destroy" this massive, deathly entity hanging over the people and "swallow" it forever (Isa 25:8). Isaiah also saw the Lord removing accusations, "the rebuke of his people."

This imagery of swallowing death matches what often happened in the sacrificial system, as noted in earlier chapters. In Leviticus 10, for example, we learn that the priestly act of eating the "sin offering in a holy place" was a symbolic enactment of atonement for the people. The priests literally swallowed death, the sacrificed animal, because in eating that death, "God has given it to you [the priests] to bear the guilt of the congregation, to make atonement for them before the Lord" (Lev 10:17).

21. Wright, *Simply*, 187.

The priests, then, made atonement by swallowing death and sin for the people, and Jesus, as high priest, would do the same in the most real, final, and complete manner.

Swallowing is a way of absorbing, but it's not the only way. Matthew sees Jesus's healing ministry as a work of swallowing or absorption, echoing the absorption of sickness depicted in Isaiah 53. As an aside, penal atonement advocates have long used Isaiah 53 as a key support for their view. Ironically, though, the passage opens by describing how the people had mistakenly interpreted the death of the suffering servant as God's direct act of condemnation, a form of divine punishment, but the passage goes on to correct that misreading: "Yet we esteemed Him stricken, smitten by God, and afflicted. But He was wounded for our transgressions, He was bruised for our iniquities" (Isa 53:4, 5). In other words, like penal atonement, the people would mistakenly believe that God was punishing Messiah, but instead, their own crimes brought about his death, the same sort of reading that we get in apostolic preaching (cf. Acts 2:23; 4:27; 7:52). "Smitten by God" was a misreading of what happened on the cross. Yes, "it pleased the Lord to bruise Him" (Isa 53:10), and "by His stripes we are healed" (Isa 53:5). But it's significant that Matthew didn't interpret this language in terms of the Father punishing the Son. Matthew understood Jesus's healing ministry, not merely the cross, as the fulfillment of "by His stripes we are healed." Matthew described it this way:

> When evening had come, they brought to Him many who were demon-possessed. And He cast out the spirits with a word, and healed all who were sick, that it might be fulfilled which was spoken by Isaiah the prophet, saying: "He Himself took our infirmities and bore our sicknesses." (Matt 8:16, 17)

Here Matthew quotes Isaiah 53 and sees in it the swallowing or absorption of illness, not stripes inflicted to satisfy the Father's justice. Healing was a gathering of sickness, an absorption, a swallowing of death because his Life overcame Death—"I have overcome the world" (John 16:33). As Peter later declared, "having loosed the pains of death, because it was not possible that He should be held by it" (Acts 2:24). He became death for us to conquer it:

> He Himself likewise shared in the same, that through death
> He might destroy him who had the power of death, that is,
> the devil, and release those who through fear of death were all
> their lifetime subject to bondage. (Heb 2:14, 15)

PART TWO: Special Blinders to the Way of the Cross

Because he was divine life, having the supreme life-in-the-blood, he could exhaust or absorb Death and Sin and rise again so that we might live. In other words, "He made Him who knew no sin to be sin for us that we might become the righteousness of God in Him" (2 Cor 5:21).

Likewise, since New Covenant followers of Christ are also a kingdom of priests and a "royal priesthood" (1 Pet 2:5, 9), we continue, as Christ's body, his act of swallowing death, bearing one another's burdens (Gal 6:2), taking in evil from the earth, and with Paul, we can "rejoice in my sufferings for you, and fill up in my flesh what is lacking in the afflictions of Christ, for the sake of His body, which is the church" (Col 1:24). Martyrdom swallows death. Imitating Christ absorbs sin. Christ's body, the church, removes evil from the world by walking in Christ's path. Restorative substitution is Christ's way. Restorative atonement is the way of the cross.

13

The Left-Right Political Distinction

Fundamental distinctions work like railroad tracks. At first, tracks look similar, but if you get on the wrong one, you can end up far away from home. Throughout redemptive history, the Lord laid down various fundamental distinctions to help direct his people and keep them from social death. From the beginning, he promised that the distinction, the *antithesis*, between the seed of the woman and the seed of the serpent would mark the primary struggle. In his law, he marked the difference between life and death through cleanliness laws. He distinguished his people from the surrounding nations and forbid them to step across that line: "You shall not go after other gods, the gods of the peoples who *are* all around you" (Deut 6:14). "For I am the LORD your God. You shall therefore consecrate yourselves, and you shall be holy; for I am holy" (Lev 11:44).

The history of God's people has often been the history of misplaced distinctions, a pattern of violated antitheses. Time passes. The lines shift. Priorities change. Much of Jesus's struggle with the scribes and Pharisees turned on how to mark large distinctions. The Jewish leadership was mistakenly convinced that the Lord was supremely concerned about guarding the lines between swearing on the temple vs. the gold of the temple (Matt 23:16) and, even more, between gentiles and Jews. They got so bound up in false distinctions they tithed on minor objects, "mint and anise and cummin, and have neglected the weightier matters of the law: justice and mercy and faith" (Matt 23:23). That's what false distinctions do. They misalign and mislead. A community stumbling about in false distinctions and priorities ultimately "strain out a gnat and swallow a camel" (Matt 23:24).

The issue of correctly marking God's antitheses didn't end with the ascension. Jesus's kingdom rewrote several key distinctions of the old, creating a new order, and, still, with great force, Paul had to remind the new believers of the antithesis:

> For what fellowship has righteousness with lawlessness? And
> what communion has light with darkness? And what accord
> has Christ with Belial? Or what part has a believer with an
> unbeliever? And what agreement has the temple of God with
> idols? (2 Cor 6:14–16)

The wrong tracks still lead one out of the kingdom.

Consider this struggle from the perspective of an enemy. A smart, strategic enemy will recognize the fundamental distinctions of a community and seek to subvert them. As we've seen, Jesus marked the fundamental antithesis for his kingdom between God and Mammon. It was the same line drawn from Eden to Rome. One could write the history of Christ's kingdom in terms of the battle over that distinction, a history of faithfulness, compromise, and plenty of diversions to get us to ignore, minimize, and look away from that antithesis. Such deceptions never have fangs. They always look well-groomed and noble.

The very modern Left-Right distinction in politics has got to be the leading candidate of this sort of wholesale misdirection. It's so common, normal, and pervasive. It shapes so much of life, even outside of politics. Its mapping of the world goes deep in people's identities. Our histories are tied up in it, and it's a very basic way of dividing up the world, carving out places to stand, selecting friends, pinpointing enemies. Yet, just a few simple questions about this modern Left-Right dogma prompts clashes with the life of Father, Son, and Holy Spirit.

How do we normally characterize the Left-Right distinction? Well, a common way sees the Left embracing the value of equality through a series of issues, and the Right doing the same with the value of freedom. So, the Left, for example, wants to rectify gross economic divergence, marginalized cultural voices, and political power with greater concern for equality as the norm. In a similar way, those on the Right stand firm on their claims about liberty and freedom so as to keep anyone from interfering with their money, their property, their guns. Equality vs. Freedom; Left vs. Right.

Norberto Bobbio suggests a different way of characterizing the Left-Right distinction. For him, it's not one continuum from the Left's equality to the Right's freedom. Instead, it's a crossed axis of equality and freedom. This axis starts, most fundamentally, with movement along a horizontal crossbeam of greater to lesser equality. The Left embraces equality, and the Right rejects it more and more. That's the basic divide, not equality to freedom, but equality to inequality. Then, he lays down the perpendicular, vertical axis that moves from freedom at the top to authoritarianism at the bottom.

This version of the Left-Right distinction divides things not into just two categories but four: the moderate Left concerned with equality and freedom; the extreme Left embracing equality and authoritarianism; the moderate Right endorsing freedom and inequality; and the extreme Right favoring authoritarianism and inequality. Or as Bobbio puts it, a "different attitude to the ideal of equality is the criterion for distinguishing left and right, and the different attitude to freedom is the relevant criterion for distinguishing the moderate wing from the extremist wing of both left and right."[1]

These two ways of dividing things both contain truth, but whichever way one cuts it, Trinitarian alarms should go off. First and foremost, neither gets the biblical antithesis right. From beginning to end, scripture exhorts us to divide faithfully between two kinds of life, two kinds of community, the faithful and the faithless, Yahweh vs. Baal, Christ vs. Beelzebub, the church vs. the world, and most significantly God vs. Mammon.

But the Left-Right distinction doesn't divide the world along biblical lines. Instead, it seeks to insert an antithesis between equality and freedom, oneness vs. manyness. This is very odd. Where did this alien antithesis come from?

Certainly Father, Son, and Spirit don't divide life between equality and freedom because the life of the Trinity expresses both values. We gladly embrace "where the Spirit is there is liberty" (2 Cor 3:17), and we've also always confessed with the Athanasian Creed that "in this Trinity . . . none is greater or less than another. But the whole three persons are coeternal, and coequal." Trinitarian life involves both the best equality

1. Bobbio, *Significance*, 69.

and the best freedom. The church, then, is obligated to adore both freedom and equality. Quite contrary to the Left-Right distortion.

In fact, the closer you look at that distinction the uglier it gets. It
calls us not just to a false antithesis; it calls us to a shattered Trinity. It's as
if the distinction aims to break apart Trinitarian Oneness and Manyness.
There's plenty of historical truth in that. The Left-Right distinction became prominent before the French Revolution. Supposedly, Left vs. Right
grew out of the seating arrangement of the French National Assembly.
Originally, the king sat in the middle, and to his right, sat the king's sup-
porters, and on his left sat his opponents and reformers.

But you can't kill the Trinity. It sneaks out somewhere. It is life. The
Enlightenment sniffed at the Trinity, but it still parasitically wanted its
values: equality and freedom, oneness and manyness. So over time, it
fractured the Trinity and set equality and freedom against each other.
But it's not a simple fracturing. The Trinity isn't a principle. The Trinity is
the mysterious union and communion of Father, Son, and Spirit—three
persons. The Enlightenment can't allow any of that, though. The Enlightenment prefers things that don't talk back or criticize, like impersonal
principles, rules, and abstractions. So during the centuries the church
faded in its Trinitarian consciousness, the secularists ran off with an im-
personalized, broken Trinity—equality vs. freedom. From that broken
Trinity you get the Enlightenment political traditions of the Left and the
Right. The Left still tends to be concerned with equality and oneness, and
the Right still focuses on freedom and individuality and firepower.

So what's a contemporary Christian to do? In practice, we dive right
into this distinction and mimic our Enlightenment lords once again.
They tell us we have to set oneness against individuality, and we say, yes
sir and divide our community into the Christian Left and the Christian
Right.

It seems so natural to us, now. We've imbibed these categories for
so long that we can't view the world without them. We can't imagine any
other way to schematize issues and life. Left-Right has seeped so deep
into our identities we think it's in our blood.

But think about it. What Kool-Aid have we drunk? A broken Trinity? What has Christ to do with a broken Trinity? A broken Trinity is
not Father, Son, and Spirit. It's some other god, or two. It's a twisted god
of equality and a warped god of freedom, both impersonal abstractions.
These aren't our gods, though. We can't pray in these names. In short,
they're idols. And by viewing the world in terms of one or the other is to

view the world through dead idols. Of course, we can use the terms *Left* and *Right* to mark out those who identify themselves that way. But if we find ourselves owning and dividing the world that way that we can be sure we ourselves dwell in deep paganism.

We shiver at the thought of viewing the world through other religious idols, but we're so comfortable with the Left-Right distinction that we don't even recognize the idolatry at work.

But try this substitution. Christians understand that Islam and Hinduism involve alien deities, anti-Trinitiarian constructs. In fact, those religions side by side (I'm simplifying, of course) have some affinities with the Enlightenment's Left-Right distinction. Versions of Hinduism have long appreciated the ultimate oneness of things, similar to that which often shows up on the Left. And Islam has long insisted on a radical individualism for the one god, a god of absolute freedom and domination, not unlike the common rhetoric for individuals on the Right. So why not interchange these terms when it comes to the so-called Christian Left and the Christian Right?

What would that sound like? That would mean that we'd divide ourselves into the perspectives of Christian Hindus and Christian Muslims. In the States, conservatives would be called Christian Muslims and liberals would be Christian Hindus. Of course, no evangelical would buy into that false dichotomy. But, that's the point. We already do that by identifying ourselves in terms of the Left-Right broken Trinity. We "Christian Muslims" have our pet issues, and we know who our enemies on the "Christian Hindu" side of things are. What insanity. How did we get backed into this Left-Right corner? How are we ever going to explain this on the Last Day?

The good news is that we don't have to bend over backward and try to carefully construct some unintuitive, complicated, artificial third way between the idolatries of the Left and Right. All we have to do is be the church. It's already a natural and supernatural third way, quite distinct from the impersonal equality and impersonal freedom of the Left and Right. We just have to imitate Father, Son, and Holy Spirit as we build the kingdom of God not by voter manipulation, firepower, or ballot-boxes but by sacrificial faith, hope, and love. We don't need any fake antithesis or impersonal idols. We just need to imitate the community of Father, Son, and Spirit within the church.

But given that the Left-Right distinction results from an idolatrous attempt to break up the Trinity, we have to reject the exclusivism of that bipolar world. Yet we also have to reject the assumption of either side that its "other" has no truth at all. Conservatives, for example, often picture any research or argument or conclusion from those on the Left as automatically false because they see the conclusions of the Left as dropping out deductively from first principles. Ann Coulter has been suckered into this idolatry: "Liberals can believe what they want to believe, but let us not flinch from identifying liberalism as the opposition party to God."[2] Coulter has a pagan antithesis, not Christian. In terms of unitarian conservatism, one need not read, listen, or watch anything from liberals or the Left because it's inherently corrupt at its root. I've seen this time and time again. I'm sure true believers on the Left return the favor. Both are disciples of the Enlightenment, not Christ. In effect, this refusal to read the other side is another way we defend ourselves from political sanctification. And if both the Left and the Right are parts of a broken Trinity, then we have to rethink this deductive rejection of the other side. If both opponents originally grew out of Trinitarian values (freedom and equality), then instead of rejecting their research a priori we should positively expect to find some truth in the other side. Both sides have to get some things right because they started off with Trinitarian concerns, and then, tragically, absolutized either equality or freedom. Still, within a Trinitarian vision, we're no longer able to dismiss the other side without expecting truth. Children of the Cold War, especially, have the greatest difficulty overcoming this. But we're not supposed to be Cold Warriors first. We're Trinitarians.

The Left-Right distinction sets up a large obstacle against seeing the way of the cross. The way of weakness favors the poor. Jesus and the prophets explicitly and repeatedly distinguished between the rich and poor. And so did Marx. One can't start making the case for the way of weakness without the Left-Right distinction closing down minds. The modern Right has largely grown up as a reaction against Marxism, and anything that comes even close to sounding like Marxism has to be ignored. That includes pronouncing blessing on the poor and woes on the rich (Luke 6). Have you ever heard a politically conservative Christian preach on Luke 6? Did it sound like Jesus at all? Blinders.

If you think about it, Marxism was a brilliant, Satanic misdirection. On the surface, it aped some key Christian concerns but then ruthlessly incarnated these via Mammon domination and self-interest. It substituted

2. Coulter, *Godless*, 22.

the domination and violence of Mammon for Christ, the Spirit, and the church. It was bound to be a seductive massacre. Capitalism and socialism are both incarnations of Mammon. Like the perfect sucker, the Christian church rode the rails as far away from Marxism as possible, spending the next century debating doctrine and missing the weightier matters of the kingdom, while the poor were enslaved and slaughtered around the world. Christians joined in prosecuting the slaughter, butchering, and imprisoning and blowing up brothers in the name of the supreme Left-Right distinction. Mammon won, and the church failed. It turned its back on the way of the cross, and it will be decades before we find the path again.

14

Impersonal Conservatism

American conservatism has been dying a slow death for some time now, but given established patterns, it will still be a decade or so before conservative Christians catch on. The biggest problem with political conservatism is the means by which it subverts the way of the cross.

In "The Fall of Conservatism," George Packer wrote about the disintegration of the conservative movement. In part, he found this epitomized in conservative leaders like columnist David Books: "Brooks had moved through every important conservative publication — *National Review*, the *Wall Street Journal* editorial page, the *Washington Times*, the *Weekly Standard* — 'and now I feel estranged,' he said. 'I just don't feel it's exciting, I don't feel it's true, fundamentally true.' In the eighties, when he was a young movement journalist, the attacks on regulation and the Soviet Union seemed 'true.' Now most conservatives seem incapable of even acknowledging the central issues of our moment. . . .They are stuck in the past, in the dogma of limited government."[1] Packer noted that the conservative "Heritage Foundation Web site currently links to video presentations by Sean Hannity and Laura Ingraham, 'challenging Americans to consider, What Would Reagan Do?'" and adds that much conservative journalism has become "calcified and ingrown."

Note those phrases: "I just don't feel it's exciting, I don't feel it's true, fundamentally true." "What would Reagan do?" Those are conservative

1. Packer, "Fall."

death knells if I've ever heard them. Indeed, "we are living in the twilight of conservatism," as conservative John Derbyshire put it.[2]

Conservatism's key drawback has always been its parasitic nature. American conservatism developed mainly in response to a dominant American liberalism of the first half of the twentieth century. As Sidney Blumenthal correctly noted, "Paradoxically, conservatism requires liberalism for its meaning. The conservatives' self-image, unchanging over time despite their hold on many office in the federal bureaucracy, is rooted in their vision of the Liberal Establishment. . . .Their shadow liberalism spurs them on, but also marks the edge of their universe; if they sail beyond it, they fear they will fall off."[3] Since conservatism developed as a response to liberalism, it did not have to produce a positive, substantive vision. It led by trying to be a photo-negative.

Even more significantly, conservatism sharpened its vision in opposition to the Soviet Union. Conservatism saw itself as representing whatever stood against the Soviet Union. That explains why it was unashamed in gathering to itself any fellow-traveler no matter how tyrannical or given to terror, as long as that dictator opposed the Soviet Union. The father of modern conservatism, the late William F. Buckley, highlighted conservatism's contrast with communism at the founding of his influential conservative magazine, *National Review*. In his "Credenda and Statement of Principles," Buckley not only defined the new magazine first and foremost in contrast to liberalism—"the intransigence of the Liberals, who run this country"—he also focused on his absolutistic contrast with communism: "The century's most blatant force of satanic utopianism is communism. We consider 'coexistence' with communism neither desirable nor possible, nor honorable; we find ourselves irrevocably at war with communism and shall oppose any substitute for victory."[4]

What happens, then, when the strong back of a dominant liberalism and the Soviet Union break? What is left of conservatism? Late in the game, Buckley himself tried to make conservatism's parasitic nature a virtue: "conservatism has been marked mostly by negative importunities against human inclinations, as is the case with the Decalogue, and with the Constitution, both of which emphasize that which ought not to be

2. Derbyshire, "Twilight."
3. Blumenthal, *Rise*, 6.
4. Buckley, "Mission."

done."[5] But man cannot live on the Decalogue alone. The apostle Paul included it within the "ministry of death" (2 Cor 3:7). The Decalogue depends on a God who substantively and positively breaks into history, intervening with a whole constructive social project of truth, beauty, and goodness. Conservatism, however, chose to build its life on vacuous opponents. This dependent conservatism isn't unique to American conservatism. The grandfather of modern conservatism, Russell Kirk, saw this as true of the older conservatism of Edmund Burke: "Throughout Europe, conservatism came to mean hostility towards the principles of the French Revolution, with its violent leveling innovations."[6] Again, conservatism defined itself in terms of what it opposed.

This parasitism has always made a definition of conservatism problematic. Buckley has spoken of the "difficulty in defining 'conservatism,'"[7] and Jonah Goldberg grants "the simple fact is that conservatives don't have a settled dogma."[8] Along the way, many conservatives have found it helpful to deny that conservatism is anything like a set of ideas, an ideology, that could be given in the form of a bounded definition. Russell Kirk tried this: "conservatism is not a political system, and certainly not an ideology. In the phrase of H. Stuart Hughes, 'Conservatism is the negation of ideology.' Instead conservatism is a way of looking at the civil social order."[9] A "way of looking," a social vision, somehow fails to count as an ideology. Kirk went on to explain conservatism in circular fashion: "although it is no ideology, conservatism may be apprehended reasonably well by attention to what leading writers and politicians, generally called conservative, have said and done."[10] In other words, conservatism is what conservatives say and do. Ronald Reagan noted that "'I think 'ideology' is a scare word to most Americans.' Republican senator Rick Santorum of Pennsylvania claimed: 'Conservatism is common sense and liberalism is ideology.'"[11]

This Santorum quote nicely highlights the benefit of denying that conservatism is an ideology. If a political doctrine is merely air, merely

5. Buckley, "Definition," 18.

6. Kirk, *Essential*, 6.

7. Buckley, "Definition," 18.

8. Goldberg, "Conservative"

9. Kirk, *Essential*, 6.

10. Ibid., 7.

11. Cited in Dean, *Conservatives*, 5.

"common sense," merely a "way of looking," then it eliminates criticism. No one can refute common sense. Denial is a rhetorical attempt to preclude objections. Certainly, history has seen how quickly those movements which lead with clearly defined propositions fail. Think of the Logical Positivists in philosophy. The clearer you are the quicker you get refuted and cast aside. Conscious obscurity gives a movement or a thinker a longer shelf life.

As tempting as a denial of its ideological nature is, in the end, conservatives couldn't resist lists of principles and axioms. They had to clarify their ideological commitments because they wanted to be, after all, an intellectual movement. They were ultimately about ideas first and foremost, not sacraments, not communal practices, not deliverance, and not shaped around Christ's character. All they had were ideas and arguments and criticisms. All they had was ideology. Even the ever-organic Russell Kirk provided a famous list of conservative ideas:

"First, conservatives generally believe that there exists a transcendent moral order, to which we ought to conform the ways of society. . . .

"Second, conservatives uphold the principle of social continuity. They prefer the devil they know to the devil they don't know. Order and justice and freedom, they believe, are the artificial products of a long and painful social experience, the results of centuries of trial and reflection and sacrifice. . . .

"Third, conservatives believe in what may be called the principle of prescription. . . . Conservatives sense that modern men and women are dwarfs on the shoulders of giants. . . .Therefore conservatives very frequently emphasize the importance of 'prescription'—that is, of things established by immemorial usage. . . .

"Fourth, conservatives are guided by their principle of prudence. . .. Any public measure ought to be judged by its probably long-run consequences, not merely by temporary advantage. . ..

"Fifth, conservatives pay attention to the principle of variety. . . .For the preservation of a healthy diversity in any civilization, there must survive orders and classes, differences in material condition, and many sorts of inequality. . . .

"Sixth, conservatives are chastened by their principle of imperfectability. Human nature suffers irremediably from certain faults. . . .To aim for utopia is to end in disaster."[12]

12. Kirk, *Essential*, 7–9.

What word stands out? Principle. Principle. Principle. This is far more significant than we usually understand. It reveals much about the heart of conservatism, even more than the actual content Kirk supplies. Conservatism loves impersonalism. It is impersonalism. It dwells in a Platonic universe of static laws, not the personalism of Trinitarianism. Love doesn't rule the conservative cosmos, abstractions do. No need for Father, Son, and Spirit. But abstractions of this sort are just old-fashioned idolatry. The Lord condemns his people who have fallen for the lack of personality, the lack of personhood of wooden and gold idols:

> They have mouths, but they do not speak;
>   Eyes they have, but they do not see;
> They have ears, but they do not hear;
>   Noses they have, but they do not smell;
> They have hands, but they do not handle;
>   Feet they have, but they do not walk;
>   Nor do they mutter through their throat.
> Those who make them are like them;
>   So is everyone who trusts in them. (Ps 115:5–8)

The impersonalism of the idols becomes manifest in "everyone who trusts in them." Conservatism and Trinitarianism can't blend.

Simple reflection on Trinitarian life quickly conflicts with what conservatives, even Christian conservatives, point to as their most basic assumptions. It's no great observation that conservatism never developed out of a self-conscious Trinitarian perspective. Like much Enlightenment thought, conservatism developed in a period of Trinitarian eclipse. In short, conservatism grew up amid brute unitarian theological categories. Ultimately, this is the church's fault for letting the truth of Father, Son, and Spirit get eclipsed, and that was an embarrassing neglect that started in the high middle ages. In fact, it's that unitarian, deistic default of the church that encouraged the backlash of the Enlightenment. "Then he goes and takes with him seven other spirits more wicked than himself, and they enter and dwell there; and the last state of that man is worse than the first" (Luke 11:26).

The figurative language in Kirk's principles above suggests that conservatism is best pictured as a deep structure, not a skeleton, not a building frame, but more like the granite underlying a mountain range. A permanent thing. It is a hard order that gives shape to everything else, an order set in the past, an order jagged and hard but adventurous. To try anything contrary or to ignore the granite is to invite disaster.

William F. Buckley also provided a list of convictions in the first issue of *National Review*. His principles are more politically specific and American than Russell Kirk's:

"a. It is the job of centralized government (in peace-time) to protect its citizens' lives, liberty, and property. All other activities of government tend to diminish freedom and hamper progress. . . .

"b. The profound crisis of our era is, in essence, the conflict between Social Engineers, who seek to adjust mankind to conform with scientific utopias, and the disciples of Truth, who defend the organic moral order. . . .

"c. The century's most blatant force of satanic utopianism is communism. . . .

"d. The largest cultural menace in America is the conformity of the intellectual cliques which, in education as well as the arts, are out to impose upon the nation their modish fads and fallacies. . . .

"e. The most alarming single danger to the American political system lies in the fact that an identifiable team of Fabian operators is bent on controlling both our major political parties. . . .

"f. The competitive prices system is indispensable to liberty and material progress. . . .

"g. No superstition has more effectively bewitched America's Liberal elite than the fashionable concepts of world government, the United Nations, internationalism, international atomic pools, etc. . . ."[13]

What stands out here is fear and panic: "protect," "profound crisis," "most blatant force," "largest cultural menace," "most alarming," "bewitched." Fear has always been a special friend of conservatism, to this very day. This is not some accidental feature. Fear roots lie deep in conservatism.

But the axiom that does all the real work in Buckley's list of convictions is a certain kind of individualism, an exaltation of the individual above all communal or corporate values and realities. This assumption underlies every single one of his convictions: an individualistic view of freedom leads to conservative opposition to the state, utopias, communism, intellectual conformity, Fabian operators, world government, as well as supporting his only positive conviction, the indispensability of the competitive price system. In fact, every one of these convictions is

13. Buckley, "Mission."

simply an expression or an application a particular notion of individu-ality, actually a rather radical individuality. In one sense, then, Buckley needn't have given us a list of seven convictions. Since they all reduce to a core principle of individualism, he might just have given us a sen-tence explaining the centrality of individualism for all of life. Whereas Kirk's principles give us the conservative mountain range that focuses on finding true and stable life only in the past, Buckley's principles glo-rify a conservatism of the billiard table: people are self-contained and fundamentally disconnected balls; they only need the felt boundaries of the state to give society its basic rectangular form. No other boundaries or connections ought to hinder the precious balls (in peace-time). That's the American way. The middle, critical section of this book examines conservatism's deep individualism.

Over the decades, conservatives have intertwined Kirk's and Buck-ley's principles in various ways. Following John Derbyshire[14] who follows Micklethwait and Wooldridge,[15] Goldberg lays out six tenets of Anglo-American conservatism:

1. deep suspicion of the power of the state
2. a preference for liberty over equality
3. patriotism
4. a belief in established institutions and hierarchies
5. skepticism about the idea of progress
6. elitism

This list tries nicely to combine Kirk's granite ridge (3,5,6) with Buckley's billiard balls (1,2,6). Goldberg likes this list because it is so partial and incomplete: "any ideology that sees itself as the answer to any question is un-conservative."

The list of conservative principles has often become shorter and more succinct as conservatives took over the power centers and needed sound bites. Michael Deaver, former aide to President Reagan, reduced conservatism to those who favor "limited government, individual liberty, and the prospect of a strong America."[16] This short list certainly captures Buckley's principles in more direct form, but, remember clarity invites criticism, and Deaver's list more blatantly shines light on one of the cen-tral contradictions of American conservatism, namely, the first two items

14. Derbyshire, "Twilight."
15. Micklethwait and Wooldridge, *Right*.
16. Cited in Dean, *Conservatives*, 4.

in his list—"limited government, individual liberty"—are not only a bit redundant but stand in strong conflict with the conservative love affair with the vast imperial military power that continues to grow after every defeated enemy. The contradiction was already there in Buckley's principles—his giant, understated qualification "(in peace-time)"—but it was buried under all his individualism.

More recent conservatives choose to make a virtue of their contradictions. Jonah Goldberg insists that to be a conservative is to be someone who finds "comfort with contradiction."[17] He sees Leftism's core value "a faith that circles can be closed, conflicts resolved." But conservatism can happily embrace contradiction because it's all about trade-offs: "the arguments of conservatives . . . are almost invariably arguments about trade-offs, costs, 'the downside' of a measure. As I've written before, the first obligation of the conservative is to explain why nine out of ten new ideas are probably bad ones." (Notice Kirk's mountain range at work.) Goldberg says conservatives get along so well (!) because "we all understand and accept the permanence of contradiction and conflict in life."

Even as the lists of conservative principles have become more succinct, conservative subgroups have splintered and multiplied. Individualism always tends to do this. Out of mere conservatives came the neoconservatives, social conservatives, theocons and more. Neoconservatives play up the military panic of the older conservatism, finding new cold wars under every rock. Social conservatives invoke secular arguments to replace religious arguments against abortion, drugs, homosexual marriage, etc. Theocons subdivide into those conservatives who invoke either natural or biblical law, but whatever the case, law is the answer, not the way of the cross. The list goes on.

While Christians need a divorce from Anglo-American conservatism, we certainly ought not replace it with liberalism, progressivism, Leftism, centrism, libertarianism, or anything else that's not the church. The church is all we need to make Trinity on earth.

Christian traditionalists shouldn't be too surprised at the call to "come out" from conservatism. Conservatives have already started making this divide. John Derbyshire notes that the "great twentieth-century conservative presidents were Calvin Coolidge and Ronald Reagan. Neither was an atheist, but neither was much of a church-goer either. Their expressions of religious belief did not venture far beyond the

17. Goldberg, "Conservative."

requirements of 'ceremonial deism.'"[18] Exactly. A perfect phrase. In more ways that Derbyshire could say, conservatism is inherently the faith of ceremonial deism. Derbyshire adds that in "scanning the names on the original masthead of *National Review*, I see several of whom it must be said that, if they had failed to show up for an editorial meeting and I had been sent out to look for them, the pews of the local churches would *not* have been my first point of call."

Similarly, Jonah Goldberg, who has grand sympathies for the Christian tradition, recognizes quite refreshingly, "Put it this way, Jesus was no conservative—and there endeth the lesson."[19] Why not? One, because conservatism "in its most naked form is amoral" and, two, he correctly recognizes that Jesus was "that revolutionary from 2,000 years ago." Conservatism is, if anything, anti-revolutionary. Goldberg contends that "any ideology that promises that if it were fully realized there would be no more problems, no more trade-offs, no more elites, and no more inequality of one kind or another is un-conservative." Minus the perfectionism, he's right that that's basically the kingdom Jesus called for. That's the kingdom the ancient prophets, like Isaiah, promised. For those still trapped in Cold War fevers, this needn't translate into a massive state. That isn't the only option. But a "fully-realized" community of justice is what Moses, the prophets, and Jesus always called for. Goldberg, understandably, recognizes that conservatism wants nothing to do with that story. Instead, like most conservatives, Goldberg wants a nice, safe, private, spiritualized Jesus: "while Christianity may be a complete philosophy of life, it is only at best a partial philosophy of government. When it attempts to do otherwise, it has leapt the rails into an enormous vat of category error." Pilate thought so too. Depoliticize Jesus. Tame him. Goldberg adds, "I don't mind at all a president who has a personal relationship with Jesus. It's just that I don't think Jesus is going to have useful advice about how to fix Social Security." End of story for conservatism. So much for their hopes.

Conservatism has no life of its own. It is a system of impersonal principles at odds with the personalism of Father, Son, and Spirit. It is a deep individualism, applying and reapplying that distortion of the Trinity. Conservatism precludes the way of the cross. How did Christian conservatives ever get seduced into this modern pharasaism? Let's please divorce the Christian story from this permanent unitarianism. We can't serve both.

18. Derbyshire, "Twilight."
19. Goldberg, "Conservative."

15

Absolute Property

Modern conservative Christians tend to agree that Jesus was just plain wrong about their property. It would be nice, for us, if Jesus had just asked that singularly deranged rich young ruler to give up his property. That would have made dismissing Jesus safe and unthreatening. But, instead he said, "Whoever of you does not forsake all that he has cannot be My disciple" (Luke 14:33). The way of the cross is also a claim about property.

Bonhoeffer reflected on how we regularly get around Jesus's commands to forsake all: "If Jesus challenged us with the command 'Get out of it,' we should take him to mean: 'Stay where you are but cultivate that inward detachment.'"[1] Bonhoeffer adds:

> How is such absurdity possible? What has happened that the word of Jesus can be thus degraded by this trifling? . . . When orders are issued in other spheres of life there is no doubt whatever of their meaning. If a father sends his child to bed, the boy knows at once what he is to do. But suppose he has picked up a smattering of pseudo-theology. In that case he would argue more or less like this: "Father tells me to go to bed, but he really means that I am tired, and he does not want me to be tired. Therefore though the father tells me to go to bed, he really means: 'Go out and play.'"[2]

1. Bonhoeffer, *Discipleship*, 81.
2. Ibid.

Yes, go out and play.

Property plays a special role in blinding us to the call of Jesus. "When the young man heard that saying, he went away sorrowful, for he had great possessions" (Matt 19:22). It's supposed to be hard for property owners to enter the kingdom of Christ, the church, after all. If it's not, then we're doing something wrong.

Instead of even questioning or rethinking property even a little, Christians have wholeheartedly joined the other side. The Enlightenment turned private property into a holy thing, a "property right," and Christians followed suit. In the early church we used to say, "Thou shalt not turn away the needy, but shalt share everything with thy brother, and shalt not say that it is thine own."[3] But now the Ron Paul Christians of the world commonly say "property rights are the foundation of all rights in a free society." But what sort of God does this modern notion of property rights presuppose?

Almost anything can count as private property—real estate, homes, factories, furniture, appliances, computers, pens, potato chips, and more. Private property generally contrasts with communal property via who has the authority to control it. Private property is usually understood to assume a right, a moral claim that allows persons or a firm to obtain, own, control, and dispose of property as the owner chooses. More specifically, traditional principles of property rights include (a) control of the use of the property, (b) a claim to any benefit from the property, (c) the authority to transfer or sell the property, and (d) the authority to exclude others from the property.

This consciously individualistic approach to property runs into immediate problems with the God of scripture. He, too, has a perspective on property ownership, and it doesn't fit well with the absolutistic and individualistic claims above.

In contrast to exclusivist claims about property, the Lord said "the silver is mine and the gold is mine" (Hag 2:8). In fact, "every animal of the forest is mine, and the cattle on a thousand hills. . . . The world is mine, and all that is in it" (Ps 50:10, 12). And, even beyond that, "To the LORD your God belong the heavens, even the highest heavens, the earth and everything in it" (Deut 10:14; cf. Ps 24:1). Even the New Testament confirms, "the earth is the Lord's, and all that is in it" (1 Cor 10:26).

---

3. Didache, 4:8 in Ehrman, *Apostolic Fathers*, 415.

If the Lord owns everything, then no other owners do. If the Lord is the absolute owner of property, then modern, exclusivistic property rights can't be legitimate. If the Lord is the only absolute owner of property, then it's something of a slap in the face for modern Christians to speak of having an absolute right to control, benefit, transfer, and exclude others from "their" property. That would be like a farm hand doing what he wants with the owner's property, without consulting the owner.

Christian individualists nod quickly, mumble about stewardship, and grant the point that only God owns all things in the way they ascribe to individuals, but then ignore the point and default to secular individualist talk about "my property" and "my money," without ever looking back to the true owner again. It's a concession without effect. Their individualism remains. Instead, God's absolute ownership of the earth and all our little plots and objects should lead us to revise our language. Instead of talking about my exclusive right to my property, we should end up talking like the early Christians: "Neither did anyone say that any of the things he possessed was his own" (Acts 4:32). And if you believe God is the only true owner of property, then you also start saying things like, "If anyone wants to sue you and take away your tunic, let him have your cloak also" (Matt 5:40), in contrast to the language of the U.S. Declaration of Independence: "He has erected a multitude of New Offices, and sent hither swarms of Officers to harass our people and eat out their substance."

As Christians, one of our first questions about property should be to think about how property would function within the life of the Trinity. Does the Trinity speak of its property like John Locke or Ayn Rand do? Does the Trinity speak of gripping "its hard-earned money" the way political conservatives do? Does the Trinity bureaucratize property the way violent socialist collectives did? Does the Trinity hold property in common or privately? Does the Holy Spirit have a right to the earth that excludes the Father and the Son? Does the Son have a right to sell the earth without the consent of the Father? Does the Father demand control of the earth without interference of the Son and Spirit? No, those sorts of claims and counterclaims better reflect Greek and Roman gods rather than the harmony of Father, Son, and Spirit. The worlds of ancient mythology capture the spirit of claim and counterclaim, war and subjugation, competition and triumph that characterize the history of private property rights. For all its goodies, the history of private property is not the history of sacrifice and self-denial. It is the spirit of individual self-interest. That is the spirit of polytheism.

Though it's tempting to complicate issues, the answers to these questions seem relatively simple in light of the relations between Father, Son, and Spirit. They share, and they don't fight or war over property. They sacrifice property for one another, and they hold it commonly, not individualistically. The Father doesn't refuse to share property with the Son or Spirit. The Spirit doesn't complain that the Son has confiscated "his" wealth. They don't threaten one another away with guns and barbed wire. They share. They hold it lightly. They love to give and not hold. Their property is the whole world, and they give it to us to handle and protect and share the way they would.

The interior life of the Trinity is the life of joyful self-denial and sharing. "The Son can do nothing of Himself, but what He sees the Father do" (John 5:19). If the Son refuses to fight for his property (Matt 5:40), he learned it from the Father. If Son refuses to worry about acquiring property (Matt 6:25), he saw it in the Father. If the Spirit leads believers to divide their goods, "as anyone had need" (Acts 2:45), then he learned it from the Father and the Son. The Trinity is a society of love and sacrifice. Ron Paul's conservative/libertarian mantra "property rights are the foundation of all rights in a free society" doesn't reflect the society of the Trinity. Exclusivism and self-interest are not the foundation of freedom in the Trinity. Love is the source of freedom. Within the life of the Trinity we do not find any of the persons withholding property from the others. We find, instead, indwelling. Each of the persons indwells the other fully, and if each indwells the other, then Father, Son, and Spirit together own the world and all it contains. It's not just the Father who owns the world to the exclusion of the Son and Spirit. Each person of the Trinity owns the whole world. They own it collectively, as one, in common. The earth is the common property of the Trinity. That is our first model of property, and if we are called to image God on earth, then that is also our goal. We are Trinitarians, not polytheists.

Old Covenant law reflected this Trinitarian sharing, as we've seen, in the distribution of the manna, such that "every man had gathered according to each one's need" (Exod 16:18), a practice echoed later in the sharing of early Acts. But even beyond this, once in the promised land, no absolute individual property rights existed. The Lord commanded farmers, "Six years you shall sow your land and gather in its produce, but the seventh year you shall let it rest and lie fallow, that the poor of your people may eat" (Exod 23:10,11). The Lord owned the land, so he could require some of the land's produce for the poor. The farmers did not have absolute property rights (Deut 24:19–22; 26:12; Lev 19:9).

Of course, more broadly, the entire land system in the promised land was a denial of individual land rights. As the centralized owner, the Lord divided the land among the various tribes. But, as individual families ran into debt and poverty, they were allowed to sell their property to ease their grief. Yet in the fiftieth year, all lands were required to return to the original families, as discussed earlier: "Each of you shall return to his possession. And if you sell anything to your neighbor or buy from your neighbor's hand, you shall not oppress one another" (Lev 25:13, 14). Notice the focus on avoiding social oppression. In other words, you could legally purchase a piece of land from a poor person and even cultivate it for several decades. Yet, you would still have to return it to the original seller, even an irresponsible seller, at the jubilee. As a legitimate and honest purchaser of that land, you ultimately lacked the final authority to transfer, use, benefit, and exclude. In short, you lacked modern property rights. This negation of Enlightenment property rights doesn't justify state socialism, but it certainly precludes the idea that the Lord is a Christian libertarian.

This rejection of absolute property rights also doesn't require that all property is commonly owned. Reflecting the Trinity, a biblical understanding of property includes both communal and individual aspects. It doesn't teach that all is held in common or that all is held individually. It precludes aspects of both.

Still, it's common for Christian conservatives to invoke the principle that "taxation is theft" and "the heart of the welfare state is theft." This simply begs the question. It assumes an individualist view of property rights. Yes, if individualism is true, and the individual alone has an absolute claim on property, then taxation is theft. But then, so is God's demand for the tithe and his gleaning laws (Lev 19:9–10; Deut 24:19–22). But, if God owns all our money, and we're merely stewards of his property, we can't automatically blurt "theft" when any transfers are required. We have to ask other questions first, about God's use of his own property, delegated authorities, etc. If, let's say, we have a crazy community that denies "that any of the things he possessed was his own" (Acts 4:32), then it's harder and more complicated to generate a simplistic charge of theft, especially if the people are willing to fight over their stuff (Matt 5:40).

It should give us some pause that scripture doesn't use the language of "government theft" to describe taxation. It speaks of oppressive taxation but not theft (e.g., 1 Samuel 8). In fact, Paul, though faced with the great oppression of the Roman Empire said, "Render therefore to all their due: taxes to whom taxes are due" (Rom 13:7). If taxes are *due* to the Roman Empire, then we have to say the empire has some right to "my" money. It's not theft, then, because God owns our money and has chosen to delegate some to a pagan empire, for whatever reason. But God owns it and permits this transfer. It's not theft. Again, once we grant that God owns all things, conservatism has lost its core.

As soon, however, as one starts questioning the holy bovine of private property, the Cold Warriors among us can't help but start stuttering about Stalin, and all the horror stories begin tumbling out all over the carpet. They are well-rehearsed. That response is instinctive because state propaganda during the Cold War catechized us into believing that our only options were the sanctioned Left or Right, or, more specifically, state capitalism or state socialism. The Cold War allowed us to think only in terms of big, national, Mammon options. The church couldn't enter into the discussion. And we turned out to be tame, obedient believers in the narrow options our pagan overlords allowed us to believe and kill for. The younger generation has a much broader imagination, willing to hear Jesus speak.

To criticize private property and ponder communal solutions isn't to endorse state socialism. As noted, socialism was just another incarnation of Mammon, as is capitalism. State socialism was about violence and domination and protecting the few at the expense of the many. Socialism, too, was about coercing self-interest by an external code. It was and is the system of Mammon. It had nothing to do with Christ or the Spirit or self-denial out of love. Love played no part in the politics of socialism. It couldn't. Only the church can do that by the power of the Spirit. The Christian attitude toward all manifestations of Mammon should be like the apostle Paul's: "For what have I to do with judging those also who are outside? Do you not judge those who are inside?" (1 Cor 5:12). In other words, why care about what Mammon solutions? State "solutions" are not the church's solutions. You cannot serve state solutions and Christ. The church is *the* city on a hill, a city competing with all expressions of Mammon. What has the church to do with presidents, parties, coercive voting, and power? That's all Mammon. Why should we care about transforming the state outside of the church? Let the Roman and American empires crumble. Let the beasts die from lack of Spirit. Let the church be the city of refuge. Let the church denounce the City of Man but not try to redeem Satan.

Oh, but the Puritans are the final word. Even they failed at some experiments in communal living in New England and that proved that private property is the only way God ordained. Of course, we can only say that if we read very narrowly. Church history has countless stories of successful communal works (not that communal living is the only option, but it helps us sort through the issues). In our own day around the U.S. and Europe and Australia, many hundreds of Christian men, women, and children live in close community with each other. Many of these have been operating with their ups and downs for decades, a period when most conservative churches have split three or four times over purely intellectual matters. The way some critics assume the automatic failure of collective church works you'd think that wealthy medieval monasteries never angered the Reformers or that multi-million-dollar-a-year Israeli kibbutzim never existed. We have to look more broadly.

Thomas DiLorenzo gives the usual answer about the Pilgrim experiments in collective farming: "Communal land ownership certainly caused problems for the Pilgrims, but, Bradford noted, 'God in His wisdom saw another course fitter for them'—and that course was private property. . . . Only a capitalist system saved the suffering American settlers."[4] But why? What was so magical about private property? The typical answer is that it avoided the free riding problem. Private property required "each individual himself bore the full consequences of any reductions in output" and each individual had "an incentive to increase his effort because he directly benefitted from his own labor."[5] In short, we say, self-interest trumped self-denial, and there's no way of ever changing that. Humans must be polytheists forever. Christ can't transform self-interest. Of course not.

Why were medieval monks able to sustain collective living for centuries but the Pilgrims only for a blink of an eye? The Pilgrims failed at collective living not because of the dictates of some unitarian, impersonal economics laws about self-interest. Their failure was much simpler than that. They lacked the habits and virtues of self-denial. Listen how William Bradford described the moral reasons for their failure. Ironically,

4. DiLorenzo, *Capitalism*, 60.
5. Ibid., 55, 56.

he began by saying those involved were "good and honest men" but then said:

> For the young men who were most able and fit for service
> objected to being forced to spend their time and strength in
> working for other men's wives and children, without any rec-
> ompense. The strong man or the resourceful man had no more
> share of food, clothes, etc., than the weak man who was not
> able to do a quarter the other could. This was thought injustice.
> The aged and graver men, who were ranked and equalized in
> labour, food, clothes, etc., with the humbler and younger ones,
> thought it some indignity and disrespect to them. As for the
> men's wives who were obliged to do service for other men, such
> as cooking, washing their clothes, etc., they considered it a
> kind of slavery.[6]

This reveals these people were spiritual basket-cases, not Christian he-roes. How could Christ-followers called to foot-washing see service as "slavery"? How could people called to embrace the public shame of the cross grumble over indignity and disrespect? How could people called to care for the weak grumble over being put on the same level as the weak? These people hadn't even passed out of Sermon on the Mount 101. They had no bodily sense of self-denial. They should never have attempted a communal project together. And yet Bradford had the gall to conclude, "Let none argue that this is due to human failing." Seriously? Mammon was already deep in their bones. They couldn't escape it, and they passed on that habitual idolatry to the American centuries that followed. Thanks for the legacy.

Afterward, we followed the Enlightenment paganism of Adam Smith and turned self-interest into a law of the universe. Unchangeable. Inviolable. Eternal self-interest before which every economic system must bow.

But isn't the whole point of the New Testament a struggle against self-interest? Sure, conservatives try to force a big difference between selfishness and self-interest, but why isn't that special pleading? Cer-tainly, simply staying alive would seem to be an innocuous bit of good self-interest. But Christians are called to the way of the cross. We're called to die: "whoever desires to save his life will lose it, but whoever loses his life for My sake will find it" (Matt 16:25). Jesus's call goes beyond both selfishness and self-interest. In the same way, the inner life of the

6. Bradford, *Plymouth*, 116.

Trinity is the life of sacrifice, not "nice" self-interest: "the Son of Man did not come to be served, but to serve, and to give His life a ransom for many" (Mark 10:45). Imaging the Trinity means moving away from the slavery of self-interest. It doesn't mean, following Adam Smith, that we now gladly embrace self-interest. It's not, as Dinesh D'Souza says, that "capitalism civilizes greed."[7] Christ's kingdom is at war with the domination of self-interest. The gospel promised freedom from sin not capitulation. Adam Smith was a pantheist, not a Trinitarian.[8] The Church needs a better class of friend.

Jesus warned "one's life does not consist in the abundance of the things he possesses" (Luke 12:15). We should be far more fascinated by people than with things. But scripture's opposition to the grip of private property is not about asceticism. It is not some Gnostic punishment for owning goods. It is about love and deliverance. The church shouldn't hate property. It should yearn to want to share. It is so giddy about warm and clean water that it should not rest until all Christians have it and much more. "When you give a feast, invite the poor, the maimed, the lame, the blind" (Luke 14:13). We want to share the goodness of God. The church should delight in making sure all her people have enough. The church cannot let a day go by satisfied until it can be said of the church international "nor was there anyone among them who lacked" (Acts 4:34). At the same time, we should not consider ourselves a loving people, living the very basics of the gospel while any Christian is in need: "But whoever has this world's goods, and sees his brother in need, and shuts up his heart from him, how does the love of God abide in him?" (1 John 3:17). We are not a loving people, sitting happy in our big houses, while other Christians struggle for food. It's a call to repentance. Is the apostle John a guilt manipulator? No, he just knows that God is love and that drives us to "hunger and thirst for justice" (Matt 5:6).

7. D'Souza, *Virtue*, 126.

8. Compare Mueller, *Redeeming Economics*; Meeks, *God the Economist*; Hirschman, *The Passions and the Interests*.

16

Nice Mammon

It seems that all the wicked rich people have disappeared from the face of the earth. What a relief. This is a tremendous development in the history of the world. They vanished a couple hundred years ago, and they won't be back. As capitalist cheerleader John Schneider explained,

> The truth is that in modern market economies the main way that people acquire wealth is not by taking it away from someone else, but by taking part in its *creation*. This is fundamentally different from the way wealth was acquired in the ancient world—and for the most part, it is what businesses and corporations do.[1]

Yes, in the bad, old world, the Lord used his prophets to harangue the rich constantly. Isaiah told the rich to "put away the evil of your doings" (Isa 1:16). Jeremiah spoke against those who had "become great and grown rich" but who did not "plead the cause of the fatherless" (Jer 5:27, 28). Amos denounced the low wages of the rich, to "sell the righteous for silver, and the poor for a pair of sandals" (Amos 5:6). In Jesus's time, he didn't even need to distinguish between the good rich and the wicked rich. He could say in an perfectly unqualified manner, "Woe to you who are rich. . . . Woe to you who are full" (Luke 6:24, 25).

But those were the bad, old days when people acquired wealth simply by "taking it away from someone else." Sure, there was Tyre, which by its "great wisdom in trade you have increased your riches" (Ezek 28:5),

---

1. Schneider, *Affluence*, 32.

but it was wildly unique, for some reason, mumble, mumble. Now, things are different.

But what if the U.S. or the entire modern West were a Tyre? What if we were far worse than Tyre ever imagined? Would the well-fed majority of us be able to see that gross injustice of the rich against the poor? Would we be able, like Ezekiel, to identify our system as Satanic? That's the question I'm intrigued by. I don't think we would. We think we'd be able to spot gross economic injustice easily, but what majority in the history of the world has ever been able to do that? Economic injustice always seems to turn invisible in the eyes of those responsible for it.

The Lord directed the prophets to speak out against the economic and political injustices of their day, but he also told them the people wouldn't listen to the obvious. He told Ezekiel, "but the house of Israel will not listen to you, because they will not listen to Me; for all the house of Israel are impudent and hard-hearted" (Ezek 3:7). Jeremiah noted that the people had "made their faces harder than rock" (Jer 5:3), and the Lord told Isaiah, "Go, and tell this people: 'Keep on hearing, but do not understand; keep on seeing, but do not perceive'" (Isa 6:9, 10). Still, Isaiah prophesied to the rulers and people in that unjust system:

> The LORD will enter into judgment
> With the elders of His people and His princes:
> "For you have eaten up the vineyard;
> The plunder of the poor is in your houses.
> What do you mean by crushing My people
> And grinding the faces of the poor?"
> Says the Lord GOD of hosts. (Isa 3:14, 15)

The plunder of the poor was right there in their houses, and yet they couldn't perceive it. How was that possible?

Well, you have to tell yourself stories and mythologies. How might that work? Imagine, for the sake of argument, that we are indeed living in a system of gross economic injustice. Just pretend.

Start small. Imagine, for example, a national system in which wealthy businesses get the government to impose regulations in order to reduce competition and raise their prices.[2] The same system provides big businesses with free land, long-term leases at below market rates, sales tax, free employee training, and more.[3] Imagine this system also allows

---

2. Carney, *Ripoff*, 107.

3. Johnston, *Free Lunch*, 101.

the rich to contribute to politicians and receive massive contracts and tax relief.[4] Imagine it's also a system in which the government protects higher-income jobs, like doctors, lawyers, and other professionals, by restricting international competitors but encourages competition for low-income occupations.[5] At times, say, this national system controls economic growth by increasing unemployment among sales clerks, factory workers, custodians, and dishwashers but not higher wage jobs.[6] Perhaps this system also provides low-interest loans, special tax breaks, and safety exemptions to middle-class business but not to dishwashers, housekeepers, and custodians.[7] In this system, let's also give special government monopolies to the rich on products that sometimes allow profit increases from 200 to 5000 percent, creating multi-billion dollar industries but no similar privileges to the poor.[8]

Imagine, now, such a system in more international terms. Imagine it needs raw materials and so begins intervening in healthy but weaker countries, over time impoverishing them beyond anything in their previous history.[9] In addition, it needs cheap labor to increase its wealth so initially it enslaves the strongest folks from those countries and forces them to mine and farm to supply raw materials for the wealthy system. Later, the system strategically and intentionally indebts these poorer nations in order keep them dependent (providing favors like military bases) and to enrich the system's corporations and the elites of those poorer countries.[10] This system might even set up a "free trade" agreement that subsidizes wealthy farmers and pushes poor farmers off their lands into cheap factory work.[11] In the end, the system consciously agrees to hold down other countries through military power and international financial organizations so that it won't have to face any serious economic competition. And, at its most effective, let's have the ruling class use economic crises, war, and disasters as an artful and quick way to transform entire countries in ways that give them even more wealth and power.[12] The re-

4. Ibid., 121.
5. Baker, *Nanny*, 26, 27.
6. Ibid., 31.
7. Ibid., 79.
8. Ibid., 47ff.
9. Wolterstorff, *Justice*, 87–89.
10. Perkins, *Confession*, 15, 16.
11. Korten, *Corporations*, 49.
12. Klein, *Shock Doctrine*.

sults of such a system keep the vast majority of the world very poor by comparison to the people benefitting from the system. On top of it, the economic system has to make itself look nice and respectable. Maybe something like this:

> The subtlety of this modern empire building puts the Roman centurions, the Spanish conquistadors, and the eighteenth- and nineteenth-century European colonial powers to shame. We Economic Hit Men are crafty; we learned from history. Today we do not carry swords. We do not wear armor or clothes that sets us apart. In countries like Ecuador, Nigeria, and Indonesia, we dress like local schoolteachers and shop owners. In Washington and Paris, we look like government bureaucrats and bankers. We appear humble, normal. We visit project sites and stroll through impoverished villages. We profess altruism, talk with local papers about the wonderful humanitarian things we are doing. We cover the conference tables with our spreadsheets and financial projections, and we lecture at the Harvard Business School about the miracles of microeconomics.[13]

Would the ancient prophets have any comment on such a rigged system? Would Jesus give it a "Woe to you who are rich"? The rich bear most of the responsibility for the poverty in such a system, much of it deliberate. It would be hard for the prophets and Jesus to condemn the rich if the problem was actually just lazy and inferior poor people. Would we call such an economic system unjust? It's hard to see what could be called unjust if something like this couldn't.

So what kind of story could one tell oneself to hide such a system?

One story we could use to avoid seeing such a system would be to eliminate or minimize any talk of classes, like rich and poor. If there are no classes, then we can't invoke Jesus's "Woe to you who are rich."

The Cold War contributed to this story. Political conservatism's parasitic vision openly resisted Marxist talk of classes and class warfare. But it's more than that. Here's the noted Christian conservative, Michael Novak, undermining talk of classes:

> To think of the poor as a class is to ignore the individual dignity of each person among them. There is at least as much complexity, subtlety, and differentiation in the individual personalities of the poor as among any other social class. . . . The attempt to simplify human reality by speaking solely in terms

13. Perkins, *Confessions*, xx.

of "class" does violence to the individuality of each human
person.[14]

To be fair, he doesn't absolutely exclude talk of classes (he says "solely"),
but he comes close—"to think of the poor as a class is to ignore the individual dignity of each." Class negates individuality. Why does that follow?
His assumption seems to be that individuals don't have any real collective
aspects, or that individuality is fundamental.

This sort of argument flows nicely from conservatism's deep individualism, a heresy many conservatives are proud of. But certainly Trinitarians aren't allowed to be closet individualists. The Trinity makes both
individuality and collectivity real, without one taking priority.

In other words, we don't have to be squeamish when Mary says God
"has filled the hungry with good things, and the rich He has sent away
empty" (Luke 1:53), or when Isaiah says "the plunder of the poor is in
your houses" (Isa 3:14).

Those are voices comfortable with classes and even class-conflict
language. But also notice how big a blinder conservative individualism
wears by wanting to eliminate class talk. All of a sudden, economic injustice on a huge scale becomes largely invisible. Classes don't exist, so we
can't see them holding down the poor. Sure, there are a few, individual
bad rich people but not entire ranks of them. Individualism is always
happy to acknowledge a few bad apples. This also explains why political
conservatives get so heated about sexual sins. Those are individual. Those
count.

Many times we avoid seeing the big system of injustice and inequality by invoking a story about zero sum thinking. Zero sum thinking is
the claim that in every exchange one person wins and one person loses.
If someone is rich, so zero sum thinking says, then someone had to be
diminished. Political conservatives and libertarians reply quickly, no, *in a
free exchange*, both parties benefit, or else they wouldn't make the trade.
So when someone gets rich, he or she has done so only because others
have freely benefitted from the exchange, too. No one has been exploited.
Hence, the system is just, after all.

For decades, a large and growing literature has documented how
wealthy nations plunder the poor via domestic and international methods. This legal plundering is the main source of the complaint about inequality, not the mere fact of differences in wealth.

14. Novak, *Liberate*, 150, 152.

Nice Mammon

In his widely acclaimed defense of capitalism, *The Virtue of Prosperity*, Dinesh D'Souza spends a chapter seemingly aimed at answering the inequality objection by rebutting zero sum thinking. "We need a new way of thinking about inequality," D'Souza says. His "new" answer comes with a drumroll: "Our examination of some of the primary causes of inequality leads to a surprising conclusion: the prime culprit in causing contemporary social inequality seems to be merit. . . .The guy who is worth little has probably produced little of value." That's new? That is the same thing conservatives have said since the first issue of *National Review*.

D'Souza comes close at one point to considering the real objection but then turns away, as if no one could actually make such a claim: "Traditionally the debate about inequality has been conducted as if the acquisition of wealth were a zero-sum game. Thorstein Veblen writes, 'The accumulation of wealth at the upper end of the pecuniary scale implies privation at the lower end of the scale.' This is the old mantra: 'The rich are getting richer and the poor are getting poorer.' Embedded in it is a big assumption, namely that the rich are getting richer *at the expense* of the poor."[15]

That's it. Don't run away now, Mr. D'Souza. That last bit is the objection. Massive legal and political plunder and special privileges for centuries—the rich getting rich at the expense of the poor due to ruling class privileges and interventions in the market.

Even conservatives agree that once law and coercion step in to benefit one side over another, then we're in the realm of zero sum possibilities. And that's the objection—that for over a century, and certainly since Bretton Woods (IMF, World Bank), Western political-economies have worked legally to transfer money and rig economic systems in favor of the wealthiest. That's what's at the heart of objection about inequality, not mere difference. You can't debunk zero sum thinking when coercion is involved.

Political conservatives, though, just glaze over and chant "no zero sum, no zero sum." Sure, maybe, in a free economy, but the complaint is hardly about inequalities resulting from free exchanges. It's about entire systems designed to keep people poor. These involve coercion. As the influential US strategist George Kennan wrote back in 1948 in a much quoted, misquoted, and debated statement,

> We have about 50% of the world's wealth but only 6.3% of
> its population. This disparity is particularly great as between

15. D'Souza, *Virtues*, 71.

ourselves and the peoples of Asia. In this situation, we cannot
fail to be the object of envy and resentment. Our real task in
the coming period is to devise a pattern of relationships which
will permit us to maintain this position of disparity without
positive detriment to our national security. To do so, we will
have to dispense with all sentimentality and day-dreaming; and
our attention will have to be concentrated everywhere on our
immediate national objectives. We need not deceive ourselves
that we can afford today the luxury of altruism and world-
benefaction. . . .

We should dispense with the aspiration to "be liked" or to be
regarded as the repository of a high-minded international
altruism. We should stop putting ourselves in the position of
being our brothers' keeper and refrain from offering moral and
ideological advice. We should cease to talk about vague and—
for the Far East—unreal objectives such as human rights, the
raising of the living standards, and democratization. The day is
not far off when we are going to have to deal in straight power
concepts. The less we are then hampered by idealistic slogans,
the better.[16]

It's in this context, a superpower systematically aiming to hold others
down, that we can talk about the inequality objection, not some mythical
free market. As conservatives, when we find ourselves tempted to answer
objections about inequality by starting with the words "zero sum game,"
we can be almost sure we're on the wrong track. That's not the objection.
We're missing it, again.

An even stronger way to avoid seeing a large system of economic
injustice is to turn on the critics of the system. Instead of granting the
immoral economic system, suggest that the critics of the system have
deep moral and psychological problems. Most specifically, the critics are
wrong because they are driven by envy and ingratitude. Yeah, that's it;
they're twisted inside. They hate success and wealth and want to destroy
it all because they can't have it or lack the talent to get it. Cite the tenth
commandment, too. Envy is explanation.

"The envious man thinks that if his neighbor breaks a leg, he will
be able to walk better himself." That, from Helmut Schoeck (1922–1993),
conservative author most noted for his 1966 book, *Envy: A Theory of Social Behavior*. Since then, conservatives have been quick to throw out the

16. Kennan, "PPS23."

charge of envy against anyone who criticizes the rich. But something's a bit too easy in this charge; it should make us a little suspicious. Even earlier, the much beloved Erik von Kuehnelt-Leddihn, writing in one of the early, sacred texts of modern conservatism, explains that the Left and critics of capitalism generally are driven by fear with "envy as its blood brother." Envy is the fear of inferiority, and "the demand for equality and identity arises precisely in order to avoid that fear, that feeling of inferiority."[17]

> In the last two hundred years the exploitation of envy—its mobilization among the masses—coupled with the denigration of individuals, but more frequently of classes, races, nations, or religious communities, has been the key to political success.[18]

This is a brilliant move. It silences all the critics. It stops us from any need of examining the details of our economic system. The facts don't matter. The accusers are sinners, full of envy and ingratitude. No need to listen. Nothing to see here. Move along.

The conservative envy charge has been convincing, but is it legitimate?

One convenient problem is that it can't be disproven. It's a charge that describes the internal state of someone, but the accuser can't see the opponent's heart. So, ideally, the charge of envy has to be based on some external evidence, some action or confession. That sort of proof would be grand if it included, say, the diary of a Leftist who confessed, "I really hate success. I really want to take down the rich." But conservatives don't point to this sort of evidence for their charge. They just assume any criticism of the rich must always stem from envy. The conservative charge of envy, then, operates much like the Left's accusation of hatred and hate crimes. Neither charge is meant to be proved. They function more as a plastic bags to trap and silence the opposition. At the very least, we need to ask conservatives who easily bandy this accusation about: what is the specific objective evidence for the internal state of envy? They bear the burden of proof.

As hinted above, the envy accusation of envy snags the nonenvious, too. Because the charge of envy is based primarily on hearing any criticism of the rich, we have to conclude that the Old Testament prophets and New Testament teachers were highly envious. "You lie on beds inlaid with ivory and lounge on your couches. You dine on choice lambs and

---

17. Kuehnelt-Leddihn, *Leftism*, 5.

18. Ibid., 6.

fattened calves" (Amos 6:4). "He has filled the hungry with good things, and the rich He has sent away empty" (Luke 1:53). "It is hard for a rich man to enter the kingdom of heaven" (Matt 19:23). "Come now, you rich, weep and howl for your miseries that are coming upon you! Your riches are corrupted" (Jas 5:1). Were Isaiah and Jesus full of envy? Did they feel inferior to the successful and wealthy? Might these opponents really not be envious but be accurately pointing out actual sins of the rich?

And what of the charge of ingratitude? Are we supposed to be grateful for the gains of injustice? For example, many conservative free market advocates have argued for decades that fractional reserve banking is thievish, inflationary, fraudulent, and immoral. How does that affect the question of gratitude?

Think about it. How much of Western prosperity has been based on fractional reserve banking? Some suggest that due to the fractional reserve system, money is multiplied six times. A $1.5 billion creation of new money will eventually result in a $9 billion increase in the total supply of dollars. Where would all the major corporations and producers be without fractional reserve banking? Would there even be a prosperous West without it? Can you imagine the West without modern business loans? And it's a wealth that touches every honest entrepreneur, even if it's just using the tools, like computers, vehicles, raw materials, etc., made possible by fractional reserve wealth.

So the conservative free-marketer is in a bit of a bind. He wants us to show our gratitude for Western wealth, and yet he agrees that much of that wealth is based on massive, systematic injustice. Do we give our wealth three grateful cheers or not? If we don't, are we being resentful and envious? In a similar way, as Stanley Hauerwas has suggested, the Mafia also produces great wealth. Should the children of Mafiosos be grateful for their family's wealth?

Anti-class individualism, zero sum "refutations," and accusations of envy and ingratitude all keep us from seeing gross economic injustice. Each avoids dealing with factual and historical claims. Each invokes conceptual masks to limit perception. The last move to consider does the same. It, too, works on the a priori level to redefine the situation such that we can't see the systematic injustice of Mammon in recent centuries. Specifically it involves the failure to distinguish between capitalism and free markets. It switches definitions. We commonly blend the two, and that's where the problem is. Historically, one involves massive government intervention, and the other minimal. One produces great wealth, and the other not so much. If we confuse the terms then we can mistake causes and hide great injustice.

The great Christians social critic, G. K. Chesterton, strongly opposed both socialism and capitalism. Chesterton explained, "When I say 'Capitalism,' I commonly mean something that may be stated thus: 'That economic condition in which there is a class of capitalists, roughly recognizable and relatively small, in whose possession so much of the capital is concentrated as to necessitate a very large majority of the citizens serving those capitalists for a wage.'"[19] He understood that capitalism was a system focused to benefit the capitalist class. Chesterton seems to have drawn on the original usage of those like Benjamin Tucker, a nineteenth-century thinker who understood capitalism was a system in which *the state intervenes in the market to benefit the capitalist class.* Government intervention for the rich, in contrast to the free market. Along the same lines, Kevin Carson said "capitalism, as distinguished from a free market, is a system in which the state represents the owners of capital and land and intervenes in the market on their behalf."[20]

In contrast, free markets are relatively small and local affairs. Farmers' markets tend to be simple and helpful free markets. No lobbyists. No legal privileges. No government subsidies. No enforced benefits. No massive transfers of wealth. No great wealth, either. It's ironic that in a book purportedly giving a *Politically Incorrect Guide to Capitalism*, the author starts off by conceding, "in this book we will examine 'pure' capitalism, even though it doesn't exist in this form today."[21] It's easy to find capitalism in the present and in history, but it's not so easy to find the free market.

Capitalism is not the free market. The history of capitalism, and the West, and the U.S., is the history of great government intervention on behalf of the wealthy. As Kevin Carson notes, "From the outset of the industrial revolution, what is nostalgically called 'laissez-faire' was in fact a system of continuing state intervention to subsidize accumulation, guarantee privilege, and maintain work discipline."[22] From Henry VIII's pillaging of the English monasteries to the genocide of some 300 million Africans and South Americans, through the government grants

19. Chesterton, *Outline*, 27.

20. Carson, *Iron Fist*.

21. Murphy, *Poltically Incorrect*, 2.

22. Carson, *Iron Fist*.

of swathes of land to the U.S. railroad corporations to the massive wealth transfers of the Cold War from the middle class to weapons manufacturers and the Bush-Obama financial corporation bailouts of 2007, the West is a history of great interventions for the rich, with legislation throughout designed to privilege and protect the financial and merchant classes.

Carson again: "Capitalism was founded on an act of robbery as massive as feudalism. It has been sustained to the present by continual state intervention to protect its system of privilege, without which its survival is unimaginable."[23] Capitalism is not a natural system. It is not something that happens without help. Its wealth production requires great amounts of special privileges and special financial favors. Without big government, big capitalism would never have survived. The modern world of Walmart, Microsoft, McDonalds, Halliburton, Boeing, and all of Wall Street could never have grown up and been sustained in a free market. They, and all of big capitalism, stay alive only by a long history of government privileges, subsidies, and protections. Capitalism turns out to be *not* an enemy of socialism, just a slight variant. Where historic socialism aimed at the poor, this socialism maintains the rich, and much more successfully. The popular criticism "socialism for the rich, free markets for the poor" remains a telling insight.

Neither the wealthiest people nor the wealthiest countries in the world gained their wealth through a history of free market exchanges. Centuries of Western wealth did not grow out of free markets. It grew out of massive transfers, protections, and special subsidies. Capitalism produces great wealth via government intervention. Who said socialism failed? It didn't in the west. Woodrow Wilson gave us the honest voice of capitalist intervention:

> Since trade ignores national boundaries and the manufacturer
> insists on having the world as a market, the flag of his na-
> tion must follow him, and the doors of the nations which
> are closed must be battered down. Concessions obtained by
> financiers must be safeguarded by ministers of state, even if
> the sovereignty of unwilling nations be outraged in the pro-
> cess. Colonies must be obtained or planted, in order that no
> useful corner of the world may be overlooked or left unused.
> Peace itself becomes a matter of conference and international
> combinations.[24]

23. Ibid.

24. Cited in Williams, *Tragedy*, 66.

Batter down those doors. That's what the marines are for, anyway. And that's what they did.

But the trick is to call centuries of capitalist intervention and government protection the "free market," or as Ronald Reagan never tired of calling it the "magic of the marketplace." Once he actually used that phrase in front representatives of the IMF and the World Bank, the very engines of state capitalism: "We who live in free market societies believe that growth, prosperity and, ultimately, human fulfillment are created from the bottom up, not the government down."[25] Talk about conservative blindness. It must be willful at that stage. The words "free market" work just like an incantation. Pronounce it in whispered tones over modern banking, military violence, or the industrial revolution, and conservatives will clap and even repeat that all you need to do is get gov'mint out of the way. The capitalists must just snicker in the background. Getting the government out of the way would be an utter disaster for Western wealth. Our world would crumble. Shout "free market" over mind-boggling economic injustice, and a white sepulcher covers the economic evil. We just won't see it. We say a priori that injustice can't occur in a free exchange, and all the wealth and poverty around us came from freely created wealth, so where is the injustice?

Schneider just gives the typical conservative conclusion: "I see nothing clearly immoral at all."[26] Exactly. You don't see.

25. Reagan, "Remarks."
26. Schneider, *Affluence*, 34.

17

American Mars

War don't ennoble men. It turns them into dogs. It poisons the soul.

– *The Thin Red Line*

Our government has kept us in a perpetual state of fear—kept us in a continuous stampede of patriotic fervor—with the cry of grave national emergency.... [O]ur country is now geared to an arms economy which was bred in an artificially induced psychosis of war hysteria and nurtured upon an incessant propaganda of fear.

— General MacArthur, 1957

No subject blinds Christians more to the way of the cross than our deep identity with national militaries. If you start asking questions and raising doubts about the goodness and benevolence of one's military, it's like Jekyll and Hyde for many Christians. They snap and turn. The anger flashes. Discussion shuts off. You are unclean. This sort of response is especially strong with Christians in the U.S. There, identifying with *the* superpower military casts an even stronger spell. Superpower military success and efficiency proves God is on our side, and to question the benevolence of U.S. military actions is to question the character of God.

Unfalsifiable. I've seen it time and again. Everyone admits, sure, military mistakes, collateral damage, a few bad apples, and some tragedies along the way. This was all unintentional, inessential. But you can't question the driving core of benevolence and good intentions of the American political/military mission. It is and always has been pure and shiny, though, of course, mistakes have happened along the way. Other nations, however, especially the former Soviet Union and now ghostly, ungraspable, omnipresent terrorists can never have good or reasonable motives. They are always essentially evil and unreasonable, even insane, but we are essentially good, despite, admittedly, a few missteps.

This identification with superpower military reaches deep within our lives, much more than we're willing to admit. Americans can't conceive of the world any other way. We can't hear any criticisms to the contrary. It is a religious *devotion*, after all, a deep loyalty, a faith, often sleeping but roused to great anger when poked. Christians can question many things, but once American Christians start questioning the essential benevolence of the military mission in the history of United States of America, blood boils. It's quite astounding to watch, and this response suggests we're dealing with some very raw idolatry at an elemental level.

Military violence and domination dwell deep in American blood. After all, war is *the* originary myth of the United States. We ourselves threw off a superpower. From war we came and to war we always return. War works. It brings closure, not a spiral. Those who live by the sword don't die by it. Most of the time we win and keep going. To put it in New Testament terms, the American colonists who waged war against the British Empire imitated first-century patriotic zealots, like Judas of Galilee, who took up arms against the Roman Empire.

> Judas the Galilean is an excellent example of these patriots. He reprimanded his countrymen as cowards for consenting to pay tribute to a pagan state and for tolerating earthly masters. Josephus says of him and Zadduk: "[They] maintained that this census would lead to nothing less than complete slavery, and they called upon the people to vindicate their liberty. They argued that, if they succeeded, they would enjoy the consequences of their good fortune, and if they failed, they would at least have the honor and glory of having shown a greatness of spirit."[1]

1. Ford, *My Enemy*, 67,68.

Patrick Henry captured the violence of the colonists this way: "Guard with jealous attention the public liberty. Suspect everyone who approaches that jewel. Unfortunately, nothing will preserve it but downright force. Whenever you give up that force, you are inevitably ruined."[2] "Downright force." Give him carnal weapons or give him death. Patrick and Judas were blood brothers. And we shed the blood of our Christian brothers, and it destined us from that day on. The United States was born not out of obedience to anything resembling the Sermon on the Mount but in a bloody feud with our Christian brothers over what?—property and finances. That's the American way.

Less than a hundred years later, the "Christian" United States lived by the sword once again in an even bloodier war between Christian brothers, North vs. South. Warring against Christians turned out to be not just a pattern for us but our special gift. It would recur again in the twentieth century. What depths of immaturity did we, do we, live in to violate the basics of following Christ? Sure, we say the other side was evil, always more evil, and those traitorous brothers threatened tyranny. Yes, maturity was needed in dark circumstances, but we followed the path of the Roman Empire while proclaiming Christ. The apostle John made all our moral rationalizations for killing fellow Christians ring hollow: "He who says he is in the light, and hates his brother, is in darkness. . . . [H]e who hates his brother is in darkness and walks in darkness, and does not know where he is going, because the darkness has blinded his eyes" (1 John 2:9–11). Perhaps that should be the slogan of the United States—"darkness has blinded his eyes." Fighting your brother is the path of darkness, not heroism. Few origins could have been more pathetic and full of shame.

The American way included not merely fighting and killing our brothers in Christ but also enslaving them. We played our part in the largest genocide in world history—African. Africa lost some 250 million of its strongest men and women at a key point in its development, and, today, the West still blames Africa for not recovering. The United States was one of the very last nations in the world to abolish slavery. Yet for generations of servitude, African slaves in the United States embraced Christ in very high numbers. Even so, we kept these covenant brothers and sisters in bondage in violation of Old Testament commands, all while convincing ourselves, over and over, that we were humane and Christ-like

2. Henry, "Speech."

masters. Frederick Douglass spoke about Christian American hypocrisy in his famous Independence Day speech of 1852.

> What, to the American slave, is your 4th of July?.... All your religious parade and solemnity, are, to Him, mere bombast, fraud, deception, impiety, and hypocrisy—a thin veil to cover up crimes which would disgrace a nation of savages. There is not a nation on the earth guilty of practices more shocking and bloody than are the people of the United States, at this very hour. Go where you may, search where you will, roam through all the monarchies and despotisms of the Old World, travel through South America, search out every abuse, and when you have found the last, lay your facts by the side of the everyday practices of this nation, and you will say with me, that, for revolting barbarity and shameless hypocrisy, America reigns without a rival.[3]

The American habit of enslaving and fighting our Christian brothers naturally turned outward as well. The drive to dominate, rather than serve, led the U.S. to begin its imperial control of the world at a very early stage. From our origins, we sought to dominate beyond our borders. This imperial eye was at work even at the early debates on the U.S. Constitution in the late 1700s. As Alexander Hamilton said, we should "concur in erecting one great American system, superior to the control of all trans-Atlantic force or influence, and able to dictate the terms of the connection between the old and new world."[4] Similarly, a few years later, even one of the most limited-government president, Thomas Jefferson, could conclude "that no constitution was ever before as well calculated as ours for extensive empire and self-government."[5]

The United States was always a deliberate empire. Most nations can live well within their borders, but from the start the United States began intervening in other countries to defend American interests, usually business interests. Our military intrusions on others' soil created this list, a partial list, unfamiliar to most Americans:

> Dominican Republic (1798–1800), Tripoli (1801–05), Mexico (1806), Gulf of Mexico (1806–10), West Florida (1810), Amelia Island (1812), Marquesas Islands (1813–1814), Spanish Florida (1814), Caribbean (1814–25), Algiers (1815), Tripoli (1815),

3. Zinn, *Voices*, 183.
4. Kesler, *Federalist*, 86.
5. Cited in Williams, *Empire*, 60; cf. Bacevich, *American Empire*.

Spanish Florida (1816–18), Amelia Island (1817), British Oregon (1818), Africa (1820–23), Cuba (1822–24), Puerto Rico (1824), Greece (1827), Falkland Islands (1831–32), Sumatra (1832), Argentina (1833), Peru (1835–36), Mexico (1836), Sumatra (1838), Fiji Islands (1840), Drummond Island (1841), Samoa (1841), Mexico (1842), China (1843), Africa (1843), Mexico (1844), Mexican War (1846–48), Smyrna (1849), Turkey (1851), Argentina (1852), Nicaragua (1853), Japan (1853), China (1854), Nicaragua (1854), China (1855), Fiji Islands (1855), Uruguay (1855), Panama (1856), China (1856), Nicaragua (1857), Uruguay (1858), Turkey (1858), Paraguay (1859), China (1859), Angola (1860), Colombia (1860), Japan (1863), Panama (1865), Mexico (1866), Nicaragua (1867), Formosa (1867), Japan (1868), Uruguay (1868), Colombia (1868), Mexico (1870), Hawaiian Islands (1870), Korea (1871), Colombia (1873), Mexico (1873), Mexico (1876), Egypt (1882), Panama (1885), Korea (1888), Haiti (1888), Samoa (1889), Argentina (1890), Haiti (1891), Bering Strait (1891), Chile (1891), Hawaii (1893), Brazil (1894), Nicaragua (1894), China (1894), Korea (1894), Colombia (1895), Nicaragua (1896), Spanish-American War (1898), China (1898), Nicaragua (1899), Samoa (1899), Philippine Islands (1899–1901), China (1900), Colombia (1901), Honduras (1903), Dominican Republic (1903), Syria (1903), Abyssinia (1904), Panama (1903–14), Dominican Republic (1904), Morocco (1904), Korea (1905), Cuba (1906), Honduras (1907), Nicaragua (1910), China (1911), Honduras (1912), Cuba (1912), China (1912), Turkey (1912), Nicaragua (1912–25), China (1912–41), Mexico (1913), Haiti (1914), Dominican Republic (1914), Mexico (1917), Haiti (1915–34), Dominican Republic (1916–24), Cuba (1917–22), Mexico (1918–19), Panama (1918–20), Soviet Russia (1918–20), Dalmatia (1919), Turkey (1919), Honduras (1919), China (1920), Guatemala (1920), Panama (1921), Turkey (1922), China (1922), Honduras (1924), China (1924–25), Honduras (1925), Panama (1925), Nicaragua (1926–33), China (1926–27), Cuba (1933), Caribbean (1940), Greenland (1941), Dutch Guyana (1941), China (1945), Trieste (1946), Italy (1947–48), Greece (1947), Philippines (1940–50), Palestine (1948), Eastern Europe (1948–56), Albania (1949–53), Korea (1950–53), Iran (1953), Guatemala (1953–54), Costa Rica (1950s), Formosa (1950–55), China (1954), Syria (1956–57), Middle East (1957–58), Indonesia (1957–58), Lebanon (1958), British Guiana (1953–64), Ecuador (1960–63), Peru (1960–65), Thailand (1962), Cuba (1962), Laos (1962–75), Brazil (1964), Congo

(1964), Vietnam (1964–75), Greece (1964–74), Bolivia (1964–75), Dominican Republic (1965), Indonesia (1965), Ghana (1966), Congo (1967), Cambodia (1970), Chile (1964–73), Costa Rica (1970–71), Australia (1975-3-75), Cyprus (1974), Angola (1975–80), Lebanon (1976), Zaire (1975–78), Nicaragua (1978–90), Jamaica (1976–80), Seychelles (1979–81), El Salvador (1980–94), Libya (1981), Sinai (1982), Suriname (1982–84), Lebanon (1982–83), Honduras (1983–89), Chad (1983), Grenada (1983), Persian Gulf (1984), Libya (1986), Bolivia (1986), Panama (1988), Philippines (1989), Liberia (1990), Saudi Arabia (1990), Iraq (1991), Zaire (1991), Kuwait (1992), Somalia (1992), Bosnia (1993), Macedonia (1993), Haiti (1993), Liberia (1996), Central African Republic (1996), Sierra Leone (1997), Afghanistan (1998), Sudan (1998), Iraq (1998), Yugoslavia (1999), Kosovo (1999), East Timor (1999), Yemen (2000), Afghanistan (2001), Kosovo (2001), Iraq (2003).[6]

The list goes on and on, as does the list of the imprisoned and dead. To become an imperial power a nation has to work long and hard to control natural resources and expand markets. That's the American way. We already noted Woodrow Wilson's market-driven claim that "the doors of the nations which are closed must be battered down" so that "no useful corner of the world may be overlooked or left unused."

During that same period, the U.S. government used the marines to carry out many of the economic missions noted above, especially in the western hemisphere. I can't help noting the oft-quoted observations of the most famous Major General of that era, General Smedley Butler (1881–1940). Here is his classic, frank description of what he led the marines to do during that time:

> I spent thirty- three years and four months in active military service as a member of this country's most agile military force, the Marine Corps I served in all commissioned ranks from Second Lieutenant to Major-General. And during that period, I spent most of my time being a high class muscle-man for Big Business, for Wall Street and for the Bankers. In short, I was a racketeer, a gangster for capitalism.

6. Grimmett, "Forces Abroad"; see also Blum, *Killing Hope*; Kinzer, *Overthrow*; Weiner, *Legacy of Ashes*.

I suspected I was just part of a racket at the time. Now I am
sure of it. Like all the members of the military profession, I
never had a thought of my own until I left the service. My
mental faculties remained in suspended animation while I
obeyed the orders of higher-ups This is typical with everyone
in the military service.

I helped make Mexico, especially Tampico, safe for American
oil interests in 1914. I helped make Haiti and Cuba a decent
place for the National City Bank boys to collect revenues in. I
helped in the raping of half a dozen Central American republics for the benefits of Wall Street. The record of racketeering is
long. I helped purify Nicaragua for the international banking
house of Brown Brothers in 1909–1912 (where have I heard
that name before?). I brought light to the Dominican Republic
for American sugar interests in 1916. In China I helped to see
to it that Standard Oil went its way unmolested.[7]

Shouldn't we be grateful for the wonderful gift of capitalistic affluence
such interventions brought us? How dare we question the blessings of
American capitalism? Or, rather, wasn't it exactly this sort of thing the
prophets and Jesus condemned so strongly? "Woe to you rich."

And U.S. military capitalism hasn't stopped. In 1998, John Maresca,
vice president of Unocal oil, testified before congress and called for a pipeline
that would transport oil southward through Afghanistan for 1040 miles to
the Pakistan coast. Such a pipeline would cost about $2.5 billion and carry
about 1 million barrels of oil per day. But there was a problem. Afghanistan
was not friendly to this move. Marescal said, "Without peaceful settlement
of the conflicts in the region, cross-border oil and gas pipelines are not
likely to be built. . . . The U.S. Government should use its influence to help
find solutions to all of the region's conflicts. U.S. assistance in developing
these new economies will be crucial to business success."[8] The George W.
Bush administration developed war plans to invade Afghanistan long before the 9/11 attacks. On October 7, 2001, the U.S. bombing commenced.
Coincidentally, the first U.S. Special Ambassador to Afghanistan was John
J. Maresca, that vice president of Unocal. The next ambassador to Afghanistan was Mr. Zalmay Khalilzad, a Unocal consultant. Four months after
the bombing, Afghanistan and Pakistan signed an agreement for a new
pipeline. Tens of thousands of Afghan civilians have died in the wake of

7. Butler, *War,* 10.
8. Gilman, "U.S. Interests."

the U.S. invasion, far more than died in the World Trade Center attacks. In Iraq, which the U.S. did not even invade for the 9/11 attacks, hundreds of thousands of civilians have died.

William Blum summarizes that in just the post-World War II interventions, the U.S. has undermined thirty populist movements fighting dictatorial regimes, provided handbooks for torture, dropped powerful bombs on the people of about twenty-five countries, attempted to overthrow more than forty foreign governments, invaded twenty sovereign nations unprovoked, and carried out assassination attempts on the lives of some forty foreign political leaders.

After all this, American leaders and people still have the gall to ask why do *they* hate us? "Most Americans are simply not aware of the impact of their culture and government's policies on the rest of the world. But, more important, a vast majority simply do not believe that American has done, or can do, anything wrong."[9] Glenn Greenwald, summarizing Air Force lecturer Robert Pape, concluded that "the prime cause of suicide bombings is not Hatred of Our Freedoms or Inherent Violence in Islamic Culture or a Desire for Worldwide Sharia Rule by Caliphate, but rather foreign military occupations."[10] In one of the most famous, recent antiwar speeches, Dahlia Wasfi argued,

> They don't hate us because of our freedoms. They hate us
> because every day, we are funding and committing crimes
> against humanity. The so-called war on terror is a cover for our
> military aggression to gain control of the resources of Western
> Asia. This is sending the poor of this country to kill the poor
> of those Muslim countries. This is trading blood for oil. This is
> genocide, and to most of the world, we are the terrorists.[11]

Terrorists? Can average, conservative American Christians even come close to asking that question? Is it even conceivable that the United States is a terrorist nation? If our identity is tied to the nation rather than Christ's church, then we can't allow ourselves to take that question seriously. It would cut too deep. Still, who are we? How could a Christian nation have such a horribly long list of war and death? It's clearly abnormal when compared to other nations. Our devotion to war and violence

---

9. Sardar, *Why*, 9.
103. Greenwald, "Occupations."
104. Wasfi, "No Justice, No Peace."

and collateral murder looks like an obsession. Our originary myths of violence must come to play.

The American origin from violence didn't start in 1776. Even by that point, we had already fought and slaughtered many. We learned it from your spiritual forefathers, the Pilgrims. One of the more noted Pilgrim slaughters came about from the Pequot natives, a tribe of freedom fighters, we might say in Reagan parlance. It seems the Pequot planned to attack and harass the Pilgrims for invading native lands and confiscating their property without permission. The Pequot concluded that the Pilgrims would at some point completely "overspread their country, and would deprive them of it."[12] The Pequot objections to the Pilgrims were basically the same as those later American colonists would use against the British. So the Pilgrims made a pre-emptive strike against the Pequot. William Bradford described his Pilgrim attack this way:

> They then made the attack with great courage, speedily forcing an entrance to the fort, and shooting amongst them. Those that entered first met with fierce resistance, the enemy shooting and grappling with them. Others of the attacking party ran to their houses and set them on fire, the mats catching quickly, and, all standing close together, the wind soon fanned them into a blaze—in fact more were burnt to death than killed otherwise. It burnt their bowstrings and made their weapons useless, and those that escaped the fire were slain by the sword—some hewn to pieces, others run through with their rapiers, so that they were quickly dispatched and very few escaped. It is believed that there were about 400 killed. It was a fearful sight to see them frying in the fire, with streams of blood quenching it; the smell was horrible, but the victory seemed a sweet sacrifice, and they gave praise to God who had wrought so wonderfully for them, thus to enclose their enemy.[13]

This "sweet sacrifice," then, nicely exposits the American Pilgrim understanding of what it means to love one's enemy: set them on fire, hew them in pieces, and give praise to God for the slaughter. It's a slight twist on the parable of the Good Samaritan, but it sold.

This moment of our national mythology merely foreshadowed what we were to become later. But our later self wasn't much different. During the "good war,"

12. Bradford, *Plymouth,* 286.
13. Ibid., 288.

On March 10 1945, the US abandoned the last rules of warfare
against civilians when 334 B-29's dropped close to half a million incendiary bombs on sleeping Tokyo. The aim was to cause
maximum carnage in an overcrowded city of flimsy wooden
buildings; an estimated 100,000 people were "scorched, boiled
and baked to death," in the words of the attack's architect, General Curtis LeMay. It was then the single largest mass killing of
World War II, dwarfing even the destruction of the German
city of Dresden on Feb. 13, 1945.[14]

Chester Marshall, the B-29 pilot flying above Tokyo that night said, "At
5,000 feet you could smell the flesh burning. . . . I couldn't eat anything
for two or three days."

What is terrorism if this isn't? Terrorism focuses on civilian deaths.
But maybe it was one of those American aberrations again. What is the
U.S. definition of terrorism? In the US Code, Title 18, Part I, Chapter
113B, we say,

> (1) the term "international terrorism" means activities that—
> (A) involve violent acts or acts dangerous to human life that are
> a violation of the criminal laws of the United States or of any
> State, or that would be a criminal violation if committed within
> the jurisdiction of the United States or of any State; (B) appear
> to be intended—(i) *to intimidate or coerce a civilian population*;
> (ii) to influence the policy of a government by intimidation or
> coercion; or (iii) to affect the conduct of a government *by mass
> destruction*, assassination, or kidnapping. (emphasis mine)

Terrorism intends to intimidate a civilian population and influence
policy by mass destruction. Well, by that definition, the United States is
not just accidentally a terrorist nation. That definition in fact describes
official U.S. nuclear policy since before the obliteration of Hiroshima and
Nagasaki. Our standing policy has always been to target civilians. To take
just one example from the past decade, our *National Security Strategy
2006* observes,

> Nuclear weapons are unique in their capacity to inflict instant
> loss of life on a *massive scale*. . . . Our deterrence strategy
> no longer rests primarily on the grim premise of inflicting
> devastating consequences on potential foes. . . . We will always
> proceed deliberately, weighing the consequences of our actions.

14. McNeill, "Night Hell."

The reasons for our actions will be clear, the force measured,
and *the cause just*. (emphasis added)

The US criminal code says targeting civilians through mass destruction is terrorism, and our long-standing nuclear policy says instant, massive loss of civilian life is sound defense policy. How can we not be a terrorist nation?

But would it matter to Christians if we were a terrorist nation? I don't think much would change. Usually, the defender shifts the question away from the immorality of killing civilians to the how we just had to do it in the case of Japan in order to save life. They simply swallow the terrorist side of the point and go on. In principle, we're not all that different from the people we label terrorists. We just have a longer track record, higher death count, and have the money and power to keep a straight face. These things "the Lord hates. . . . hands that shed innocent blood, a heart that devises wicked plans, feet that are swift in running to evil" (Prov 6:16–18).

In speaking of World War I, the great American Presbyterian J. Gresham Machen said, "Imperialism, to my mind, is satanic. . . . The war for humanity, so far as its result is concerned, looks distressingly like an old-fashioned land-grab."[15] In a similar vein in the 1960s, Martin Luther King, Jr. continually exhorted the young men that listened to him to reject violence:

> They asked if our own nation wasn't using massive doses of
> violence to solve its problems, to bring about the changes it
> wanted. Their questions hit home, and I knew that I could nev-
> er again raise my voice against the violence of the oppressed in
> the ghettos without having first spoken clearly to the greatest
> purveyor of violence in the world today—my own government.
> For the sake of those boys, for the sake of this government,
> for the sake of hundreds of thousands trembling under our
> violence, I cannot be silent.[16]

The greatest purveyor of violence in the world? King gained even more opponents with that line. But was he wrong? Was Machen wrong to speak of the powers involved in World War I as Satanic? Of course not. Both followed the ancient prophets. Consider the Roman Empire. Rome certainly saw itself through its emperors as "the savior of the whole human

15. Stonehouse, *Gresham Machen*, 279.
16. King, "Break Silence."

race." The official imperial propaganda of the time spoke glowingly of the Roman Empire:

> Land and sea have peace, the cities flourish under a good legal
> system, in harmony and with an abundance of food, there is
> an abundance of all good things, people are filled with happy
> hopes for the future and with delight at the present.[17]

But, as noted earlier, Daniel described Rome as "exceedingly dreadful, with its teeth of iron and its nails of bronze, which devoured, broke in pieces, and trampled" (Dan 7:19). The book of Revelation picks up Daniel's imagery of the beast of Rome, describing it as a monstrous creature who received its power, throne, and authority from "the dragon" (Rev 13:2) or Satan himself (Rev 12:9). In quite subversive terms, Jesus unveiled the Roman Empire as Satanic. That went contrary to all the official pictures of Rome as the world's great benevolent peacemaker. But if Rome was Satanic, and the United States perpetrated evils far beyond those that ancient Rome ever dreamed of, is it not possible that the United States could justly be called Satanic? Surely, other nations would qualify as well, the Soviet Union and the British Empire. And if the United States is properly a Satanic nation, then our dismissal of Christ and the way of the cross at least becomes more understandable.

The influential French Reformed pastor Jean Lasserre preferred to describe Christian devotion to the military in terms of loyalty to the war god, Mars, rather than Satan. He wrote in terms of what he had seen in World War II among European Christians. Lasserre says Mars is a deity with wide appeal.

> He hides for a while, puts on a skillful disguise, and penetrates
> into the Church of Christ. Christians go on chanting their Savior's praises and victory without realizing that their hearts have
> already been delivered up unresisting to the domination of omnipotent Mars. They sincerely love Christ, but in their churches
> and cathedrals stand the names of those who have given their
> lives for their country. They glorify Christ, but are flattered
> when their sanctuaries are adorned with ex-servicemen's flags.
> They preach Christ, but exalt the greatness of their country
> and the nobility of its heroic defenders. They teach love of one's
> neighbor, but enjoin military service. They say you cannot
> serve God and Mammon, but they themselves serve God and
> Mars. Mars laughs quietly, sure of his triumph—from which

17. Cited in Wengst, *Pax*, 9.

> Mammon too will emerge not without profit. Mars knows he
> can rely on Christians' passive obedience when D-Day comes,
> and he despises the puny sovereignty of Christ, knowing that
> Christ's so-called disciples have already bowed the knee before
> him, Mars.[18]

It certainly takes a deep spirituality like this to explain American devotion to war and violence. It is too strange without it. American Christians still proudly send their sons off to fight for Mars. How can one be part of such a Satanic system and serve Christ? We could turn the question, too: would we be willing to bear the social shame if Christ really did forbid us to take part in the military of a Satanic nation? But didn't he? How much more do we actually need to hear from Jesus beyond the obligation to love our enemies? You may not obey that command of Jesus in any military. You may not give bread and drink and seek the good of your enemy during combat. You cannot seek to kill your enemy and follow the way of the cross.

---

18. Lasserre, *War*, 16.

18

Broad Way Illusions

"Being a Christian should just scare the hell out of us."

– STANLEY HAUERWAS

It's overwhelming. What the Lord requires us *not* to believe in order to follow the way of the cross is just too much. It seems too much not just in terms of actual sacrifice but also in terms of dismissing so much "obvious" knowledge. Just consider the few issues discussed in previous chapters. If the way of the cross is something like what I've sketched and argued for, then we're called to dismiss traditional applications of providence, sin, heaven, atonement, fundamental political axioms, handy conservative principles, cemented assumptions about property, the prosperity of the west, the benevolence and honor of U.S. military history, the simple pattern of middle class living, centuries of individualist indoctrination, and all the trillions of dollars spent in advertising and government propaganda to catechize more and more in the ways of Mammon. It would require living contrary to the testimony of thousands of well-loved theologians, politicians, economists, historians, satisfied middle class people, Christian family, and friends. And each generation of Christians would have to renew that renunciation in its own era. It's just too much. The slogan "let God be true though every man a liar" would take on unbearable social weight. The broad way works so hard to keep us from the truth.

Dostoevsky recreates this unbearable sense of the "narrow way" with the murder evidence brought against Dmitri Karamazov. Dostoevsky already set us up for doubting the cost of following the narrow way earlier in the novel in the Grand Inquisitor's discussion. There we learned that the church had to explain to Jesus that the way of the cross required too much freedom and responsibility. It wasn't a light yoke at all. So the church "fixed" it and made on the broad way of destruction the normal way. It was a reasonable decision. Then later in the novel, Dostoevsky brilliantly forces this same decision on the reader. The evidence against Dmitri is overwhelming. Even Dmitri recognizes this. He even admits evidence against himself. He had hated his father and threatened to kill him. He was lurking in the shadows that night. But he didn't kill Fyodor. But all the reasonable and dignified people can't see the truth. The evidence is too strong the other way. Dostoevsky gives us long, blind speeches from both the prosecution and defense that confirm the tedious broad way. To believe in Dmitri's innocence requires isolation and insanity. But the reader knows the truth. And still, we would have had to join all the mediocre minds in condemning Dmitri, and Jesus. So much authority and academic insight and imperial power condemned Jesus. How could all that credentialed power be so blind? But it was.

Winston in Orwell's *1984* faced a similar wholesale deception. He knew the truth, but it was an exceedingly narrow path. Every public and private social pressure in his totalitarian world rejected the simple truths he knew. To counter them required unbelievable insight and courage. Winston tried to live his narrow path secretly.

> He wondered, as he had many times before, whether he himself
> was a lunatic. Perhaps a lunatic was simply a minority of one.
> At one time it had been a sign of madness to believe that the
> earth goes round the sun. . . . But the thought of being a lunatic
> did not greatly trouble him; the horror was that he might also
> be wrong.[1]

"Perhaps a lunatic was simply a minority of one." Isn't that phrase just a shade away from Jesus's "narrow is the gate and difficult is the way which leads to life, and there are few who find it" (Matt 7:14)? Few. Not many find it. They have to see past all the piles of counterevidence and tasty

---

1. Orwell, *1984*, 70, 71.

propaganda that warms and fills us. As Bonhoeffer said in mock resignation, "Well, then, let the Christian live like the rest of the world, let him model himself on the world's standards in every sphere of life, and not presumptuously aspire to live a different life under grace."[2]

The greatest of the broad way blinders isn't something as dark as a murder trial or a totalitarian nightmare. It's something as simple and pervasive as the assumptions of middle class life. If we're living the pleased and grateful middle class life, buying and selling, embracing and eating, then hearing Jesus's words about the way of the cross just can't be as radical as all that. He loves middle class people and has a wonderful plan for our lives. And so many of us believe the same version of the Christian story. We just have to believe in Jesus's death and go about our normal middle class lives, just being sure to hate evolutionists, abortionists, and homosexuals. That's all that's required. All our friends and sister denominations have confirmed this for decades. We have fixed the gospel.

But did Jesus allow Christians to live normal, modern middle class lives? Are we allowed to ask that question? What if the answer were, no? What if Jesus, as part of his repudiation of the broad way, asked his followers not to lead, normal middle class lives? What if he had exhorted us, instead, to live very differently, to not be part of the normal career and mortgage and vacation system? Would we be able to hear him?

He seems to have done just that, didn't he? In the parable of the sower, Jesus laid out the narrow vs. broad way in visual terms. The sower sowed his seed in four places, the wayside, on rocks, among thorns, and in good soil. Satanic theft and persecutions frightened away the first two sorts of believers, whether rich or poor. Then the thorns get some of the others: those who "are choked with cares, riches, and pleasures of life, and bring no fruit to maturity" (Luke 8:14). Does this group, "choked with cares, riches, and pleasure," include modern middle class people like us? No, we say. Look, we hold true beliefs about Jesus and the Christian worldview in our heads, contrary to those cowardly liberals who quiver before Enlightenment idols. And besides, the people in the parable are extremes, "choked" with life concerns. Not us. We have to work hard to pay our bills and send the kids to college, but that's not being choked. Those choked are people beyond us, Christians who have houses and cars much bigger than our own. Never us.

2. Bonhoeffer, *Cost*, 44.

But, in the Sermon on the Mount, Jesus explained what it was to be choked by cares of this world. He set the bar much lower than the super rich: "Therefore I say to you, do not worry about your life, what you will eat or what you will drink; nor about your body, what you will put on. Is not life more than food and the body more than clothing?. . . Therefore do not worry, saying, 'What shall we eat?' or 'What shall we drink?' or 'What shall we wear?' For after all these things the Gentiles seek" (Matt 6:25ff.). The first way we deflect this exhortation is to reduce it, again, to questions about excess anxiety. Jesus was just talking about excess worry, and we don't do that, especially if we're good Protestant stoics. So the verse can never stick against us. As long as we're not anxious, we can be as deeply enmeshed in cares and bills as we like.

Jesus, though, spoke to people who had real worries about food and clothing. That would be the lower classes, who followed him about, fishermen and such. Modern middle class folks aren't desperate for food and clothing. We have those, though it sometimes takes some budget-ary hand-wringing at the end of the month. And if he's exhorting lower classes on these points, then middle class folks are already firmly in the realm of those "choked with cares, riches, and pleasure." We seem already to have been written off. We don't show up in his audience. "For after all these things the Gentiles seek." That's the group we fall in with. And to us in that group, he says, How hard it is for those who have plumbed water, electricity, a good sewage system, a mortgage, and a running car to enter the kingdom of God.

Again, Jesus is not against wealth and property, just unsacrificial ways of holding it. He's against those who gather wealth for their own families and not the whole body. He's against individual and family self-ishness, the heart of modern middle class living. His solution is not to give up wealth or steel our wills with stoic psychology but to seek the church: "Seek first the kingdom of God and His righteousness, and all these things shall be added to you" (Matt 6:33). His kingdom somehow supplies our electricity, clean water, and clothes, not our own family-focused careers. The believers in Acts eliminated the anxiety over food and clothes, not by psychology but by sharing: "Nor was there anyone among them who lacked." The kingdom removed individual anxiety by becoming a strong, economic center.

Whatever ways in which the church-kingdom becomes that eco-nomic center, it is not typical middle class life. It is not the typical, mun-dane world of the gentiles, "choked with cares, riches, and pleasure."

Christ does not want us serving God and the middle class system. He wants a kingdom of radical freedom, not one enslaved by individualized wealth. This new kingdom takes great imagination and adventure, with plenty of trial and error. Middle class living is extremely easy and seductive.

But to go against the middle class vision requires too much courage, too much imagination and energy and a driving love to deliver. Contrary to all evidence, we have to believe Dmitri was innocent. Like Winston, we have to be some kind of lunatic minority.

That sort of talk provokes the sorts of doubt that Jesus did. After preaching, one of Jesus's followers asked, "Lord, are there few who are saved?" (Luke 13:23). Think about that question. Generally, our preaching doesn't provoke that sort of challenge because for us all that matters is believing the right truths about Christ. Middle class folks can do that rather easily. Cheap grace like that doesn't require any real sacrifice, since that sounds like works and works are arrogant. End of discussion. But Jesus's warnings against the typical system of wealth provoked the question, "Who then can be saved?" (Luke 18:26). If "successful" people don't fit comfortably within the way of Jesus's church, then who can? Again, Jesus pointed them back to the very different nature of his kingdom-church (Luke 18:29,30).

Maybe we can find a better way to avoid the narrow-way teachings of Jesus. Instead of granting that Jesus's way is always for a few, perhaps we've misunderstood those verses. What ways have we made to minimize Jesus's dichotomy between the narrow and broad?

We often try to get those verses to work within our intellectualized version of the gospel. We say that to follow the narrow way is the path of believing unbelievable things that millions of Christians believe but a majority of non-Christians can't. We believe in Adam and Eve, the virgin birth, and resurrection, whereas non-Christians don't. The problem with this answer is that Jesus didn't speak of unbelievers in those contexts. He had only believers in mind. In the parable of the sower, he spoke of four kinds of believers, not unbelief. Similarly, in the Sermon on the Mount, his talk of narrow and broad sits in the context of "Not everyone who says to Me, 'Lord, Lord,' shall enter the kingdom of heaven." Christians make up the broad path. Christians who have preached, exorcized demons, and performed miracles (Matt 7:22).

Others recognized the Christian context of the verses but looked to hard doctrine to divide the narrow and broad ways. Spurgeon was notorious for this move. He put all his intellectual opponents in the broad way and kept the narrow way for hard-minded, doctrinal people like himself: "at this time, to be popular one must be broad—broad in doctrine, in morals, and in spirituals. . . . Lord deliver me from the temptation to be 'broad,' and keep me in the narrow way though few find it!"[3] On the contemporary scene, the Westboro Baptist sorts—"God hates fags"—do something similar. Sure, they follow a narrow way that stirs up opposition, but it's not in obedience to Jesus's commands to love their enemies. They hate their enemies. Jesus spoke of the narrow way in the context of visible fruit not mere ideas (Matt 7:16) and active obedience: "whoever hears these sayings of Mine, and does them, I will liken him to a wise man who built his house on the rock" (Matt 7:24). One doesn't "do" hard beliefs, say like double predestination or limited atonement. The closest one can *do* "hard doctrine" is perhaps to hold it smugly, contrary to intellectual "cowards." But the commands Jesus had just given focused on living against Mammon, against violence, against hating enemies, and more. We can easily hear these and not do them. That captures most Christians.

Sometimes we explain away the dichotomy of narrow and broad by limiting Jesus's application to the first century. We say Jesus wasn't describing the church through the centuries but just the problematic of the first century. He didn't have millions of modern Western Christians in mind, just the narrow remnant of first-century Jews. That's certainly one angle he applies, especially in Luke 13:22ff. But that can't be the whole answer, since the Jewish remnant isn't invoked in the Sermon on the Mount. As we've seen, those on the broad way preached and did miracles in Jesus's name (Matt 7:22), Christians not Jews, and the disciples' question, "Who then can be saved?" (Luke 18:26) came in response to Jesus's comments on the rich in general: "How hard it is for those who have riches to enter the kingdom of God" (Luke 18:24). That's not a comment about first-century riches alone. It's a universal warning.

Some also minimize the narrow-way teaching by holding up prophetic passages about the worldwide success of Christ's gospel. Habakkuk prophesied, "the earth will be filled with the knowledge of the glory of the LORD, as the waters cover the sea" (Hab 2:14). That clearly doesn't sound like a narrow way. Waters cover the sea in the broadest way imaginable. In the same way, Daniel prophesied that Christ's kingdom would become "a great mountain" and fill "the whole earth" (Dan 2:35). Jeremiah, too,

---

3. Cited in Greenman, *Sermon*, 186.

prophesied of the New Covenant that "they all shall know Me, from the least of them to the greatest of them" (Jer 31:24). That seems to be an exact reversal of the broad way and narrow way. So how do these passages fit?

Of course we have to always keep in mind the operatic or apocalyptic language of the prophets. They often captured realities that appear exaggerated on earth. Describing Babylon's fall, Isaiah said, "For the stars of heaven and their constellations will not give their light; the sun will be darkened in its going forth, and the moon will not cause its light to shine" (Isa 13:10), and when Ezekiel described the fall of Egypt he said the Lord would, "cover the heavens, and make its stars dark. . . and the moon shall not give her light" (Ezek 34:7–8). Many of us readily recognize the apocalyptic exaggeration in these negative passages, and we're obligated to remember the same answer works for the positive passages, too.

But Jesus captured the best of both worlds—optimism and the way of the cross—in his reply to the disciples who had given up all for him:

> Assuredly, I say to you, there is no one who has left house or
> brothers or sisters or father or mother or wife or children or
> lands, for My sake and the gospel's, who shall not receive a
> hundredfold now in this time—houses and brothers and sisters
> and mothers and children and lands, with persecutions—and
> in the age to come, eternal life. But many who are first will be
> last, and the last first. (Mark 10:29–31)

"Receive a hundredfold now in this time." He promises astounding material and social blessings to those who follow the way of the cross, to those who have taken up the way of deliverance and sharing. Through life of the kingdom-church, we can share in great wealth. Again, the saints in early Acts showed this in concrete terms. They actually gained wealth as a whole, and later monastic movements became very wealthy, too. We want to make sure all in need grow in shared wealth. But, notice, in the midst of these very real and tangible kingdom riches, hundredfold people and lands, Jesus promises that "persecution" will continue. We sometimes imagine the optimistic future promised by the prophets as a time of Christian state domination, where we control all political, artistic, and economic power. But that's not Jesus' vision. That's just Mammon with a Christian label. Isaiah's vision of a blessed future wasn't of a bustling, powerful Christian metropolis but rather a basic peasant's, Hobbits' existence. In the world where the "the wolf and the lamb shall feed together" (Isa 65:25), we see simple, non-luxurious life:

They shall build houses and inhabit them;
They shall plant vineyards and eat their fruit.
They shall not build and another inhabit;
They shall not plant and another eat;
For as the days of a tree, so shall be the days of My people,
And My elect shall long enjoy the work of their hands.
They shall not labor in vain,
Nor bring forth children for trouble. (Isa 65:21–23)

And even in that serene scene, Jesus promised continuing persecution. It will not go away entirely. Jesus promised. And we should be highly suspicious when the church's godly repudiation of Mammon doesn't provoke persecution.

The great Christian leader, Oscar Romero famously observed before his 1980 assassination, "a church that suffers no persecution but enjoys the privileges and support of the things of the earth—beware!—is not the true church of Jesus Christ."[4] He explained,

a church that doesn't provoke any crises,
a gospel that doesn't unsettle,
a word of God that doesn't get under anyone's skin,
a word of God that doesn't touch the real sin
of society in which it is being proclaimed—
what gospel is that?
Very nice, pious considerations that don't bother anyone.[5]

The way of the cross is the way of persecution. Jesus promised. And if we live in a society, like the modern west, where the church isn't persecuted—no, secular taunts don't count—then either we're a thoroughly Christianized culture or we've been thoroughly co-opted by Mammon. We are not a threat to the dominant system. As Romero said, we preach a "very spiritualized word, a word without any commitment to history, a word that can sound in any part of the world because it belongs to no part of the world."[6] The narrow way is a hard way. Few find it. It takes overwhelming courage to reject the broad way. Few want to see the narrow way. It's easier to insulate ourselves from its demands and just talk about doctrine and interpreting the Bible forever. "You search the Scriptures,

4. Romero, *Love*, 125.
5. Ibid., 44.
6. Ibid., 18.

for in them you think you have eternal life; and these are they which testify of Me" (John 5:39).

But if the narrow way is hard, requiring us to give up our lives, then what about Jesus' promise that his way was easy? On the one hand, Jesus told us to take up, daily, the way of public humiliation, self-denial, and death, the way of the cross, and yet he also said his burden was light:

> Come to Me, all you who labor and are heavy laden, and I
> will give you rest. Take My yoke upon you and learn from Me,
> for I am gentle and lowly in heart, and you will find rest for
> your souls. For My yoke is easy and My burden is light. (Matt
> 11:28–30).

As good moderns, we often immediately privatize this and hear Jesus talking about our individual lives. But a yoke was a way of describing an oppressive political system. The Lord described Israel's slavery in Egypt as a yoke: "I have broken the bands of your yoke and made you walk upright" (Lev 26:13). He then threatened his people that he would make them "serve your enemies" or "put a yoke of iron on your neck" (Deut 28:48). Jeroboam pled with Rehoboam against his father's, Solomon's tyranny: "Your father made our yoke heavy; now therefore, lighten the burdensome service of your father, and his heavy yoke which he put on us, and we will serve you" (1 Kgs 12:4).

In contrast to the politics of the Roman Empire and the Jewish Temple, Jesus promised a kingdom-church that would be a refuge for the oppressed. It would be a place where the least would be lifted up and protected. It would be the kingdom which lived in accord with the Sermon on the Mount and exemplified the beatitudes. That was great news, deliverance from the kingdom of Mammon. Jesus' kingdom is a place of initial and continuing deliverances from dominations and slavery, external and internal—"I will not be brought under the power of any" (1 Cor 6:12).

The apparently conflicting commands of the great cost of the way of the cross and the easy yoke also come from different perspectives. From the perspective of the world and Mammon, the way of the cross is a great burden. We have to give up everything Mammon holds precious—self-interest, unsacrificial wealth, effectiveness of violence, honor, and glory. But from within Jesus' kingdom those things are demonic oppressors. They are principalities and powers that weigh us down. Jesus' yoke, then is indeed easy from within the life of the Trinity. Self-denial is the adventure of great freedom. The way of the cross is a dance through the Red Sea.

PART THREE

Constructing
the Way of the Cross

19

Being the Kingdom-Church

A round AD 382, after a severe drought hit Cappadocia (modern east-ern Turkey), the church father, Gregory of Nyssa wrote of the poor that had flooded the capital city, Caesarea (Mazaka):

> We are not lacking in sojourners and exiles, and pleading
> hands are extended to us everywhere. These people's shelter is
> the open sky. . . . They wear rags for clothing; their only harvest
> is the goodness of those who give them alms.[1]

The bishop of the city, the noted father Basil of Caesarea, moved the church in several significant ways to serve the refugees. In a more per-manent way, Basil established a genuine Christian city on a hill, outside of Caesarea, later known as the Basiliad. Under his direction, the church there created

> a large complex of buildings that provided shelter for travelers,
> medical care for the ill—especially those, such as lepers, whom
> society at large despised—food for the hungry, and occupation
> for many who otherwise would be unemployed.[2]

Clergy oversaw the day-to-day administration of the new town. It had an early hospital, residences for the poor and clergy, "small factories or workshops for teaching and practicing trades. Some of these were either

1. Cited in Gonzalez, *Faith and Wealth*, 174. See also, Holman, *Wealth and Poverty* and Holman, *Hungry*.

2. Gonzalex, *Faith and Wealth*, 182–83.

entirely unprecedented, or at least relatively novel, for their day."[3] The town had some precedents and appears to have been connected to other similar projects in the Caesarea area. The project grew quickly.

> As the Basileias grew, it attracted poor immigrants from many other places, quite distant, who upon their arrival were also enrolled in its program of charity and work.[4]

The Basiliad went on to influence other churches in other regions for many years. Here, finally, was a city on a hill that captured the way of the cross. In many ways, whatever its details and failings, Basil's work stood out as a wonderful symbol of Christ's gospel.

Christ's gospel is the story of deliverance, a release from a spiritual-material tyranny, the principalities and powers of Satan/Mammon. The church is the new kingdom of refuge: "He has delivered us from the power of darkness and conveyed us into the kingdom of the Son of His love" (Col 1:13). We too often understand Paul's summary in purely spiritual-intellectual terms, but for the weak the church is an actual place of refuge and freedom. It is supposed to be a move from an unjust and uncaring domain into a kingdom of support, justice, and friends. It is the move from one political entity to another, and if that move is incomplete or merely about "worldview," then we haven't yet been delivered from the kingdom of Mammon. We're called to create a whole, competing city, not just a lecture room. Segundo Galilea expressed some of the simple joy of this sort of kingdom building in his description of the opening of a new medical clinic in a "miserable little village of the Andes" in Peru—"no hospital, no medicines, no doctors or nurses." The people of the village have no money to travel to the city. Many of them suffer greatly from their illnesses and die early. In the same village, "there is also a group of families in more comfortable circumstances. They can afford to travel to the city for medical care. Finally, one day, the church sets up a well-staffed and well-equipped medical clinic. The poor can receive treatment right there in their village, and the clinic offers its services and medicines for free.

> Now comes the day of the formal opening. A priest is asked to bless the new facility. He says—this minister of Christ: "You are happy ones today, you, the poor of this village. For this clinic is yours. It belongs to you."

3. Holman, *Wealth*, 269.
4. Ibid.

At first glance it may seem that the priest's assertion is not precisely accurate. Actually, the clinic is for everyone, is it not? . . . So why does the priest mention only the poor?

> For a very good reason. It is the poor who have the most reason to rejoice, most reason to be "happy" about the clinic. For the poor, more than for those of the village in more comfortable circumstances, the clinic is the fulfillment of an ancient promise. It is "good news." It is a great source of help. True, the clinic is not for them alone. It is for the rich and poor alike. *But its primary beneficiaries are the poor.*[5]

"For theirs is the kingdom of heaven" (Matt 5:3). And it is a kingdom, growing whole and complete, and it's not aping Mammon's way: "Render therefore to Caesar the things that are Caesar's, and to God the things that are God's" (Matt 22:21).

I raise the Basiliad and the medical clinic, here, in this chapter to mark it as a visual goal for a constructive vision. The first part of this book sought to offer a constructive scriptural narrative for the way of the cross, rooted in the Old Covenant and expressed most fully in Christ. The book's second part focused more critically on special blinders that keep us from seeing the way of the cross. But one can't start either of those discussions before sympathetic minds quickly begin to ask for practical suggestions and ideas for local churches. That's what this chapter aims to do in a weak way.

It would be far more convincing and helpful for me to be able to draw on several decades of my own practice to make such suggestions. But that was nowhere near my life, though I search for it now. As much as I'd like to avoid this chapter, the argument can't end with the second part. I will certainly be pointing to and drawing from those who have many decades of working in churches and projects that have aimed to incarnate the way of the cross. Their experience is invaluable and nonromantic. But for folks on my end of things, I still think I might have something to contribute. Consider, then, this closing attempt at constructive, practical thinking as a yearning that might be helpful to others struggling with the baby steps. It aims in broad ways to show the direction local churches might start going, and it offers some qualifications and explanations not found earlier.

5. Galilea, *Beatitudes*, 14–15.

Basil's city, though, starts off as a visual goal to which the way of the cross points. It was an actual city of mercy, not developed along the lines typical of Mammon then or now. It was a city focused on weakness, deliverance, and sharing. But most importantly, it was in principle a city competing against the cities of Mammon. This doesn't mean that is was in practice holding forth an explicitly, libertarian-individualist sort of hostility to anything from the state. Sometimes churches and local government officials can work together wonderfully. But the ideal Jesus holds up, as described in earlier chapters, is a kingdom-city that aims in certain ways to be self-sufficient from the ways of Mammon, a cruciform city centered in the beatitudes and the Sermon on the Mount, Christ's unprincipled "constitution" of virtues and instincts and habits and Spirit.

Most churches now don't see themselves even moving in the direction of becoming full-orbed cities for mercy, manufacturing, farming, education, etc. Churches generally act more like think tanks, where people go for weekly inspirational encouragement. We might do some marginal mercy work, some charity, and the like, and give plenty of Bible studies. But that's it. We don't think of Christ's kingdom heavily involved in manufacturing and creativity and rescue. Yet work, for example, is one of the primary ways of catechizing Christians. But work's very spiritual training, outside the church's influence, is usually catechizing in Mammon. If we're called to renounce Mammon, then we have to create or encourage business and occupations where Christians can seek first the kingdom, not profit, the bottom line, and self-interested pricing. We need to create a city on a hill that imitates Christ.

I've mentioned local churches several times because I see them as the heart of Christian politics. I don't think we should any serious or concerted interest in national politics, candidates, and parties. I can't remember the last year I voted in a national or state election. Would the apostles really have spent so much time, signatures, lobby groups, and money to bring to power the Roman emperor that sounded most friendly to Christians? That was the world of Mammon, as is ours. Christians getting excited about the latest figure-head president, whether Left or Right, are Christians who have a very narrow view of Christ's kingdom. Why help Mammon build its kingdom or try to redeem Mammon? Church and state solve problems differently. The state has no promise of the Spirit and the depths of the human heart. The state can only look on the surface, and that's not God's way. The state can only deal with externals, and that will always be halfway and ineffective. The state excels at coercion and violence, even when implied, and that's not Christ's way. Christ's kingdom works in the realm of interior virtues and love. The state can have no grasp of that world. In many ways, the church-state contrast is like that of the Old and New Covenants. "For the law was given through Moses, but grace and truth came through Jesus Christ" (John 1:17). To imitate or use the state now is to return to immaturity.

National programs and parties have merely been ways to distract Christians from building Christ's kingdom. The distraction has worked quite effectively. Imagine if Christians in Western nations had instead spent their money and time and lobbying developing hundreds of thousands of small, competing "cities" within the world that positively embodied our values, instead of begging governments to impose, powerless external codes to curtail outward behaviors of nonbelievers. We would have been much more effective and much more of a threat. "If there had been a law given which could have given life, truly righteousness would have been by the law" (Gal 3:21). Trusting in external codes for morality moves in the direction of greater immaturity. That was the Old Covenant without the Spirit. And we fell for it in modern times and supported those candidates that lied to us decade after decade. All the while, churches became less relevant and moved farther away from Christ's kingdom because we'd joined the opposing project. It was all a masterful misdirection.

If we start thinking more in terms of building Basiliads, that require churches to use all the skills in the congregation—administrative, manufacturing, aesthetic, mathematical, business, and more—all within the way of the cross, then we will be building Christ's city on a hill.

But churches have to be at the center of such a shift. It is not a calling for individuals alone. As argued earlier, the Sermon on the Mount seems designed to crush enthusiastic individuals who want to give up all their stuff and become radical hermits all on their lonesome. Christ doesn't need any more hermits. We're called to make Trinity here, and that means he has called communities of disciples to live his kingdom. Sometimes this takes time and many transitions. Sometimes churches themselves will be the biggest obstacles. But lone rangers who read a book and burn to be radical will not last long. We need like-minded communities, dedicated to patience, love, and self-denial.

Carrying out the kingdom in this way will require the freedom to experiment and fail. It will require the looseness to forgive over and over, to learn more and more. Such faithfulness is not romantic. Historically, as groups of believers have tried to come together and live the kingdom in the Sermon on the Mount, they have faced far more trials and temptations than they ever experienced before. Most moves to do this faced great internal pressures to fail and many times violent reactions from without. We can never appreciate the power of the Sermon on the Mount until a community really tries to live it. Then all hell seems to break lose. Historically, too many practitioners seemed clueless at the vengeance they would encounter from simple experiments in challenging nice Mammon. The proud, the glory-hungry, the romantics almost always implode or get crushed. Movements scatter. Leaders die. Christ's kingdom is not for the squeamish, and it's that danger that confirms Christ's constant warning about taking up his cross. Jesus regularly warned people away from his kingdom. But it promised far greater life than that pushed by those chanting "we have no king but Caesar."

20

Getting There

If something like Basil's project was the right direction, then how do
we transition there? It's easy for some of us to delay by over-intellec-
tualizing the situation. We sometimes don't make simple moves because
we need to have all the details worked out beforehand. Sure, we'll run
into complications and obstacles peculiar to each of our situations, but
we must always keep in mind that Jesus's commands are indeed pretty
simple and straightforward. Yes, we've covered them in centuries of rationalizations and distractions, but once free of those the Lord welcomes us
into a world of trial, error, and failure as we relearn his basics.

In making our move along the path of the cross, the church should
shape our planning and practice. Jesus promised the Spirit to the church,
not to lone individuals or parachurch organizations, as helpful as these
will be at times. So, if you're an individual Christian, outside of church
leadership roles, then perhaps the easiest path would be to find a congregation or community already committed to various expressions of the
way of the cross. The world is full of them, once you start to look around.
Over the past ten to twenty years, more and more congregations have
been waking up to the ways of the cross, and many have decades of experience. Go and listen. Go and serve. Go and apprentice.

Of course, this simple advice assumes few connections to family and
work. It's a direction for youth. Many of us can't just get up and go where
the action is because we're turning around later in life. We are devoted
wives and husbands, with kids and a mortgage. We're heavily involved

with the system of Mammon and an immediate break would be unfair to those we're connected to. They didn't originally sign on for this "new" way (neither did we). They may some day be persuaded, but, then again, they may not. We're called to serve and love them and still aim to be disciples of Christ.

We have to grant that people bound in these situations are similar to those to whom Jesus said, "Follow Me," and we replied, "Lord, I will follow You, but let me first go *and* bid them farewell who are at my house" (Luke 9:61). Jesus didn't look too kindly on that response. He said, "No one, having put his hand to the plow, and looking back, is fit for the kingdom of God" (Luke 9:62). How do we escape the dilemma? How do we sacrifice our lives for our families and heed Jesus' call? Maybe confession? We can confess our predicament and plead for mercy. We can confess being enmeshed with idols and pray for persuasion, patience, and opportunities to open up that would be accommodating. And I think we also need to be open to hear Jesus's judgment that we may not be "fit for the kingdom of God." If I can see where Christ wants me to go, and I can't get there in the time and manner he would seem to require, then I should be willing to accept his sentence. He's a just judge, and I will follow after him in my crippled manner from a distance, even if he needs to cut me out of the kingdom. I'll accept it and keep praying for a door.

Others of us might already be serving in some form of church leadership, perhaps deacons, elders, pastors, or other staff. You have to weigh your situation even more carefully, because you are part of the institution called to lead people in the way of the cross. You have to weigh your situation carefully and honestly evaluate your influence, voice, and opportunity. Should you seek to reform or seek another more cross-friendly work? The typical American-Protestant way is to take the alleged high ground and create another split church. Throw a fit, play the prophet, and convince the other leaders and congregants that they definitely want nothing to do with the way of the cross. That's tiresome and bears little fruit.

In most circumstances, the move to raise the questions in the way of the cross produces quick and visible resistance. It becomes clear instantly that discussion shuts down and walls go up. Should you spend the next decade trying quietly and peacefully to persuade folks who clearly have no interest in even talking about these issues? Situations will differ. Some might make that choice, especially if you're younger. But older believers need to seriously consider the cost. Does Jesus really want us to spend decades wasting time, begging to get a word in now and then? In most situations that seems like a bad call. Jesus didn't spend all his time trying to politely woo the religious establishment. They had the training and responsibility to be more teachable than the flock. Jesus didn't waste time. He went, instead, to those in real need. Avoiding the very strong temptation to prophetic self-righteousness, we have to be ready at some point to hear Jesus's command: "And whoever will not receive you nor hear your words, when you depart from that house or city, shake off the dust from your feet" (Luke 10:14). Move on. Find a more fruitful way to serve elsewhere.

If you're higher in leadership, perhaps a lead pastor, and you come to these convictions and no one else around you does, then you need to guard your commitments to the people around you carefully. If it took you decades to see the way of the cross, you can't expect others to see it overnight. But you might have more leeway than others to preach and try to lead your people into the way of Christ. Depending on your relationship to other leaders and members, this might go fruitfully for a while. But, remember, we're dealing with deep spiritual, sometimes idolatrous commitments in these issues, and most often you should expect things to go sour. You can't expect other people to be as excited as you are, and it's difficult work turning around an aircraft carrier. Look for the writing on the wall, the circling of wagons. If you can spot it far enough ahead, then be sure to develop some "tent-making" abilities. As Wendell Berry once reportedly said to a group of seminary students, one of the drawbacks of having a church salary instead of tent-making pay is that church-salaried leaders can't tell the truth to their congregants. Telling the truth requires some financial independence, but if leaders and a congregation can threaten us financially, then we pull our punches. Plan ahead.

Maybe that's not your situation. Maybe you're a lead pastor, and the people around you have been happily urging you down this path for years. You finally come around, and you're now in the middle of a like-minded leadership willing and eager to change. You're in a good position, and you can move more quickly. Still, you don't want to trample congregants who may not be where you and your leaders are. Self-denial and empathy are still key.

Instead of expecting a majority of a congregation to turn around quickly, even with good teaching, consider setting up experimental ministries, small works that head in the right direction, even imperfectly. Many people's resistance to the way of the cross stems from fear. Fear of the poor. Fear of change. Fear of leaving the broad way. Sometimes, these people overcome their fears when they can see a once-worrisome mercy project do good work in a short space of time. Choose a mercy work small enough that doesn't redirect the church in a completely new direction at first and distant enough to the worriers that they're not immediately threatened. Lord willing, over time and with good fruit from the work, they'll pick up on the call, too.

One direction to avoid, however, would be the typical, risk-free sort of mercy ministries that conservative churches are happy to do. Aim for a work with more at stake. We want to avoid being those rich who merely give out of their abundance. Jesus had no interest in them. Those sorts of ministries allow us to stay the same and keep the poor at a safe distance. Sometimes food banks, pregnancy clinics, second-hand clothing stores can do this. Not all, especially those connected to ministries with other more sacrificial works in place. The key in establishing pilot ministries would be to set them up in ways that require more sacrifice and identity with the poor. Maybe it involves planting a small church, with a way-of-the-cross core group in a low income area. Maybe it involves trying to setup a real sister-church relationship with an existing minority church. Lead with confession and much listening. Be sure to be very familiar with those who have successfully walked these deeper paths, especially folks like Mark Gornik—*To Live in Peace: Biblical Faith and the Changing Inner City*; and Robert Linthicum—*Building a People of Power;* and the New Monastics—*Schools for Conversion: 12 Marks of a New Monasticism;* and David Platt—*Radical Together: Unleashing the People of God for the Purpose of God;* and Ron Sider's reflections on several fruitful and wholistic works—*Bread of Life: Stories of Radical Mission.*

Then follow their footnotes, but don't read forever. Jump in and start making your own mistakes.

With an enthusiastic leadership, one of the first things to do would be to reprioritize the typical budget, following patterns suggested in Acts. Instead of focusing a church budget with middle-class goals (buildings, audio ministries, expensive web pages, comfortable salaries, etc.), the church could refocus its goal on direct works of deliverance. Small churches can encourage tent-making funding for all full-time elders and pastors. At the same time, it might seek full-time pay for those in diaconal or mercy positions. The last shall be first. As a church moves from the traditional teaching-obsessed model to one more service-centered, members will need to take over more and more work, women and men, young and old.

With a church budget prioritized around the way of the cross, many things that were marginal become central, and vice versa. One of the goals is to create a community situation where Jesus's seemingly crazy exhortation against savings—"Do not lay up for yourselves treasures on earth"—makes sense. Imagine a situation where members need not fear living check to check. In an American context, people regularly face bankruptcy from medical emergencies. The church should be able to relieve that fear and others like it, like unemployment. Ideally, a large diaconal fund should be able to cover member medical, education, and even housing costs at some point. Remove those items from a typical American-Christian budget, and members will start having some serious money to use for building the kingdom.

Within an enthusiastic church, one of the biggest (and most worrisome) goals would be to get the leadership and some members headed in the direction of living on half their incomes. This comes from the example of Zacchaeus. It's not an absolute rule, but it's a great aim. It might start off as a smaller percentage. It might end up larger. But we know Jesus was pleased with Zacchaeus's half. For some, such a move will be easy. For others, it will take years. Many will need to find ways to get free from all their debts. If you have any very wealthy members, maybe they could seed a jubilee-type of ministry dedicated to subsidizing and freeing members from debt, with written commitments never to go there again. All of this will involve some strategic planning, perhaps involving sale of houses, changes of job, and moves to more modest housing. This should all be voluntary and driven by great love and joy. Leadership needs to live this first and learn the hard transition solutions.

Imagine a church diaconal fund made up of half the incomes of its families. That community can, then, start down the path of some serious kingdom projects. Of course, churches that go this particular route should be extremely transparent about book-keeping. Make it easy for every members to see every move, even daily if need be. Overall, leadership in this sort of congregation will generally have to be much more open, democratic, delegating, receptive, and communal than traditional teaching-centered churches. Building a Christ's kingdom requires all of the gifts of the body, not just teaching.

Different churches could organize the funds in numerous, imaginative, legal ways. Many gather it in a common but transparent purse.

Other traditions build mutual aid societies. Whatever way works best. Once we help free our own people from Mammon, the more we'll be able to follow the way of the cross and reach out with serious relief to those around us. Again, there's no lockstep order to these kinds of steps. Some may start with delivering outsiders and then turn within.

In the midst of reprioritized Zacchaeus types of sharing and tent-making, a majority of the congregation needs to aim to disconnect from their dependence on Mammon's eight-hour or more work days. This may take years, too. But Christians waste too much kingdom time serving Mammon's bottom line. We live in a world of competing kingdoms. Why spend so much time serving businesses that don't contribute to direct kingdom work? Sure, we tell ourselves we earn plenty of money at a good corporation so we can donate to the kingdom. But is that what Jesus asked? Isn't that what the rich at the temple were doing in Jesus day? He sniffed at that. At the last day, Matthew 25 doesn't have the Lord praising those who donated big chunks of change but those so dedicated to the weak that they didn't even know they were doing it. We're called primarily to clothe and feed, not finance. I speak of long-term goals, not transitional funding.

In our current teaching-focused context, to urge members toward more church work means they need more education so they can teach. But in a broader kingdom model, we don't need so many teachers. We need what members are already good at in their prior professions and trades. If we're encouraging people out of serving in the system of Mammon, that doesn't mean we don't want them building and manufacturing. Churches need to encourage those same activities within the activities of the church. As in the Basiliade, churches need to take the trades seriously. We need to get into manufacturing so that, for example, we don't have to force the Third World poor to work for slave wages to make our clothes. Churches need to learn to make their own clothes. We need to create humane places for work, with shorter work days and kingdom goals. The church needs to lead in this since we failed our Third World brothers and sisters so miserably. Of course, we need to go beyond making clothing, though that would be gigantic in itself, requiring many talents. Churches need to expand into other areas given up to Mammon as well: furniture, farming, financial institutions, and more.

Smarty-conservatives will balk at taking over clothing manufacturing. They like to say (in zero-sum fashion) that making our own clothing will create more poverty by removing much-needed jobs. This omits the point that American business interests helped rig world systems to force our overseas brothers and sisters into unjust jobs. And a better solution isn't to leave them in the sweat shops for generations but to create more Basiliads in those countries. Create good work places in those countries, and get Christians in the West to pay much more for clothing. Or bring those brethren into our Basiliads, until we all reach a point of equity (1 Corinthians 8). We've got a long way to go by any of these paths.

Small congregations don't have to worry about rescuing the world. Start small. Create sister relations with just one low-income church nearby. Then, soon afterwards, involve those two churches in adopting one overseas church. Aim for equity among all three. When the diaconal fund is large enough, have the church fund regular travel between those churches, getting sheltered Americans out to the Third World, and bringing Third World sisters and brothers to the West in regular cycles, not just short-term visits, never to be repeated. We're to be involved in each others' lives, knowing names and bearing burdens.

For some churches in hardened Mammon areas (e.g., suburban United States), instead of wasting so much time trying to beg middle-class people to come to church, churches might, at some point, need to consider moving the church to another part of town where real needs exist. Jesus didn't come for the "healthy," and we have to be willing to admit those are the only people we've generally been interested in. We need to get to the point where we can say that about the Western middle class. The early church wasn't locked in service to "many wise, mighty, or noble" and neither should we think first of serving the educated, the influential, the comfortable. Those of us in the group of the educated, influential, and comfortable need to learn to deliver others. That's our purpose. But some churches find themselves with no one in the vicinity to deliver, except other middle-class people. Think big. Think about moving where the Spirit can work. It need not require moving into utter poverty, especially for the soft. Most communities just have to look a little farther than their immediate neighborhood to find people who would be hungry for Christ's whole kingdom. Go to them. Be free enough to turn your back on the middle class.

Loving our enemies includes groups that our ancestors abused. As white Westerners look for places to serve, we want to look for those our ancestors wronged. White Americans should seek out native Americans, African Americans, and Latino immigrants and workers. Western nations will never seriously consider the questions of reparations for our destruction of Latin American and Africa, a destruction that will still take centuries from which to recover (even if we were to stop undermining them immediately). States and citizens are generally too individualistic to think generationally, but churches can. Churches can begin thinking in terms of reparations and restitutions, especially if we go one church at a time. At the same time, we don't want to repeat mistakes of the past. We don't want to go into local distressed areas talking and talking about mercy, only to dominate and remove more power. Leading with repentance instead of "solutions for the backward poor" will go farther. Again, the Gorniks and Linthecums of the world (mentioned above) provide invaluable advice.

If the Lord blesses our hunger to deliver our friends and enemies, churches should obviously get into the housing side of things. We might start by purchasing duplexes and whole apartment complexes. We might even build them. Perhaps at some point we can build houses so that no member has to go into lifetime debts for mortgages. Thinking about housing prompts questions about having members live together or in close proximity. Again, hundreds of Christian works have already moved in this direction. Some live in common, some live close. More and more are moving out of radical individual housing styles, where members are separated by long drives. The variations on this can vary by region and the personalities involved. The goal is break with Mammon's atomism and to learn to live in genuine community with one another, face to face, at work, rest, service, and not just at worship and Bible studies. This has and will take a much richer understanding of self-denial. But our calling is to make Trinity here, and we can't do that while serving the system of Mammon.

In the past and today, many Christian groups who begin to live together and with greater sharing will sometimes turn largely inward and cut themselves of in separatist ways. The temptation that direction is great, especially for resentful conservatives. But turning inward rejects the way of deliverance. Separatism isn't the way of the cross. The way of the cross is very much directed toward loving and serving all those outside the church, bringing tangible mercy and hope in a new kingdom. The temptation to turn inward will also increase as well-intentioned churches face rejection and troubles from the communities they have so excitedly sought to serve. The way of the cross is not the way of romanticism. It is the way of death and self-denial and rejection. That is the only path to true life.

Churches that head down the Basiliad path will be open to creating many different institutions to deal with all aspects of the kingdom. At the same time, Christians have to become more familiar with the natural dynamics and negative directions institutions naturally follow over time. The history of the church is the history of institutions that turn on their original excitement. We need to be constantly wary of how institutions quench the Spirit and kill themselves. We need to study more and draw on many resources that have examined this perennial problem in and out of the church. Sometimes the Spirit genuinely seems to give up on an organization, even one that isn't so bad. The Spirit leaves but the institution trudges on in a coma. Perhaps one way Christians, at least, can rethink institutions is to revisit the land-rest requirements of the Old Covenant. The Lord wanted the land to rest every seventh year, and perhaps we can find some analogies there. Perhaps we should build institutions light enough to do that. Perhaps we should build into their bylaws that they will automatically shut down after six years, only to be revived after much prayer, fasting, and majority voting. We have to be dynamic enough to let our pet institutions die. Christians waste so much time desperately trying to keep dead institutions alive, many times because people's salaries and identities are caught up in them. Jesus's command to give up all should also include unhealthy Christian institutions. Plan to dismantle them and build something new. Most often, institutions reflect the personalities of their makers, and yet those people grow old, change, and die. Build them to take on new personalities, as painful as that might be. As people of the Trinity, with equal concern for past, present, and future, we can't be a people who privilege the past over the future.

As our churches grow in the way of the cross, seeking to deliver, share, commune, and love our enemies, we will continue to expand our prophetic voice. As with everything, we want to address the household of faith first. Throughout, we'll have to be calling on Christians to give up the dreams of Mammon, including careers that are indifferent to Christ's kingdom. We'll have to call and train ourselves to love the seemingly unlovable, until we see their superiority. At the same time, resisting Mammon will naturally lead more and more Christian leaders to call on Christian men and women to get out of the imperial military. We will no longer encourage our youth to serve the immoral interests of Western governments, especially Britain and the United States. This will be highly unpopular, and that's an understatement. But why do we call Jesus Lord and yet butcher our enemies? The time has come for millions of

Christians to withdraw from the military and do something constructive in Christ's kingdom. Perhaps that alone might slow centuries of invasion and death. Some have observed that if nice, conservative German Christians had refused to fight on behalf of Hitler, he could never have taken his first steps.

Over time, the way of the cross will naturally provoke more and more resistance to the church. We need to count the cost beforehand. As the church repudiates all the ways of Mammon, the church will appear more freakish and unnatural to the surrounding world. The greatest resistance will first come from those within the church herself. It always does. The broad way will show itself pervasive in the church, and we will hear accusations of heresy, treason, cowardice, extremism, Marxism, un-Americanism, envy, resentment, and all the other tiresome tricks. You will lose friends and gain friends. You will lose institutions and gain them. These issues of the way of the cross go deep into people's identities, and you can't criticize idolatrous identities without provoking wrath, however peacefully you might do it. Jesus promised this would happen. To resist Mammon is to invite bloodshed. Count the cost. "Whoever does not bear his cross and come after Me cannot be My disciple" (Luke 14:27).

The life of Christ's church is a delegated life. The church isn't called to wait and beg for Jesus in heaven to do something. We're not called to lay back and let Jesus set up his kingdom from heaven. We're not supposed to hang out with Mammon and hope that God's providence will naturally extend Christ's kingdom over time. That's our job. Jesus delegated the kingdom to the church: "I bestow upon you a kingdom, just as My Father bestowed one upon Me" (Luke 22:29). When someone hands you a kingdom you have a responsibility to bring it to its goal. Christ's kingdom is the good news of refuge and deliverance. It is the solution to the problem of evil and injustice in the world. That's not the Trinity's job. That's the church's job. He handed over to the church the ministry of reconciliation (2 Cor 5:18). The church is Christ's body on earth (1 Corinthians 12), and we're called to restore, heal, feed, clothe, manufacture, farm, educate, and worship in order to bring all the ancient promises to fulfillment. We're called to do all the things he did when he was on earth—deliver, renounce, share, love, perceive, and commune. Like Christ, the church is to feed on evil and absorb it. That's what resurrection life does. We can touch the unclean and the dead. We are to become sin so that more may have life. That is the way of the cross. "But why do you call Me 'Lord, Lord,' and not do the things which I say?"

21

The Spirituality of Descent

I have been, I think, rightly hard on the individualisms, among other things, that have distorted our understanding of Christ, his gospel, and kingdom. My arguments have been directed at remembering and incorporating the centrality of the communal. We have very deep cultural holes to get out of. I haven't argued that the disagreement is between individual vs. communal but rather individual vs. communal/individual. The goal isn't to deny individuality but rather to include the communal.

In the rush of works and ministries, it would be easy to forget this. It would be easy for those with a more communal or social bent to neglect the individual in our attempt to overcorrect misleading traditions. But Christ was clearly concerned about the actual transformation of individual persons and individual souls. He gave us paths on which to transform individuals from egocentric or unitarian individuals into Trinitarian persons, indwelling one another and God himself.

One can't talk, then, about "how to get there," to Christ's cross-shaped city on a hill, without grasping the crucial work of transforming individuals. I've highlighted and assumed this from the beginning of this work, and here I want to make it more explicit. We can't create and sustain Christ's kingdom without the simultaneous maturing of individual souls. Simultaneity is important. I certainly don't think it's a question of just fixing the individual first and then the social will work itself out or a question of resolving social sin and hoping individual souls will follow suit. We need both at the same time, and we're destined to fail if we follow only one of those paths (as we have for centuries). The literature of mercy work is full of stories of those who focused on deliverance, sharing, and love of enemies who imploded after a while. Often, they had immature souls, too immature to go far on the way of the cross. Christ's way requires radical communal and radical individual reshaping by the Spirit.

In other words, churches that grow convinced of the centrality of the way of the cross in its kingdom dimensions ought not to run off toward social self-denial and mercy work until they develop a commitment to transform their souls. History shows us that the demands of serious kingdom work cannot be borne by the weak and spiritually immature. It involves too much failure and heartbreak for the typical Westerner, especially the typical American. We have been catechized in the opposite direction for too long. As Jesus explicitly warned, "he who received the seed on stony places, this is he who hears the word and immediately receives it with joy; yet he has no root in himself, but endures only for a while" (Matt 13:20, 21). We are those who have "no root" in ourselves.

Opposition to Mammon is not a game. It is an invitation to death. It is a move against some of the deepest spiritual forces on earth. To take on Mammon is to take on serious and entrenched darkness. "We wrestle not against flesh and blood" (Eph 6:12). But "against the rulers of the darkness of this age." Do we believe that? Do we really believe that pursuing the way of the cross will infuriate comfortable darkness? Just look at church history. Every Christian group that has tried something as seemingly innocuous as trying seriously to live out the Sermon on the Mount has conjured up wrath for itself. The nicest people on the block have turned ballistic. These issues go deep. They touch our deepest identities, and when you start questioning these identities, you find out how fundamentally connected they are to the spiritual realm.

Our first glance should never be at the deep-seated problems in others, though. We have to grapple first with our own twisted spiritualities, my own. The basic problem is this: we can't hope to wrestle with Mammon in the world around us without first conquering the Mammon that has so long gripped our souls. It's futile and pointless. Unless we exorcise the Mammon that shapes our normal habits, we will fail to overcome it in our communities. We will always default to our natural, comfortable Mammon ways of solving problems and setting goals. Our kingdom-churches will fall.

Happily, Jesus showed us how to be delivered from our Mammon souls. Most of our modern Christian traditions have little familiarity with his methods because we've reduced the gospel to an intellectual ticket into heaven. Once we have that ticket, we assume soul transformation here and now isn't important. Actually following and imitating Jesus drops out of our picture because all we have to do is give mental assent to his work on the cross, and we're in.

What's most strange is that Jesus didn't preach this message, our message. He didn't preach primarily about trusting in his shed blood on the cross. He focused on real transformation here and now. Think about it this way: we try and convince people to be interested in Jesus because of his finished work on the cross. True and good. But how did Jesus gain thousands of followers and disciples and apostles even *before* that later message was clear? What was attractive about Jesus's message before the cross? What message did he teach so that people followed him even before his resurrection? Cynthia Bourgeault posed this question wonderfully:

> For these first disciples, the ones who listened and said "yes" to Jesus, *the outcome was as yet unknown*. Both crucifixion and resurrection lay ahead. . . . What caused them to say "yes" to Jesus? It must have been very different from what now, twenty centuries later, is our normal understanding of the situation. We may say "yes" to Jesus because we know now that he is the Son of God, that he died and rose again, and that in union with him we hope to do likewise. They didn't know this. What said "yes"?[1]

The Sermon on the Mount and similar passages, for example, make up Jesus's kingdom preaching, and yet such passages say nothing about shed blood on the cross. Jesus focused on something else in these messages, not atonement. Yet, they are hugely attractive messages in and of themselves. Sure, some followed him for shallow reasons, but why did the many, devoted, faithful follow? What made people want to follow Jesus's way? Following Bourgeault, we could call this Jesus' "guru" message. A guru message is about living life here and now. It is wisdom for the good life on earth. What made people choose Jesus as a guru instead of countless other Jewish gurus wandering around first-century Palestine?

The strange thing is that Jesus's preaching seemed terribly *un*attractive. He kept talking about death. Consider trying to attract a crowd with this sort of teaching:

1. Bourgeault, *Wisdom*, 9,10.

> Most assuredly, I say to you, unless a grain of wheat falls into
> the ground and dies, it remains alone; but if it dies, it produces
> much grain. He who loves his life will lose it, and he who
> hates his life in this world will keep it for eternal life. (John
> 12:24–26)

What a strange message. Could any teaching be more off-putting? Why did people want to follow this?

In the midst of all his talk about death, Jesus also promised genuine life and freedom. "I have come that they may have life, and that they may have it more abundantly" (John 10:10). "If you abide in My word, you are My disciples indeed. And you shall know the truth, and the truth shall make you free. . . . If the Son makes you free, you shall be free indeed" (John 8:31–36). Death and life and freedom? How did this guru teaching all fit together? On the surface, it must have seemed pretty confusing.

The key to unlocking Jesus's teaching involves a strange view of the self, in fact, selves. We can't understand Jesus's or apostolic teaching if we view ourselves as one self. Moderns have a particularly difficult time with this, but to understand Jesus's teaching, we have to see every individual in terms of his or her two selves.

Consider how Jesus' paradoxical language about death assumes two selves: "Jesus said to His disciples, 'If anyone desires to come after Me, let him deny himself, and take up his cross, and follow Me'" (Matt 16:24). From one angle, this sort of command doesn't make sense. We've heard it so often that we might miss the confusing bit. On the one hand, he says the self must die, but, on the other hand, something has to follow him and take up a cross. If the self died, what is carrying the cross? A nonself? What part of us "follows" him? A mere body? It seems Jesus calls on individuals to deny and affirm a self at the same time. He seems to assume we can have a self and not have a self simultaneously.

The way through this paradox is to picture a person with two selves, one to deny and one to follow Jesus. This two-selves understanding actually has a long history within scripture and the church, especially in medieval spirituality. If we don't think in terms of two selves, we run into other confusions. We tend to see Jesus's command as a denial of individuality. Maybe, we think, we're supposed to deny our individuality and take on Jesus's own individuality. We die, and somehow his particular personality lives in us. Apart from being impossible, it runs contrary to all the later teaching about the importance of different individualities and gifts that make up the body of Christ. Other times we avoid the two-selves picture by reducing Jesus's language until it's minimized to nothing, a mere figure. Perhaps we think Jesus just means we should just put others first and ourselves second. There's truth in that, of course. But he doesn't mention others in these commands, and he speaks of denial and humiliation, not just a respectable second place.

The two-selves picture brings its own complications. But Jesus and the New Testament writers invoke the two-self language in important ways. Listen for the distinct two-ness expressed in the following passages:

"The spirit indeed is willing, but the flesh is weak." (Matt 26:41)

"Do not let your left hand know what your right hand is doing." (Matt 6:3)

"It is not you who speak, but the Spirit of your Father who speaks in you." (Matt 10:20)

"For what profit is it to a man if he gains the whole world, and loses his own soul?" (Matt 16:26)

"He said to him, 'Come out of the man, unclean spirit!'" (Mark 5:8)

"It is the Spirit who gives life; the flesh profits nothing." (John 6:63)

"He who eats My flesh and drinks My blood abides in Me, and I in him." (John 6:56)

"At that day you will know that I am in My Father, and you in Me, and I in you." (John 14:20)

"Abide in Me, and I in you. As the branch cannot bear fruit of itself, unless it abides in the vine, neither can you, unless you abide in Me." (John 15:4, 5)

"That they all may be one, as You, Father, are in Me, and I in You; that they also may be one in Us." (John 17:21)

"Our old man was crucified with Him." (Rom 6:6)

"But now, it is no longer I who do it, but sin that dwells in me." (Rom 7:17)

"For the good that I will to do, I do not do; but the evil I will not to do, that I practice." (Rom 7:19)

"For those who live according to the flesh set their minds on the things of the flesh, but those who live according to the Spirit, the things of the Spirit. For to be carnally minded is death, but to be spiritually minded is life and peace. Because the carnal mind is enmity against God; for it is not subject to the law of God, nor indeed can be. So then, those who are in the flesh cannot please God." (Rom 8:5–8)

"If anyone is in Christ, he is a new creation." (2 Cor 5:17)

"Walk in the Spirit, and you shall not fulfill the lust of the flesh. For the flesh lusts against the Spirit, and the Spirit against the flesh; and these are contrary to one another, so that you do not do the things that you wish. But if you are led by the Spirit, you are not under the law." (Gal 5:16, 17)

"Therefore put to death your members which are on the earth." (Col 3:5)

"Put off, concerning your former conduct, the old man which grows corrupt according to the deceitful lusts, and be renewed in the spirit of your mind." (Eph 4:22, 23)

"You have put off the old man with his deeds, and have put on the new man." (Col 3:9, 10)

And even Matthew 25 suggests this interesting duality. Part of them somehow didn't "know" what the other part was doing:

"When did we see You hungry and feed You, or thirsty and give You drink? When did we see You a stranger and take You in, or naked and clothe You? (Matt 25:37, 38)

Some have tried to explain this duality in terms of the transition between unbelief to belief or unregeneration to regeneration by the Spirit, but the passages don't allow such a simple line. For Paul, quite explicitly, the battle between flesh and spirit is a battle Christians fight their entire lives. "Walk in the Spirit, and you shall not fulfill the lust of the flesh." Others try to make sense of these passages within one soul. They assume an individual soul is always a mix of natural tendencies to sin and some Holy Spirit in the margins. One can never mature on such a view. Or we divide the soul into parts, one part is sinful and that pollutes a well-meaning will. Jesus and the New Testament call on a self to die, but we can't just kill a part of the soul. The New Testament assumes a stronger duality here, two selves.

As we've seen, Paul famously marks this divide as that between flesh and spirit, which captures that aspect of life not revived by the spirit (flesh = merely material, without the Holy Spirit, also the Old Testament law and unbelievers) and the spirit (that aspect of life animated by the Holy Spirit). Needless to say, hopefully, by now, we know Paul wasn't contrasting material vs. nonmaterial, as in ancient Greek or Platonic fashion. The body and the material world are good and holy creations, as is the spiritual dimension. But either dimension without the Holy Spirit lacks the most important kind of life, divine life. Paul's division lines up better with the shift between Old and New Testaments, namely, life before Pentecost and life after Pentecost—flesh vs. spirit.

Within Christ's followers, then, there remains a struggle between a pre-Pentecost self and a post-Pentecost self, and these press against one another—"flesh lusts against the Spirit, and the Spirit against the flesh." Thomas Merton and others have helpfully characterized this flesh/spirit duality in the language of true self vs. false self.[2] In terms of the language used in this book, we can also speak of the flesh or false self as our Mammon self, and the spirit or true self as our Christ self. Within each of us, our Christ-self aims to overcome our Mammon-self.

Reformation Protestants get worried about this talk because we find it important that nothing pure or good goes on inside humans. We get a little nervous with talk that suggests there might be something very pure deep down inside of us. But here we're letting our Reformation tradition subvert scripture. For example, when Paul says, "I have been crucified with Christ; it is no longer I who live, but Christ lives in me" (Gal 2:20), are we really going to say that the Christ who lives in us is sinful? No, it's Christ himself, after all. Still, "no good thing dwells in me," we say. But notice how the apostle himself qualifies that language in terms of two selves: "For I know that in me (that is, in my flesh) nothing good dwells" (Rom 7:18). Yes, nothing good dwells in one of his selves, the flesh, but Christ-in-him is his deep self, and that is holy. To confirm this, following this claim, he speaks of the holiness of his "inner man"—"For I delight in the law of God according to the inward man" (Rom 7:22).

What are these two selves, then? Look at Paul's interesting language again: "I have been crucified with Christ; it is no longer I who live, but Christ lives in me" (Gal 2:20). He speaks of an I that is crucified and dead, and a surviving I and me in which Christ lives. Part of our difficulty with New Testament psychology is that we don't really believe that the divine truly indwells us. The apostles really believed this, as did most of church history. After the Reformation, we turned into default demythologizers about divine indwelling. We retreated and made it mere decorative, figurative language. Indwelling became a legal fiction, a mere concept. "Christ in us" became something of an ethical ideal, a goal, a shared hope. But our notion was not the genuine divine indwelling that Jesus so explicitly promised and prayed for: "that they all may be one, as You, Father, are in Me, and I in You; that they also may be one in Us" (John

2. A helpful, evangelical introduction to this topic is Benner, *Gift*.

17:21). Trinitarian oneness is not a fiction. It involves true, metaphysical indwelling.

What are the two selves, then? One is our self made in the image of God, the original Spirit within us, now as believers indwelt by Christ. One of ourselves is our individuality permeated or in real communion with Christ, always distinct, yet truly indwelt. This is the life that Jesus promised. It is eternal life within us now, as John said: "Let what you heard from the beginning abide in you. If what you heard from the beginning abides in you, then you too will abide in the Son and in the Father" (1 John 2:24; cf. John 6:53–55; John 17:2–4; 1 Tim 6:12; 1 John 1:2; 3:15; 5:11; 5:20). Most importantly, this Christ-self finds its identity first and foremost in the knowledge that God deeply loves it. Just as the Father declared his love for the Son—"This is My beloved Son, in whom I am well pleased" (Matt 3:17)—so the Father says the same for our true selves. That love becomes the basis of our identity: "An identity ground in God would mean that when we think of who we are, the first thing that would come to mind is our status as someone deeply loved by God."[3]

What is our *other* self, then? In short, the flesh. In contrast to the Spirit or true self or Christ-self. A study of Paul's use of "flesh" is intriguing, and I won't go into it here in detail. Sometimes Paul uses "flesh" rather neutrally as mere body or persons, and other times he picks out especially the natural limitations of the body, and yet other times the term clearly takes on negative moral connotations.[4] Most interestingly, in both Paul and John, our flesh-self is connected to deception and lies and the world. There is something untrue and artificial about the flesh. It's not natural. It's artificial and constructed. Paul speaks of the flesh as if it were a covering or a burden over the true self: "if I do what I will not to do, it is no longer I who do it, but sin that dwells in me" (Rom 7:20). The flesh is a lie in that "you do not do the things that you wish" (Gal 5:17). John speaks of the flesh as "For all that is in the world—the lust of the flesh, the lust of the eyes, and the pride of life—is not of the Father but is of the world" (1 John 2:16). These are all deceptions and lies about the real. The flesh and the world are in close communion and both are false depictions of life. This comes as no surprise, since the world and Mammon are Satan's kingdom, and Satan is a deceiver and the father of lies (John 8:44). Paul also discusses the two selves in terms of what they obey. They follow

---

3. Benner, *Gift*, 49.

4. See James Dunn's helpful survey in *Theology of the Apostle Paul*, 51ff.

laws and systems: "with the mind I myself serve the law of God, but with the flesh the law of sin" (Rom 7:25), the law of Satan and Death.

John's connection between the flesh and the pride of life are especially helpful. We can know more about the false self by its connection to the world. We lose something in the dynamic of maturity, if we just understand the flesh or false self as emphasizing all sin generically. Satan and the world have priorities. Certain sins stand out, and so we should expect the same of the false self. If the flesh is a construct, an artifice made up of lies from the world, then, from our earlier discussion about Satan's temptation of Christ, we know what its priorities are. In fact, Satan's temptation now takes on added significance at the individual level. Mammon and its three Ps, the needs of prestige, power, and possessions, is not just a corporate system. It duplicates at the individual level in our flesh, too. Our flesh-self, like Satan and the world, is obsessed with our own individual perceived needs for domination, honor, respect, security, control, and all main vices of Mammon. Satan attempted to cause Christ to fall to these temptations of the false self, but Jesus was already grounded in the Father and Spirit. Our calling, now, is to grow free of the same temptations, and that usually takes a lifetime.

In the end, both our corporate and individual lives struggle between Christ and Mammon. At the individual level, the struggle between our two selves is a struggle between lies—"world, lust of the flesh, pride of life" (1 John 2:16); and the truth—"Christ in you, the hope of glory" (Col 1:27). The false self is a body of lies about ourselves. It is unreal but powerful. It fights for our dignity, popularity, and wealth. The Mammon self lies at the root of all grasping and infighting and selfishness and international wars. In contrast, the true self is real. It is not a construct. It will last. It is Christ in us. It is our true identity, but we stray from it. We struggle against it and often fall back into the false self's values. We strayed from our true self most significantly in Eden, and, as Paul says, we are now renewing the original image, that true self, the Spirit in us: "Do not lie to one another, since you have put off the old man with his deeds, and have put on the new man who is renewed in knowledge according to the image of Him who created him" (Col 3:9,10).

Notice Paul's connection between lying and the false self, the old man. That is what it does. It lies and accuses and fights for the three Ps in us. The flesh is the deepest slavery, and Christ the truest freedom.

Now, with the New Testament's two-self portrait in mind, we can make much better sense of Jesus's guru message and the spirituality of descent. With the two selves in the background, Jesus promised his followers freedom and abundant life, both to be lived in a new, alternative community. But the way to freedom and abundant life was the path of death. How do the two selves explain this?

In short, we kill our false selves and live more and more in our true selves. We abandon Mammon and develop Christ in us, all by the gifts and power of the Spirit. In other words, Jesus preached that those who desire true freedom and divine power, need to deny their powerful but artificial worldly selves, taking up the path of descent through self-denial, and abide in indwelling Christ self. This is Jesus's guru message—freedom and abundant divine life. Strip your souls of the longings for Mammon (needs for power, prestige, possessions) and find your identity in the actual indwelling of God. We could reword Paul's two-self claim this way: "Through self-denial I have put to death my false self, my flesh; it is no longer my flesh who lives, but Christ lives in and through my true self" (Gal 2:20).

Living a genuinely abundant life as an individual requires reversing the values of Mammon. Living the good life means being free of Mammon's spirituality of ascent and greatness and domination, free from the chains of prestige, power, and possessions. Jesus promised that happiness and blessedness and true freedom come from being loosed from Mammon's burdens at the very center of our being. This message ran counter to both the way of Rome and the Jewish leadership. They sought domination and the best seats, but Jesus said the path to real freedom was in letting go of those sorts of needs. Where Mammon seeks ascent, Jesus teaches descent. Let go and be free.

Putting to death the false self doesn't mean rejecting those main Mammon ideas merely intellectually. We have to get them out of our bones and souls. They go deep within us, though. Whenever we're personally offended by someone's inadvertent slight or insult, that's a sign we're living out of our false self. We subtly picture ourselves as deserving respect and honor. We don't want anyone to question us. We want to be popular and be able to control situations. We want to be the best. Those are all signs that we're living out of our needs for prestige, power, and possessions. As David Benner says, "The more we identify with our psychologically and socially constructed self, the more deeply we hide from God, ourselves, and others."[5] Whole Christian institutions, as well

---

5. Benner, *Gift*, 88.

as individuals, continue to live out of their false selves. Jesus needed only the approval of the Father, not anyone else. His identity was in the Trinity, and so he didn't respond in anger when personally insulted or disrespected. Roman soldiers could spit on him and he didn't retaliate with biting words. He was free of all the petty needs for popularity and tiny power, and so the Lord would exalt him. He was poor in spirit, free of a false self, free from any Mammon within his soul.

We can summarize Jesus's guru message in three words: freedom, indwelling, and refuge. He returns to these three topics over and over. You can find some version of them in almost every episode in the gospels. He promised true freedom through denying the false self. He promised true life by finding your identity and life in the indwelling of God. And these two together would create a new world, a new kingdom, the church made up of people not bound by the slavery of their false selves but living richly with God dwelling at the center of their being. "Unless a grain of wheat falls into the ground and dies, it remains alone; but if it dies, it produces much grain."

In Philippians, Paul famously sketches Christ's entire mission in terms of the spirituality of descent. Christ, as the second person of the Trinity, sat at the right hand of the Father, exalted from eternity. Yet, he descended to serve. He descended and rejected all the trappings of Mammon and the flesh, and we are to imitate his spirituality—"Let this mind be in you":

> Christ Jesus, who being in the form of God, did not consider it
> robbery to be equal with God, but made himself of no reputa-
> tion, taking the form of a bondservant, and coming in the
> likeness of men. And being found in the appearance of man, he
> humbled himself and became obedient to the point of death,
> even the death of the cross. Therefore God also has highly ex-
> alted him and given him the name which is above every name.
> (Phil 2:6–9)

This is our prime model of descent. This is the way of the cross, and we are to imitate his path both individually and corporately. Death before resurrection. Self-denial before exaltation.

And yet it's not just generic self-denial in the spirituality of descent. Jesus didn't call on us to follow in the path of descent on our own strength. Ultimately, the spirituality of descent would be a dead end apart from the cross and resurrection and Pentecost. Jesus's guru teaching cannot succeed without those final events interventions. Without the victory of the crucifixion and resurrection, we would still be enslaved by all the powers of Death, Sin, and Satan. But "death no longer has dominion" (Rom 6:9). We might try the path of descent all we like, but without the overthrow, without the absorption and exhaustion of all those forces, without Christ's disarming of Satan (Col 2:15), Christ's life breaking the power of death in resurrection, we would be most miserable and lost. We would not be able to break the hold of the false self on us, and without Pentecost we would never mature; we could never know real union with God. But because of these events, we now live in a new cosmos, a new heaven and earth, promising freedom and indwelling now.

Those revolutionary events, however, do not bring immediate maturity. At a much greater and cosmic level, they resemble God's freeing the Israelites from the oppression of Pharaoh. We have passed through the Red Sea and stand in the wilderness pointed toward the promised land. It has all been grace. No human works freed us from Pharaoh. God acted and delivered us by grace alone. Now he calls us through the wilderness of self-denial. The wilderness reshapes us and sanctifies us. We face Satanic temptation there, like Jesus did. Even when various tribes of the church might reach the promised land, new trials and temptations await. Wilderness and promised land continue as places of transformation, of dying to self and rising in resurrection. We should excel much more than the saints of old. They had the glory of the law, but we have the Spirit of God himself dwelling in us, transforming us, maturing us. We are truly in a different world than the Old Covenant.

Living the spirituality of descent creates continuing conversions throughout our lives. God continues to surprise us. He continues to bring water out of rocks and pour new wine into old wineskins. We have to be alert, or we'll be left behind in the wilderness. Even Jesus's promise of divine indwelling is not a static, once-and-done event. There is ebb and flow. We need the Spirit to cause our true self, our Christ-self, to grow within us. This may sound strange, but Paul uses this language of growing the indwelling Christ already in us: "My little children, for whom I labor in birth again until Christ is formed in you" (Gal 4:19). They have Christ within them, and yet he is still not fully formed in them. It is a process, a lifelong process of transformation.

But how do we get the divine person to dwell in us even more? It's certainly not just adding more information and knowledge. The intellect is just a surface. And it's not just controlling our will to be more moral. That should be an effect, a symptom, but not the core. In truth, we have to transform the deepest part of our being, our soul. How does one transform a soul? All aspects of life contribute to this—intellectual, emotional, volitional, providential—but ultimately we change a soul, in part, by having it live in the direct presence of God.

The greatest gift God has given us for growing in the presence of God is prayer. Prayer connects us directly to God, directly to abundant and eternal life. Prayer, in its most mature form, is union with God. That's why prayer stands out as so central in the history of the church. Prayer, above all disciplines, forms the heart of the spirituality of descent.

In our overly intellectualistic traditions, we tend to reduce prayer to mere asking, mere petitioning. But prayer is often much deeper than conscious requests. Paul spoke of several categories of prayer—"supplications, prayers, intercessions, and giving of thanks" (1 Tim 2:1). We tend to reduce all these to petitions and verbalized requests, but something more is going on. For example, Paul speaks here of "intercessions," and he elsewhere spoke of this sort of prayer in rather mysterious terms—"the Spirit Himself makes intercession for us with groanings which cannot be uttered" (Rom 8:26).

In the Psalms, prayer often consists in simply watching and waiting silently in the presence of the Lord.

"Truly my soul silently waits for God; from Him comes my salvation." (Ps 62:1)

"My soul, wait silently for God alone, for my expectation is from Him." (Ps 62:5)

"Lead me in Your truth and teach me, for You are the God of my salvation; on You I wait all the day." (Ps 25:5)

"Rest in the LORD, and wait patiently for Him." (Ps 37:7)

"I wait for the Lord, my soul waits, and in His word I do hope. My soul waits for the Lord more than those who watch for the morning—yes, more than those who watch for the morning." (Ps 130:5, 6)

In the Gospel account of busy Martha and resting Mary, we find in Mary as an influential model in church history of the importance of resting in the presence of Christ—"Mary, who also sat at Jesus' feet and heard His word" (Luke 10:39). Christ defends Mary's "waiting" and contemplation—"But one thing is needed, and Mary has chosen that good part" (Luke 10:42).

Jesus himself "often withdrew into the wilderness and prayed" (Luke 5:16), and it's interesting near the time of his crucifixion that Jesus rebukes his disciples for their inability to "watch and pray": "What!

Could you not watch with Me one hour? Watch and pray, lest you enter into temptation. The spirit indeed is willing, but the flesh is weak" (Matt 26:40, 41). They apparently lacked the discipline to sit just one hour waiting in the presence of the Father. Jesus expected more from them.

But how does waiting, watching, and contemplation transform the soul? David saw his waiting on the presence of the Lord as a means of strengthening his innermost being: "Wait on the Lord; be of good courage, and He shall strengthen your heart; wait, I say, on the Lord!" (Ps 27:13–14). Subsequent centuries of saints have testified the same. Waiting on the Lord is supernatural therapy for us. It renews. Devoted, silent prayer presents before the Lord the deepest parts of our soul and invites him to purge and change us at our core. One cannot leave the presence of God without undergoing transformation, and once God does his gracious work on our souls as we meditate and long for him, we grow up, slowly. We overcome the flesh. God disciplines our souls for greater use in his kingdom. He prunes our souls, freeing us more and more from our flesh and false lies, so that we become more like his Son, more willing and skilled and empowered to walk in the way of the cross.[6]

So Christ's people must be a people of prayer, not just petitions, but prayer of deep, contemplative union with God. We have to be a people who learn to live constantly in the presence of God, a people, in other words, who "pray without ceasing" (1 Thess 5:17; Rom 12:12).

Now we can see why the broader mercy work of the kingdom and the spirituality of descent have to go hand in hand. One can't do Christ's mercy work with a Mammon soul. Many have tried and failed. Many have tried to set up Christian churches and close-knit communities without dedicated focus on putting to death their Mammon selves. Such projects are doomed. "That they all may be one, as You, Father, are in Me, and I in You; that they also may be one in Us" (John 17:21). We cannot manifest the life of the Trinity on earth, without the self-denial and indwelling at the heart of the Trinity.

And that is Christ's mission for us: to incarnate the life of the Trinity on earth. "Thy kingdom come on earth as it is in heaven." The means

---

6. The revival in contemplative prayer has produced many helpful texts, including Richard Foster, *Sanctuary of the Soul: Journey into Meditative Prayer*; Jan Johnson, *When the Soul Listens: Finding Rest and Direction in Contemplative Prayer*; R. Thomas Ashbrook, *Mansions of the Heart: Exploring the Seven Stages of Spiritual Growth*; Ruth Haley Barton, *Invitation to Solitude and Silence: Experiencing God's Transforming Presence*; Cynthia Bourgeault, *Centering Prayer and Inner Awakening*.

and goal is the way of the cross, the way of imitating Jesus here and now. The way of the cross is the way of weakness, renunciation, deliverance, sharing, enemy-love, foolishness, and community in both individuals and communities. This path manifest the love of Father, Son, and Spirit on earth.

The main question, then, that Christ continues to press upon us today as in the first century remains—"why do you call Me 'Lord, Lord,' and not do the things which I say?" (Luke 6:46).

Appendix A

A Short Retelling of Romans

To many Protestants, the Book of Romans presents a completely different world than that given by Jesus. To put it simplistically, we have often seen Jesus concerned with the kingdom and life on earth, while Paul took off in an entirely different direction, one concerned primarily with the Augustinian mechanics of will and subtle nuances about the stages of how an individual soul gets into heaven before God. And Protestants have generally preferred to follow this narrow picture of Paul. Generally, that has meant jettisoning Jesus's main teachings, primarily the Sermon on the Mount and all is kingdom applications throughout the Gospels. Of course, a bifurcation like that can't be true. Jesus and Paul have to be talking about the same thing.

The Book of Romans has been a key battleground in this kingdom vs. cross discussion over the centuries. I've interacted with portions of Romans in my main text, but that usually won't help unless we have a different and bigger picture of Paul's goals in Romans. Without that, we keep slipping back into thinking he's talking about individual salvation and automatic steps into heaven. In fact, Paul has very little concern with heaven. In the place or places he mentions it, he immediately talks of judgment of our works. Even those New Perspective sort of theologians, over the past few decades, still seem too stuck in the older picture of what Paul is doing in Romans. They've moved things a bit, but the New Perspective reading of Romans still doesn't sound much like the topics

Jesus raised. This is a generalization. They are New Testament scholars; I am not.

I suspect one way to begin loosening the old picture of Romans as a treatise on individual salvation is to read it, as Paul himself frames it, in the book of Habakkuk. Let Habakkuk's issues become Paul's issues, and see if that helps us connect Jesus and Paul. We can go further. If we read Romans through not just Habakkuk, but also the concerns of Isaiah and the Psalms and Hosea, all the Old Testament passages he cites, then the mission of Jesus and Paul blend wonderfully and quite surprisingly. That's my proposal, and I've tried a very short version below, just to get a taste of what this might look like, within my own serious limits.

Paul's Main Thesis: If God is for you gentiles, who can be against you? Contrary to the apparent success of Roman-Jewish domination and denigration of you, God, through the new world of Christ and the Holy Spirit, has vindicated and adopted you once-despised, once-rejected and weak gentiles as glorious sons.

I am writing to you persecuted, denigrated, and despairing Roman gentiles to help you see, contrary to all the appearances around you, that God has indeed sided with you at this momentous shift in history, and he has vindicated you despised gentiles, adopted you as his true sons, and not with your dominant opponents, Roman or Jewish, whatever they say. You will despair less over your situation if you view it through the prophets, especially Habakkuk. The righteous few in Habakkuk's time lamented as you do. They, too, lived under the powerful domination of an evil and idolatrous Babylon, and they, too, struggled against hypocritical temple leaders within the covenant.

But God was not on the side of ancient Babylon or Israel's corrupt rulers of that day. God was wrathful against all such rulers and instead sided with those Abrahams who were loyal to him without the temple works and rituals, like you. You have always been the true Jews, the true Abrahams. God has always desired mercy, not sacrifice. And this persecution from falsely righteous but corrupt leadership has long been a pattern to recognize in Israel's history. In the Psalms, David repeatedly spoke from your position against a corrupt leadership on behalf of the righteous sufferers. Habakkuk and David had to persevere and recognize that God hadn't abandoned them, even though it clearly looked like it.

Your current story repeats their laments, yet they recognized God was on their side. You have to see this, too, and be encouraged.

In fact, your situation is gloriously better than either Habakkuk's or David's. The revelation and work of Jesus Christ has shown that God has all along favored Abraham's way over Moses's way. The Lord called Abraham originally as a gentile, just like you. Abraham's way of sonship, without the temple rituals and such, was the original way, but the Lord inserted Moses's way to heighten and expose their rebellion for a while. But Moses's way was never intended to be the unchangeable system forever, and your persecutors err in believing it so. God always wanted Abraham's way of sonship and obedience without the rituals of Moses. Abraham's way comes from the heart, and Abraham recognized God's ways contrary to sight, like you need to, and God embraced father Abraham like he embraces you now.

Moses's way didn't bring life but wrath and more sin. Since Adam's disobedience, Sin and Death and Condemnation was a universal beast that held everyone in its grip, even you. It made you exiles and hostile to God, while it had you in its grip. Into that oppressive world system, the Lord introduced the Mosaic system, in part, to make things worse and speed them along, to bring resolution quicker. As such, Moses's way was never supposed to last. God's people were always supposed to return to Abraham's way, as we experience now. Christ loved his enemies, even in their exile under the rule of Sin and Death, and he returned Jew and gentile to that original path by cleansing us with this life-giving blood, by defeating the reign of the universal beast of Sin-Death-Condemnation-Law. His work freed you from the beast so that you could live even better than Abraham in the new reign of Christ and the Spirit. You were rescued from the domination of principalities and powers and now you serve Christ.

Can't you see how superior our new situation is? Moses's way, though holy and just, never had any power to overcome the domination of Sin. Only the Spirit in this new world can do that. Without the Spirit we would still be powerless but now you can see the Spirit's work in your own lives, and you don't see it in the lives of those who persecute you. That should encourage you, too. They still try to live in the old, temporary world of Moses, and that's death. The work of the Spirit in your lives is even more evidence that God is truly on your side and not your persecutors. And if God is truly on your side, who can do anything permanent against you?

I understand this is all too difficult to see in your present distress, but you and your opponents should have already seen it throughout the prophets. The prophets over and over testified that God worked through weakness and remnants. The prophets even promised that God would turn and adopt gentiles alongside that remnant. We all should have known this. We all should have seen this coming, though now the shift stumbles many and even makes you doubt. But listen to the prophets. They promised an unbelievable change would come, a great stumbling block that many would not see. But you should see. You are the great recipients of God's turn. And since true Israel has always been a remnant, then God has kept his promise to save all true Israel. God uses foolishness and surprise to accomplish his goals; who can truly fathom his great wisdom?

Since you are no longer under the bondage of Sin or Moses's way, you must stand out as true sons of God, vindicated from your former shame, adopted from your history outside of God's family. Live the new kingdom Christ preached, a kingdom of life, full of service, sharing, love, mercy, non-retaliation, and still more persecution. But you can no longer take your persecution as God's displeasure with you, despite what your detractors say. Don't live like them. Don't take up arms against the Roman Empire. Don't dominate weak people in your midst. Christ was merciful to you. Imitate him. Suffer and bear shame like he did, and yet he knew God was still on his side. Learn from Habakkuk. If God is for you, who can be against you? Obey like Abraham. See through the lies. Imitate Christ. Let God deal justice to your persecutors.

Appendix B

The Way of the Cross and the Reformed Tradition

In my earlier discussion, I briefly mentioned how very similar descriptions of the way of the cross show up across varying Christian traditions. This intriguing unity suggests a basic clarity to the way of the cross. At the same time, observers within those traditions will often strongly resist the vision, and some will even want to deny any thematic connections between their tradition and the way of the cross. I suspect some critics within my own conservative Reformed and Presbyterian tradition may not, at first, see any connections between it and the way of the cross. Since it's a more parochial concern, an appendix seemed appropriate to address this. Though many of my Reformed compatriots will usually quickly apply a dismissive label—"Anabaptist!"—to this sort of discussion of the way of the cross (that's how we generally "argue" in my circles), I rather think it was a combination of traditional Reformed distinctives that encourged me in the direction of the way of the cross, emphases that provide deep motivations, shape, and boundaries which prompted me to reflect along the lines of the traditional way of the cross. Below, I'll sketch several of those Reformed themes that naturally push one in the direction of the way of the cross.

On the surface, the Reformed tradition clearly hasn't been very friendly to way of the cross themes. We certainly don't have a strong tradition of way of the cross thinking, though it's growing and certain names stand out (earlier I mentioned some of those Reformed thinkers who made great contributions to way of the cross acts and thoughts). Perhaps that's why scripture warns us against the traps of traditions. Looking broadly at all Christian traditions, we each have strong and weak points. I suspect we each get about 30 percent of our vision correct and are blind in the rest. The same with the Reformed tradition. If that's right, then we're forced to look for the good in other traditions, and we would all expect some blindness on most issues. At least it's a helpful rule of thumb that might keep us listening instead of labeling.

As I grew in my understanding of the way of the cross, it became clear that it didn't directly contradict traditional Reformed thinking much at all. Most of the time, the Reformed tradition simply had either avoided or omitted way of the cross issues. No contradiction was possible. Then on other issues, I found not a contradiction but a change in priorities. Teachings that used to seem so central and essential to my theological thinking slowly appeared rather unimportant. They lost significance. If one tries to stick close to the teachings of Jesus, no matter what, then one finds that many traditionally important subjects fall to the side, simply because Jesus never talked about them much or at all. As we strive to match our theological priorities to Jesus's concerns, many former obsessions turn pale. For example, within the Reformed tradition, the topics of predestination, providence, and free will loom huge. In our creeds, they take up entire chapters and statements. Volumes and more volumes have been written about all the intricacies of predestination. Josephus says these were also hot topics in the first century, with the Essenes playing the part of Calvinists, the Sadducees as libertarians, and Pharisees as open theists. Given the overwhelming weight given to this subject in the Reformed tradition, it's certainly odd to find Jesus say so little about it—mainly, if anything he gave some throw-away observations. He talked much more about loving our enemies, but that topic never merited a whole chapter in our creeds and confessions.

The topic of predestination simply doesn't do any heavy lifting for Jesus. Not much is gained or lost with it. We can still obey the Sermon on the Mount without having to figure out the details of any one view. In day-to-day practice, high solutions to the questions of predestination don't show up much. Sure, we Reformed overuse providence as a solution to too many problems, as argued earlier, but when it comes to concrete actions we don't choose between predestinarian and, say, semi-Pelagian behaviors. If I decide to mow my lawn, I don't invoke some special predestinarian reasons to do it. I just do it, and it doesn't feel predestined at all. I act quite like the libertarian or open theist. I could strictly embrace all the deepest arguments from Calvin, the Westminster Confession, and the Canons of Dordt, and yet I still start my mower just like the Pelagian or open theist. Well, then, that applies to all my decisions and everyone's decisions. We always act as if we're free, even if that's not true. But if that's true, then all the long defenses of predestination must be generally talking about that secret aspects of predestination that have little to nothing to do with day to day life.

Even more, then, how did such an irrelevant topic become so absolutely central in some traditions like the Reformed? How did such a marginal discussion come to dominate such a large part of Christian thought after Augustine and especially through the Reformation and today? One has to back and figure out the motives that first prompted those debates.

The discussion's genealogy seems to go back to a focus on individual salvation. That was clearly one of Augustine's concerns, but it wasn't Isaiah's or Habakkuk's. The discussion of individual salvation raises the question of individual faith, and because the church early on misread Paul as being more concerned about the mechanics of individual salvation rather than contrasting the way of Abraham to that of Moses, we naturally had to try to reduce the amount of works involved in individual salvation. The developed discussion grew out of a worry about avoiding human effort, a noble motive. The discussion sought to protect the giftedness of grace and the honor of God. The Pelagians, semi-Pelagians, and Arminians stood their ground on freedom, and the Reformed tried to take the moral high ground by saying that even an individual's faith was a predestined gift from God. It had nothing to do with us. There. No works at all. But that answer already seems to have bought into the Pelagian or Arminian categories. It's already granted that particular acts of human faith are what bring about salvation, but it just says those individual acts were given by God. Again, the model of the exodus might help out. Instead of granting the non-Augustinian picture, the exodus removes human action from situation entirely. The Israelites were in slavery to Pharaoh. What did they do to escape his dominion? Nothing. It was all of grace. The Lord heard their cries, and he came down and started harassing Pharaoh with supernatural disruptions. He told Moses what to say, and then God did all the dirty work, blood, frogs, hail, etc. At the Red Sea, the Lord did all the work, again. Human effort didn't enter into any of the main work of deliverance. It showed up much later, in the wilderness, in questions about loyalty.

Given the exodus scenario, questions about whether the Israelites' faith was Reformed, God-given or their Arminian own can't even get started. The whole discussion is simply misplaced. It wasn't a human effort situation in the first place. The same thing seems to be happening in the New Covenant. Christ did all the work of salvation, destroying the tyranny of Sin, Death, and Condemnation, and then he turned to us in the wilderness. We didn't help him take in Sin on the cross, rise from the dead, or ascend. It was all grace. And yet, we've wasted so much time and paper trying to get the details about such largely marginal subjects. It turned out to be yet another distraction from Jesus's priorities. If Jesus didn't find it important enough to restate and expound upon in detail, then why should we? The way of the cross messes mightily with priorities. We spend centuries tithing the details of providence and predestination and have missed the weightier matters of justice and mercy. Most traditions do this sort of thing, not just the Reformed. We all get distracted from the truly important things like the way of the cross. Theological distractions seem built in to warnings about the broad path. We search the scriptures for centuries and still miss Jesus.

What about the constructive connection between the Reformed tradition and the way of the cross? Quite apart from the traditional five points of Calvinism, the Reformed tradition has also stood out in it emphasis and work concerning the universal lordship of Christ, covenant structure of redemptive history, the reality of the kingdom, theological antithesis, the unity of scripture, the importance of the Old Testament, the supremacy of Christ, the centrality of the church and sacraments, and the historical reality of the kingdom of God. All of these can prod people toward Jesus's priorities in the way of the cross, and I love and am grateful for all of them in the Reformed-Presbyterian tradition.

The Reformed tradition has been good at emphasizing the world-encompassing scope of Christ's claims. This has encouraged many adherents, especially in the Dutch Reformed tradition, to seek out Christian perspectives in all areas of life. At least it's not a strange question to ask in Reformed circles. That plays nicely into the absolutistic call of the way of the cross. Christ asks for us to surrender all of life, including economics, home life, and foreign policy. Christ is Lord of every inch.

The Reformed tradition has long recognized the importance of covenants throughout biblical history. Covenant theology helps explain the progress, continuities, and discontinuities in redemptive history. It helps to give a coherent narrative of the whole, from Adam to Christ.

Redemptive history isn't just a random collection of disconnected heroes. It's a continuous, interlocking story. The way of the cross grows out of the ongoing covenantal mission of God, and it was through covenantal thinking that the Reformed faith started taking the Trinity more seriously. The move from Trinity to the way of the cross is even more direct, but it took all traditions a while to think seriously about the Trinity in just the last century.

Kingdom is very central to the way of the cross, and the Reformed tradition long had that category open but central. The tradition understood the kingdom in different ways, but it generally didn't have to be persuaded that the kingdom was a real presence on earth and not just a heavenly future. Much of the Reformed tradition also saw earthly manifestations of the kingdom as expected and genuine, though we often confused the kingdom with national idols and movements.

For me, the Reformed tradition has always been good at least in looking for the antithesis in history—seed of the woman vs. seed of the serpent, the people of God vs. the enemies of God. We have often misidentified that antithesis in horrible ways. But we knew how important it was. Too many questions hinge on the answer for it to be ignored. In the way of the cross, Christ offers us the antithesis between God and Mammon, and I've tried to sketch that in big, Reformed ways.

The Reformed tradition has been driven to preserve the unity of scripture. We're always on guard against Marcion and recognize the importance of the Old Testament. Many traditions dismiss the Old Testament, but the Reformed will always wrestle with it. We will disagree about how much continuity and discontinuity there is, but at least that's a good worry for us. Jesus said he wasn't jettisoning the old, and that is a key constraint of the Sermon on the Mount. That sort of constraint has forced some of us to see the roots of the way of the cross in the Old Covenant, the way of deliverance and sharing and enemy love. It's all there.

The Reformed tradition also inadvertently sets the stage for the way of the cross through its emphasis on the centrality of Christ himself. His reign is not only universal Lord, he is the center of everything. This is the key to the way of the cross, and it was, for example, Barth's Christological emphasis that led Bonhoeffer to the way of the cross.

John Calvin has often been called the theologian of the Holy Spirit. Among non-charismatic traditions, the Reformed pay special attention to the work of the Holy Spirit. He is not marginal but central in individuals and society, sanctifying, enlightening, and maturing God's people.

The Reformed have often recognized the place of the Spirit in the transition from Old to New Covenants, and that sets up the depths and heart obedience expected in the Sermon on the Mount. The world works by Spirit, not mechanics.

Finally, where other traditions sometimes marginalize the church, the Reformed have always recognized its centrality. We disagree about how central it is, sometimes rightfully, as I've argued, identifying the church as the kingdom, other times letting the church serve as a lecture factory. At the same time, thanks largely to Calvin, the Reformed have recognized the power and importance of the sacraments. Because in varying measure, we recognize that the Holy Spirit works decidedly through baptism and the Lord's Supper, these have always played heavily into our view of God's work. Such an emphasis sets us up for an even greater ecclesiology and communality in the way of the cross.

These are just some of the ways the Reformed tradition connects to the way of the cross, and I long to see all of us in that tradition grow so that in a couple hundred years people will see the way of the cross as an even more natural outgrowth of the Reformed-Presbyterian tradition. May that be true of all our traditions.

Acknowledgments

T hough they should in no way be blamed or harangued for this book, I want to thank many friends who encouraged and/or challenged me on this project as it developed over the past few years. Thanks to the students in the last class I taught at New St. Andrews College on early versions of these subjects. What a trip that was. Thank you Michael Harkin, Greg Fields, Joshua Appel, Brendan O'Donnell, Justin Hughes, Joshua Gibbs, Brad Littlejohn, Dave Hatcher, Lisa Beyeler, Austin and Laura Storm, Jayson Grieser, Gregory Soderberg, Seth Toebben, Naing Thang, Wes Callihan, Rusty Olps, Neville Graaff, Chris Aberle, Steve Fawver, and the special blessing of Kayla Fry. Thanks to Peter Leithart and Toby Sumpter for the extra work they put in on the manuscript, and for Peter's too-kind foreword. What a great gift. Thanks even more, Peter, for providing a safe place for discussion and for your encouraging attempts to help me reconnect. You are a gift from God. Special thanks and admiration for regular discussions with the amazing Patch Blakey. Patch you are a friend who's too good to be true. Thanks for always being there. Thank you so much Donny Linnemeyer for your friendship and perseverance week in and week out as we chewed on so many books and issues. May the Lord use you mightily. Thank you very much KC Rumrey for your vision, support, crazy co-travels, and encouragement. Wish we lived closer. Extra thanks to Brad Belschner for your risk-taking and trust. Without you this book would never have been completed. Of course, many thanks to Christian Amondson and Rodney Clapp at Cascade Books for letting this book see the light of day. Thanks to the late Greg Bahnsen for giving voice decades ago to several key instincts contained here. Deep thanks to Doug Wilson for nearly two decades of wonderful and creative reshaping that gave me fresh direction in so many areas, even though we've ended up on different paths. Thanks eternally, my friend. Thanks Mom and Dad for your support, confidence, love, and great lunches. Thanks Mom especially for your unending prayers. Thanks to my sis, Lucy, for reading the manuscript multiple times and for insisting we go to that great Justice Conference in Portland. But most of all, thanks for being a devoted cheerleader on this project at the right times. I'm forever grateful. Thanks beyond words to my wife Paula, to whom this book is dedicated, for your passion, loyalty, and tough questions throughout. I adore your humor, honesty, and many talents that have given our family so much life. I kiss your lips forever. And many thanks to my children—Amanda, Chelsea, Mac, Eric, Gabe—for fascinating discussions about these things around the house and for letting me read strange stuff aloud and show you twists and turns. You are amazing people who continue to surprise me in the best ways. As Bill Murray's character says in Lost in Translation—"It's the most terrifying day of your life the day the first one is born . . . And they turn out to be the most delightful people you will ever meet in your life."

Bibliography

Alcorn, Randy. *Heaven*. Carol Stream, IL: Tyndale, 2004.

Ashbrook, R. Thomas. *Mansions of the Heart: Exploring the Seven Stages of Spiritual Growth*. San Francisco: Jossey-Bass, 2009.

Athanasius of Alexandria. *St. Athanasius on the Incarnation of the Word*. Crestwood, NY: St. Vladimir's Seminary Press, 1993.

Bacevich, Andrew. *American Empire: The Realities and Consequences of U.S. Diplomacy*. Cambridge, MA: Harvard University Press, 2002.

Baker, Dean. *The Conservative Nanny State: How the Wealthy Use the Government to Stay Rich and Get Richer*. Washington, DC: Center for Economic and Policy Research, 2006.

Barton, Ruth Haley. *Invitation to Solitude and Silence: Experiencing God's Transforming Presence*. Downers Grove, IL: InterVarsity, 2010.

Belousek, Darrin. *Atonement, Justice, and Peace: The Message of the Cross and the Mission of the Church*. Grand Rapids: Eerdmans, 2012.

Benner, David. *The Gift of Being Yourself: The Sacred Call to Self-Discovery*. Downers Grove, IL: InterVarsity, 2004.

Berdyaev, Nicolas. *Spirit and Reality*. London: Centenary, 1949.

Blum, William. *Killing Hope: U.S. Military and CIA Interventions Since World War II*. Monroe, ME: Common Courage, 2004.

Blumenthal, Sidney. *The Rise of the Counter-Establishment: The Conservative Ascent to Political Power*. New York: Union Square, 2008.

Bobbio, Norberto. *Left and Right: The Significance of a Political Distinction*. Chicago: University of Chicago Press, 1996.

Boettner, Lorraine. *The Reformed Doctrine of Predestination*. Phillipsburg, NJ: P&R Publishing, 1979 [1932].

Bonhoeffer, Dietrich. *The Cost of Discipleship*. Translated by Richard Pevear and Larissa Volokhonsky. New York: Simon and Schuster, 1995.

Bourgeault, Cynthia. *Centering Prayer and Inner Awakening*. Cambridge, MA: Cowley, 2004.

———. *The Wisdom Jesus*. Boston: Shambhala, 2008.

Bradford, William. *Of Plymouth Plantation*. San Antonio, TX: Vision Forum, 2009 [1909][1650].

Buckley, William F. "Mission Statement," *National Review*, November 19, 1955. Online: http://www.nationalreview.com/articles/223549/our-mission-statement/william-f-buckley-jr.

Bibliography

———. "Toward a Definition of Conservatism." *National Review*, August 17, 1992, 18.

Bunyan, John. *The Pilgrim's Progress*. Carlisle, PA: Banner of Truth, 2009 [1896; 1676].

Butler, Smedley. *War Is a Racket*. Port Townsend, WA: Feral House, 2003 [1935].

Campbell, Charles. "The Folly of the Sermon on the Mount." In *Preaching the Sermon on the Mount*, edited by David Fleer and Dave Bland, 59–68. St. Louis: Chalice, 2007.

Cardenal, Ernesto. *Love: A Glimpse of Eternity*. Brewster, MA: Paraclete, 2006.

Carney, Timothy. *The Big Ripoff: How Big Business and Big Government Steal Your Money*. New York: Wiley, 2006.

Carson, Kevin. *The Iron Fist Behind the Invisible Hand: Corporate Capitalism as a State-Guarantee System of Privilege*. Nanaimo, BC: Red Lion, 2002. Online: http://www.mutualist.org/id4.html/.

Chesterton, G. K. *The Outline of Sanity*. Norfolk, VA: IHS, 2002 [1926].

Coulter, Ann. *Godless: The Church of Liberalism*. New York: Crown Forum, 2006.

Dean, John. *Conservatives Without Conscience*. New York: Viking, 2006.

Derbyshire, John. "Twilight of Conservatism: We are Living in False Hope." *National Review Online*, May 10, 2005. Online: http://old.nationalreview.com/derbyshire/derbyshire200505100802.asp.

DiLorenzo, Thomas. *How Capitalism Saved America*. New York: Crown Forum, 2004.

Dostoevsky, Fyodor. *The Brothers Karamazov*. New York: Farrar, Straus and Giroux, 2002.

D'Souza, Dinesh. *The Virtue of Prosperity: Finding Values in an Age of Techno-Affluence*. New York: Free Press, 2000.

Dunn, James. *Theology of the Apostle Paul*. Grand Rapids: Eerdmans, 2006.

Ehrman, Bart, editor. *The Apostolic Fathers I*. Loeb Classical Library. Cambridge, MA: Harvard University Press, 2003.

Ferguson, Niall. *The Ascent of Money*. New York: Penguin, 2008.

Flood, Derek. "Substitutionary Atonement and the Church Fathers." *Evangelical Quarterly*, 82.2 (2010) 142–59.

Ford, J. Massynbaerde. *My Enemy Is My Guest: Jesus and Violence in Luke*. Maryknoll, NY: Orbis, 1984.

Foster, Richard. *Sanctuary of the Soul: Journey into Meditative Prayer*. Downers Grove, IL: InterVarsity, 2011.

Galilea, Segundo. *The Beatitudes: To Evangelize as Jesus Did*. Maryknoll, NY: Orbis, 1984.

Gilman, Benjamin (chairman). "U.S. Interests in the Central Asian Republics." Hearing Before the Subcommittee on Asia and the Pacific of the Committee on International Relations. House of Representatives. February 12, 1998. Online: http://commdocs.house.gov/committees/intlrel/hfa48119.000/hfa48119_0.htm.

Gnuse, Robert. *You Shall Not Steal: Community and Property in the Biblical Tradition*. Maryknoll, NY: Orbis, 1985.

Goldberg, Jonah. "What is a 'Conservative'?" *National Review Online*, May 11, 2005. Online: http://old.nationalreview.com/goldberg/goldberg200505111449.asp.

Gonzalez, Justo. *Faith and Wealth: A History of Early Christian Ideas on the Origin, Significance, and Use of Money*. San Francisco: Harper and Row, 1990.

Gornik, Mark. *To Live in Peace: Biblical Faith and the Changing Inner City*. Grand Rapids: Eerdmans, 2002.

Bibliography

Greenman, J. et al. *The Sermon on the Mount Through the Centuries*. Grand Rapids: Brazos, 2007.

Greenwald, Glenn. "They Hate Us for Our Occupations." Salon.com, October 12, 2010. Online: http://www.salon.com/2010/10/12/terrorism_28/.

Grimmett, Richard. "Instances of Use of United States Forces Abroad, 1798–2001." In *Congressional Research Service Report for Congress*. Washington, D.C.: Library of Congress, 2002. Online: http://www.dtic.mil/cgi-bin/GetTRDoc?AD=ADA463153.

Hannity, Sean. *Let Freedom Ring: Winning the War of Liberty Over Liberalism*. New York: Regan, 2002.

Hengel, Martin. *Crucifixion: In the Ancient World and the Folly of the Message of the Cross*. London: SCM, 1977.

Henry, Patrick. "Speech in the Virginia Ratifying Convention." June 5, 1788. Online: http://www.madisonbrigade.com/p_henry.htm.

Hirschman, Albert. *The Passions and the Interests: Political Arguments for Capitalism Before Its Triumph*. Princeton, NJ: Princeton University Press, 1997.

Holman, Susan. *The Hungry Are Dying: Beggars and Bishops in Roman Cappadocia*. New York, Oxford University Press, 2001.

———. *Wealth and Poverty in Early Church and Society*. Grand Rapids: Baker Academic, 2008.

Jeffery, Steve, et al. *Pierced for Our Transgressions: Rediscovering the Glory of Penal Substitution*. Nottingham, England: Inter-Varsity, 2007.

Johnston, David Cay. *Free Lunch: How the Wealthiest Americans Enrich Themselves at Government Expense*. New York: Penguin, 2007.

Johnson, Jan. *When the Soul Listens: Finding Rest and Direction in Contemplative Prayer*. Colorado Springs: NavPress 1999.

Kavanaugh, Denis, translator. *Fathers of the Church: A New Translation. Saint Augustine*. Vol. 11. Washington, DC: Catholic University Press of America, 2011.

Kelly, G. B. and F. B. Nelson. *Dietrich Bonhoeffer: A Testament to Freedom: The Essential Writings of Dietrich Bonhoeffer*. San Francisco: HarperSanFrancisco, 1990.

Kesler, Charles and Clinton Rossiter. *The Federalist Papers*. New York: Signet Classic, 2003.

Kennan, George. "PPS23." In *Foreign Relations of the United States*, 1948, volume 1, part 2 (Washington DC Government Printing Office, 1976), 524–525. Online: http://en.wikisource.org/wiki/Memo_PPS23_by_George_Kennan.

King, Jr. Martin Luther. "A Time to Break Silence." Delivered 4 April 1967, Riverside Church, New York City. *Online: http://www.stanford.edu/group/King/liberation_curriculum/speeches/beyondvietnam.htm.*

Kinzer, Stephen. *Overthrow: America's Century of Regime Change from Hawaii to Iraq*. New York: Henry Holt, 2006.

Kirk, Russell. *The Essential Russell Kirk*. Wilmington, DE: Intercollegiate Studies Institute, 2007.

Klein, Naomi. *Shock Doctrine: The Rise of Disaster Capitalism*. New York: Picador, 2007.

Korten, David. *When Corporations Rule the World*. San Francisco: Berrett-Koehler, 1995.

Kuehnelt-Leddihn, Eric von. *Leftism Revisited: From De Sade and Marx to Hitler and Pol Pot*. Washington, DC: Regnery, 1991.

Lasserre, Jean. *War and the Gospel*. London: James Clarke, 1962.

Bibliography

Linthicum, Robert. *Building a People of Power.* Colorado Springs: Authentic, 2005.

McNeill, David. "The Night Hell Fell from the Sky." *The Asia Pacific Journal,* March 10, 2005. Online: japanfocus.org.

Mead, William Russel. Charlie Rose interview. *Charlie Rose,* PBS, May 23, 2003.

Meeks, M. Douglas. *God the Economist: The Doctrine of God and Political Economy.* Minneaspolis: Fortress, 2000.

Micklethwait, John and Adrian Wooldridge. *The Right Nation: Conservative Power in America.* New York: Penguin, 2004.

Mueller, John. *Redeeming Economics: Rediscovering the Missing Element.* Wilmington, DE: Intercollegiate Studies Institute, 2010.

Murphy, Robert. *The Poltically Incorrect Guide to Capitalism.* Washington, DC: Regnery, 2007.

Nouwen, Henri. *In the Name of Jesus.* New York: Crossroad, 1989.

Novak, Michael. *Will It Liberate?* New York: Paulist, 1986.

Oden, Thomas, editor. *The Parables of Kierkegaard.* Princeton, NJ: Princeton University Press, 1978.

Orwell, George. *1984.* New York: Harcourt Brace, 1983 [1949].

Owen, John. *The Death of Death in the Death of Christ.* London: Banner of Truth, 1959.

Packer, George. "The Fall of Conservatism." *The New Yorker* (May 26, 2008) 47–55.

Packer, J. I. "The Logic of Penal Substitution." In *Celebrating the Saving Work of God: The Collected Shorter Writings of J. I. Packer,* 85–123. Vancouver, BC: Regent College Publishing, 1998.

Parsons, Wilfrid, translator. *Fathers of the Church: A New Translation. St. Augustine: Letters.* Washington, DC: Catholic University of America Press, 1955.

Perkins, John. *Confessions of an Economic Hit Man.* San Francisco: Berrett-Koehler, 2004.

Platt, David. *Radical Together: Unleashing the People of God for the Purpose of God.* Colorado Springs: Multnomah, 2010.

Reagan, Ronald. "Remarks at the Annual Meeting of the Boards of Governors of the World Bank Group and International Monetary Fund." September 29, 1981. Online: http://www.reagan.utexas.edu/archives/speeches/1981/92981a.htm.

Roberts, Alexander and James Donaldson. *The Ante-Nicene Fathers.* Vol. 1. Grand Rapids: Eerdmans, 1957.

———. *The Ante-Nicene Fathers.* Vol. 3. Grand Rapids: Eerdmans, 1957.

———. *The Ante-Nicene Fathers.* Vol. 4. Grand Rapids: Eerdmans, 1957.

Rohr, Richard. *Falling Upward: Spirituality for the Two Halves of Life.* San Francisco: Jossey-Bass, 2011.

———. *Radical Grace: Daily Meditations.* Cincinnati: St. Anthony Messenger, 1995.

———. *Things Hidden: Scripture as Spirituality.* Cincinnati: St. Anthony Messenger, 2008.

Rohr, Richard and John Feister. *Hope Against Darkness: The Transforming Vision of Saint Francis in an Age of Anxiety.* Cincinnati: St. Anthony Messenger, 2001.

Romero, Oscar. *The Violence of Love.* Farmington, PA: Plough, 1998.

Rosner, Brian. *Greed as Idolatry: The Origin and Meaning of a Pauline Metaphor.* Grand Rapids: Eerdmans, 2007.

Rutba House. *Schools for Conversion: 12 Marks of a New Monasticism.* Eugene, OR: Cascade, 2005.

Bibliography

Sardar, Ziauddin and Merryl Wyn Davies. *Why Do People Hate America?* New York: Disinformation, 2002.

Schneider, John. *The Good of Affluence: Seeking God in a Culture of Wealth.* Grand Rapids: Eerdmans, 2002.

Sider, Ron. *Bread of Life: Stories of Radical Mission.* Marion, IN: Triangle,1996.

Stott, John. *The Cross of Christ.* Downers Grove, IL: InterVarsity, 2006.

Stonehouse, Ned B. *J. Gresham Machen: A Biographical Memoir.* Carlisle, PA: Banner of Truth, 1987.

Thomas a Kempis. *The Imitation of Christ.* Translated by A. Croft and H. Bolton. New York: Dover, 2003.

Wasfi, Dahlia. "No Justice, No Peace." http://www.youtube.com/watch?v=SLoINj48IP8.

Watson, Thomas. *All Things for Good.* Carlisle, PA: Banner of Truth, 1986 [1680].

Weiner, Tim. *Legacy of Ashes: The History of the CIA.* New York: Anchor, 2007.

Wengst, Klaus. *Pax Romana and the Peace of Jesus Christ.* London: SCM, 1986.

Williams, William Appleman. *The Tragedy of American Diplomacy.* New York: Dell, 1962.

———. *Empire as a Way of Life.* Brooklyn, NY: Ig Publishing, 1980.

Wolterstorff, Nicholas. *Until Justice and Peace Embrace.* Grand Rapids: Eerdmans, 1983.

Wright, N. T. *Simply Jesus.* New York: HarperCollins, 2011.

Zinn, Howard and Anthony Arnove. *Voices of a People's History of the United States.* New York: Seven Stories, 2004.

Recommended Reading on
Way of the Cross Themes

Alexander, John. *Being Church: Reflections on How to Live as the People of God*. Eugene, OR: Cascade, 2012.

————. *Your Money or Your Life: A New Look at Jesus' View of Wealth and Power*. Eugene, OR: Wipf and Stock, 2005.

Arpin-Ricci, Jamie. *The Cost of Community: Jesus, St. Francis and Life in the Kingdom*. Downers Grove, IL: InterVarsity, 2011.

Ashbrook, R. Thomas. *Mansions of the Heart: Exploring the Seven Stages of Spiritual Growth*. San Francisco: Jossey-Bass, 2009.

Augsburger, David. *Dissident Discipleship: A Spirituality of Self-Surrender, Love of God, and Love of Neighbor*. Grand Rapids: Brazos, 2006.

Barton, Ruth Haley. *Invitation to Solitude and Silence: Experiencing God's Transforming Presence*. Downers Grove, IL: InterVarsity, 2010.

Belousek, Darrin. *Atonement, Justice, and Peace: The Message of the Cross and the Mission of the Church*. Grand Rapids: Eerdmans, 2011.

Benner, David. *The Gift of Being Yourself: The Sacred Call to Self-Discovery*. Downers Grove, IL: InterVarsity, 2004.

Bercot, David. *The Kingdom That Turned the World Upside Down*. Amberson, PA: Scroll, 2003.

Berdyaev, Nicolas. *Spirit and Reality*. London: Centenary, 1949.

Bonhoeffer, Dietrich. *The Cost of Discipleship*. New York: Touchstone, 1995.

Bourgeault, Cynthia. *Centering Prayer and Inner Awakening*. Cambridge, MA: Cowley, 2004.

Boyd, Greg. *The Myth of Christian America: How the Quest for Political Power Is Destroying the Church*. Grand Rapids: Zondervan, 2007.

Camp, Lee. *Mere Discipleship: Radical Christianity in a Rebellious World*. Grand Rapids: Brazos, 2008.

Cavanaugh, William. *Being Consumed: Economics and Christian Desire*. Grand Rapids: Eerdmans, 2008.

————. *Migrations of the Holy: God, State, and the Political Meaning of the Church*. Grand Rapids: Eerdmans, 2011.

————. *Theopolitical Imagination: Christian Practices of Space and Time*. New York: T&T Clark, 2003.

Recommended Reading on Way of the Cross Themes

———. *Torture and Eucharist: Theology, Politics, and the Body of Christ*. Malden, MA: Blackwell, 1998.

Chan, Francis. *Crazy Love: Overwhelmed by a Relentless God*. Colorado Springs: David C. Cook, 2008.

Claiborne, Shane. *Irresistible Revolution*. Grand Rapids: Zondervan, 2006.

Clapp, Rodney. *A Peculiar People: The Church as Culture in a Post-Christian Society*. Downers Grove, IL: InterVarsity, 1996.

Dickau, Tim. *Plunging into the Kingdom Way: Practicing the Shared Strokes of Community, Hospitality, Justice, and Confession*. Eugene, OR: Cascade, 2010.

Duckworth, Jenny and Justin. *Against the Tide, Towards the Kingdom*. Eugene, OR: Cascade, 2011.

Ellul, Jacques. *Anarchy and Christianity*. Grand Rapids: Eerdmans, 1988.

———. *Money and Power*. Eugene, OR: Wipf & Stock, 2009.

———. *The Presence of the Kingdom*. Colorado Springs: Helmers and Howard, 1989.

———. *The Subversion of Christianity*. Grand Rapids: Eerdmans, 1986.

Fleer, David and Dave Bland, editors. *Preaching the Sermon on the Mount*. St. Louis: Chalice, 2007.

Foster, Richard. *Sanctuary of the Soul: Journey into Meditative Prayer*. Downers Grove, IL: InterVarsity, 2011.

Galilea, Segundo. *The Beatitudes: To Evangelize as Jesus Did*. Maryknoll, NY: Orbis, 1984.

Gonzalez, Justo. *Faith and Wealth: A History of Early Christian Ideas on the Origin, Significance, and Use of Money*. San Francisco: Harper and Row, 1990.

Gorman, Michael. *Cruciformity: Paul's Narrative Spirituality of the Cross*. Grand Rapids: Eerdmans, 2001.

Gornik, Mark. *To Live in Peace: Biblical Faith and the Changing Inner City*. Grand Rapids: Eerdmans, 2002.

Greenman, J. et al. *The Sermon on the Mount Through the Centuries*. Grand Rapids: Brazos, 2007.

Hauerwas, Stanley. *After Christendom: How the Church Is to Behave If Freedom, Justice, and a Christian Nation Are Bad Ideas*. Nashville: Abingdon, 1991.

———. *The Peaceable Kingdom*. Notre Dame, IN: University of Notre Dame Press, 1991.

———. *Unleashing the Scripture: Freeing the Bible from Captivity to America*. Nashville: Abingdon, 1993.

Hays, Richard. *The Moral Vision of the New Testament: Community, Cross, New Creation, A Contemporary Introduction to New Testament Ethics*. New York: HarperOne, 1996.

Horsley, Richard and Neil Silberman. *The Message of the Kingdom*. Minneapolis: Fortress, 2006.

Johnson, Jan. *Invitation to the Jesus Life*. Colorado Springs: NavPress, 2008.

———. *When the Soul Listens: Finding Rest and Direction in Contemplative Prayer*. Colorado Springs: NavPress 1999.

Kaufman, Ivan. *"Follow Me": A History of Christian Intentionality*. Eugene, OR: Cascade, 2008.

Kraybill, Donald. *The Upside-Down Kingdom*. Harrisonburg, VA: Herald, 2011.

Kuyper, Abraham. *Christianity and Class Struggle*. Translated by Dirk Jellema. Grand Rapids: Piet Hein, 1950.

Lasserre, Jean. *War and the Gospel.* London: James Clarke, 1962.

Leithart, Peter. *Against Christianity.* Moscow, ID: Canon, 2003.

———. *Between Babel and Beast: America and Empires in Biblical Perspective.* Eugene, OR: Cascade, 2012.

Linthicum, Robert. *Building a People of Power.* Colorado Springs: Authentic, 2005.

Myers, Ched. *Binding the Strong Man: A Political Reading of Mark's Story of Jesus.* Maryknoll, NY: Orbis, 2008.

Nouwen, Henri. *In the Name of Jesus.* New York: Crossroad, 1989.

Rohr, Richard. *Falling Upward: Spirituality for the Two Halves of Life.* San Francisco: Jossey-Bass, 2011.

———. *Things Hidden: Scripture as Spirituality.* Cincinnati: St. Anthony Messenger, 2008.

Romero, Oscar. *The Violence of Love.* Farmington, PA: Plough, 1998.

Rutba House. *Schools for Conversion: 12 Marks of a New Monasticism.* Eugene, OR: Cascade, 2005.

Schroeder, C. Paul. *On Social Justice: St. Basil the Great.* Crestwood, NY: St. Vladimir's Seminary Press, 2009.

Sider, Ron. *Bread of Life: Stories of Radical Mission.* Marion, IN: Triangle,1996.

Sobrino, Jon. *The Principle of Mercy: Taking the Crucified People from the Cross.* Maryknoll, NY: Orbis, 1994.

Stassen, Glenn. *Living the Sermon on the Mount.* San Francisco: Jossey-Bass, 2006.

Stock, Jon, Tim Otto, and Jonathan Wilson-Hartgrove. *Inhabiting the Church: Biblical Wisdom for a New Monasticism.* Eugene, OR: Cascade, 2006.

Trocme, Andre. *Jesus and the Nonviolent Revolution.* Maryknoll, NY: Orbis, 2003.

Wengst, Klaus. *Pax Romana and the Peace of Jesus Christ.* London: SCM, 1986.

Willard, Dallas. *The Divine Conspiracy: Rediscovering Our Hidden Life in God.* New York: HarperOne, 1998.

———. *The Spirit of the Disciplines: Understanding How God Changes Lives.* New York: HarperOne, 1990.

Wilson-Hartgrove, Jonathan. *God's Economy: Redefining the Health and Wealth Gospel.* Grand Rapids: Zondervan, 2009.

———. *The New Monasticism.* Grand Rapids: Brazos, 2008.

Wink, Walter. *Jesus and Nonviolence: A Third Way.* Minneapolis: Fortress, 2003.

Wright, Christopher. *Old Testament Ethics for the People of God.* Downers Grove, IL: InterVarsity, 2011.

Wright, N. T. *Simply Jesus: A New Vision of Who He Was, What He Did, and Why He Matters.* New York: HarperOne, 2011.

Yoder, John. *The Politics of Jesus.* Grand Rapids: Eerdmans, 1994.

Yoder, Perry. *Shalom: The Bible's Word for Salvation, Justice, and Peace.* Nappanee, IN: Evangel, 1998.

York, Tripp, editor. *A Faith Not Worth Fighting For: Addressing Commonly Asked Questions about Christian Nonviolence.* Eugene, OR: Cascade, 2012.